AF560595

HISTORY OF INDOLOGICAL STUDIES

PAPERS OF THE 12TH WORLD SANSKRIT CONFERENCE
Vol. 11.2

HISTORY OF INDOLOGICAL STUDIES

Edited by
KLAUS KARTTUNEN

MOTILAL BANARSIDASS PUBLISHERS
PRIVATE LIMITED • DELHI

PAPERS OF THE 12TH WORLD SANSKRIT CONFERENCE HELD IN HELSINKI, FINLAND, 13-18 JULY 2003
VOL. 11.2

General Editors:
PETTERI KOSKIKALLIO & ASKO PARPOLA

First Edition: Delhi, 2015

ISBN: 978-81-208-3994-6

Also available at:
MOTILAL BANARSIDASS
41 U.A. Bungalow Road, Jawahar Nagar, Delhi 110 007
8 Mahalaxmi Chamber, 22 Bhulabhai Desai Road, Mumbai 400 026
203 Royapettah High Road, Mylapore, Chennai 600 004
236, 9th Main III Block, Jayanagar, Bengaluru 560 011
8 Camac Street, Kolkata 700 017
Ashok Rajpath, Patna 800 004
Chowk, Varanasi 221 001

Printed in India
by RP Jain at NAB Printing Unit,
A-44, Naraina Industrial Area, Phase I, New Delhi–110028
and published by JP Jain for Motilal Banarsidass Publishers (P) Ltd,
41 U.A. Bungalow Road, Jawahar Nagar, Delhi-110007

PREFACE

Completing this book turned out to be much more difficult than I originally supposed. At the beginning, I was very happy to be able to organize a section at the Helsinki Conference dealing with the history of Indology, one of my favourite subjects since the 1970s. To my disappointment, some cancellations made the section much smaller than I had planned. Nevertheless, we had an interesting morning with some useful papers and fruitful discussion. But when I looked at the matter after the conference, I saw that the planned book would be very thin indeed. After some further pondering and consultation with Prof. Parpola, I decided to fill it out with other material. I had myself an unpublished paper which seemed very well suited to the purpose as it gave a sort of background to the history of later Western Indology. I also thought that a bibliography of printed material about the history of Indology in general and Indological traditions of various countries in particular would add value to the book. When Prof. Zysk, who had not been able to attend the conference, agreed to provide his unpublished (though available as net version) paper about the history of Indian studies in Denmark, I saw that I had succeeded in collecting what seemed to me a nice volume. Here it is.

As the papers included in this volume only discuss some rather narrow parts of Indology, I have prepared as an introduction a short summary showing the main trends in the past of Indology. Prof. Garzilli continues her studies of the contacts of some Western Indologists with Nepalese scholars. My own papers have two quite different topics. The first is about the role of Indian pandits and scholars in the early history of Indology, while the second traces the development of Indian studies in Sweden. Prof. Serebriany presents an interesting attempt of combining Indology in Russia with some trends in Russian cultural history. Dr. Zavhorodniy's contribution about the Ukrainian translations of Indian classics contains much little-known information. The article of Prof. Zysk was mentioned above and the book concludes with a bibliography of the history of Indology.

Finally, I must thank Professor Asko Parpola and Motilal Banarsidass for their patience in waiting for this volume. Margot Whiting has kindly checked the English of the Preface and Introduction.

KLAUS KARTTUNEN

CONTENTS

CONTRIBUTORS

ENRICA GARZILLI
Asiatica Association
Via V. Bellini 4
20122 Milano
ITALY
e-mail: garzilli@asiatica.org

KLAUS KARTTUNEN
Department of World Cultures
P.O. Box 59
00014 University of Helsinki
FINLAND
e-mail: klaus.karttunen@helsinki.fi

SERGEI D. SEREBRIANY
E. M. Meletinsky Institute for Advanced Studies in the Humanities
Russian State University for the Humanities
6 Miusskaya Square,
125993 Moscow
RUSSIA
e-mail: s.serebriany@gmail.com

YURIY ZAVHORODNIY
G. Skovoroda Institute of Philosophy
National Academy of Sciences of Ukraine
4 Tryokhsviatytelska Street
01001 Kyiv
UKRAINE
e-mail: zavhorodniy@ukr.net

KENNETH G. ZYSK
Department of Cross-Cultural and Regional Studies
University of Copenhagen
Karen Blixens Vej 4, Bygn. 10,
DK-2300 Copenhagen S
DENMARK
e-mail: zysk@hum.ku.dk

ABBREVIATIONS

(More specific abbreviations are given in the bibliographies)

ABORI = *Annals of the Bhandarkar Oriental Research Institute*, Poona
AO = *Acta Orientalia*, Leiden/Copenhagen
BDCRI = *Bulletin of the Deccan College Research Institute*, Poona
BSO[A]S = *Bulletin of the School of Oriental [and African] Studies*, London
GGA = *Göttingische Gelehrte Anzeigen*, Göttingen
JA = *Journal Asiatique*, Paris
JAOS = *Journal of the American Oriental Society*, New Haven
JASB = *Journal of the Asiatic Society of Bengal*, Calcutta
JRAS = *Journal of the Royal Asiatic Society*, London
MO = *Le Monde Orientale*, Stockholm
OLZ = *Orientalistische Literaturzeitung*, Leipzig
WZKM = *Wiener Zeitschrift für die Kunde des Morgenlandes*, Vienna
WZKS = *Wiener Zeitschrift für die Kunde Südasiens*, Vienna
ZDMG = *Zeitschrift der Deutschen Morgenländischen Gesellschaft*, Wiesbaden

MS(S) = manuscript(s)
Nep. = Nepalese
NGMPP = Nepal-German Manuscript Preservation Project
RV = *Ṛgveda*
Skt = Sanskrit
V.S. = *vikrama saṃvat*, Vikrama era (= AD 56/57–)

Introduction

KLAUS KARTTUNEN

This introduction is intended to offer an outline of ideas and trends in the history of Indian Studies. There are, in fact, two entirely different ways of considering this history. On the one hand, it can be seen from the viewpoint of the growth of knowledge (when errors and distortions should also be included) of Indian literature, history and civilization, but on the other hand, it can be seen as a sort of a continuation of ancient Indian science. As the majority of the articles in the present book deal with Western Indology, I have taken the first viewpoint in this introduction, while the second will receive some light in my first article in this book.

1. PREHISTORY[1]

The beginnings of Western knowledge of India lie in Graeco-Roman Antiquity. This can be roughly divided into three periods: The early period before Alexander and his expedition to India, the Hellenistic age from Alexander to the first century BC and the Roman imperial period. Important authors for the early period are Herodotus and Ctesias. In the next period follow the historians of

[1] In a survey like this, definite time limits are misleading, more or less symbolic. The years I have selected as turning points are 1786, the year of Sir William Jones' famous address, 1852, the year of Burnouf's death, 1914, the beginning of the First World War, and 1978, the year of the publication of *Orientalism* by Edward Said.

Alexander, especially Nearchus and Onesicritus, and soon also the diplomat Megasthenes and his fragments. The extant authors, such as Strabo, Pliny and Arrian, belong to the Roman period, while the *Periplus of the Erythraean Sea* and Ptolemy's *Geography* are important for geographical and trade history. Towards the end of antiquity, there are still important authors such as Pseudo-Palladius and Cosmas Indicopleustes.

The conception of India in the classical period went through certain changes. In the beginning, it was the land of fabulous riches and wonders of nature on the rim of the known world. From the time of from Alexander's expedition, it was the land of naked philosophers with their rigorous ascetism, but also a real geographical and political entry and, especially in the Roman period, a source of various luxury items.

In the Middle Ages, the continuation of the classical heritage is the dominate trait in the accounts of India. The direct contact between Europe and India almost stopped with the rise of Islam.[2] Medieval literature was characterised by a lack of historical sense, still conspicuous in the 16th century. Thousand years old accounts were deemed in the same way, or even as more valuable and credible than the contemporary ones. India was more a literary conception than a real country.

Nevertheless, we can mention some medieval travellers: Marco Polo and others saw India on their way to China or on the way back. The Dominican missionary Jordanus spent years on the Malabar coast in the early 14th century and wrote a book about 'The Wonders of India'. Niccoló de' Conti (1395?–1469) told his story to the papal secretary Poggio Bracciolini, who published it in his *De varietate fortunae*. The Russian merchant Afanasij Nikitin visited India around 1470 and wrote a perceptive account which was only published in 1819.

---

[2] As I am here attempting an outline of the history of Western Indology, the important contributions in Arabic (e.g., al-Bīrūnī) and Chinese (e.g., Xuanzang) fall outside my survey.

The early modern age, from the 16th to the early 18th century, saw the beginnings of colonialism and direct trade between India and Europe. From the present viewpoint, it was the time of missionaries and travellers. Both wrote accounts, often full of prejudices, errors and incorrect conclusions, but also containing many interesting details.

From the 16th century on, there were numerous Catholic missionaries working in India and many were also literarily active. The English Jesuit Thomas Stephens (1549–1619) was a notable Marāṭhī scholar. Jacopo Fenicio (1558–1632) wrote an account of Hinduism. Sebastian Manrique (1590?–1669) visited many little-known places. The Jesuit Roberto De' Nobili (1577–1656) adopted Indian customs and became the Christian guru in Madurai. The German Jesuit Heinrich Roth (1610–1668) was an early Sanskrit scholar, and Constantino Beschi (1680–1747) is still remembered as a Tamil scholar and author. The Austrian Jesuit Joseph Tieffenthaler (1710–1785) prepared a geographical description of India, mainly based on his own surveying. The French Jesuits Jean Calmette (1692–1740), Jean François du Pons (1698–1752) and Gaston-Laurent Cœurdoux (1691–1779) may already be listed among the pioneers of classical Western Indology. Jean-Antoine Dubois (1766–1848) was long appreciated until he turned out to be just a copyist, wholly dependent on the work of N.-J. Desvaulx (1745–1823). The Italian Carmelite Paulinus a Sancto Bartholomaeo (1748–1806) in Kerala and Rome was a pioneer of Sanskrit philology.

We can also name a few Protestant missionaries: Bartholomäus Ziegenbalg (1683–1719) did much for Tamil studies. He was followed by Benjamin Schulze (1689–1760) who wrote grammars of Hindustani and Telugu. Johann Philip Fabricius (1711–1791) collected a useful dictionary of classical Tamil. Note that Abraham Roger (1609–1649), who wrote a famous account of Hinduism, was no missionary, but the minister of a Dutch factory in South India as was also Philippus Baldaeus (1632–1671).

Early lay travellers include Ludovico di Varthema (beginning of the 16th century), Duarte Barbosa (d. 1521) and Tomé Pires (d. 1524). The Venetian merchants Cesare de Federici and Gasparo Balbi visited India in the late 16th century. The Dutchman Jan Huyghen van Linschoten (1563–1611) worked in Goa, but collected information about all Asia. The first Britons visited India at the end of the century.

In the 17th century, the French physician François Bernier (1620–1688) wrote on contemporary Mughal history as he had himself observed it. The jeweller Jean Baptiste Tavernier (1605–1689) visited India no less than six times. India was also included in the travels of Thomas Coryat, Pietro Della Valle, Jean Chardin and Adam Olearius.

The number of travel accounts is already so great in the 18th century that we can mention only a few important ones. Abraham Hyacinthe Anquetil-Duperron (1731–1805) visited the Parsis in Surat and became the pioneer of Avesta studies. Pierre Sonnerat (1749–1814) served in the French Navy in Asian waters.

The last important travel books hail from the beginning of the 19th century. These include the books of Francis Buchanan Hamilton (1762–1829), Bishop Reginald Heber (1783–1826), William Moorcroft (1765–1825) and Mountstuart Elphinstone (1779–1839).

2. THE EARLY PERIOD 1786–1852

The story of early Calcutta Indology has been told often. In the beginning, N. B. Halhed translated the legal compilation from the Persian intermediary (1776), but Charles Wilkins (1749–1833) was already capable of rendering the *Bhagavadgītā* and the *Hitopadeśa* directly from Sanskrit (1785 and 1787). Sir William Jones (1746–1794) achieved much in a relatively short time. He founded the Asiatic(k) Society, translated the *Śakuntalā* and Manu and discussed the questions of history and linguistics. Henry Thomas Colebrooke (1765–1837) began the development of Indology into a formal discipline. Among other things he was the first to present Vedic literature, Pāṇini and the six schools of Indian philosophy to Western readers. The Baptist missionaries of Serampore, especially William Carey (1761–1834), published grammars and even some texts.

The Orientalist paradigm sees the will to subjugate the country as the main motivation of these early Indologists, but this is too simple an explanation. Undoubtedly, such a motivation was involved, when the government subsidized Indological studies, but a reading of the texts of those early scholars often reveals genuine enthusiasm. They really admired the classics of Sanskrit literature and sought to obtain important information about ancient history in general. Of course, some had also more practical (legal and missionary) interests.

Nevertheless, Sir William Jones and his contemporaries were not only pioneers of the new approach. They also had their background in the earlier period and were still much dependent on such ideas as the outlines of ancient history derived from Old Testament stories and legends. Sir William Jones was not the founder of comparative linguistics. He foreshadowed it, but his own ideas on the development of languages and relations between them were still rather primitive.

All this soon also echoed in Europe. A number of Calcutta publications were soon reprinted and translated into French and German. This was the age between enlightenment and romanticism, of philosophers and poets. Johann Gottfried von Herder (1744–1803), Friedrich Wilhelm Joseph Schelling (1775–1854) and Arthur Schopenhauer (1788–1869) were all positively interested in India, but criticism was offered by Friedrich Hegel (1770–1831) – but from the viewpoint of Indology they were all poorly informed dilettantes. Friedrich Schlegel (1772–1829) wanted to be the founder of a new discipline but his work still contains much fantasy. Johann Wolfgang von Goethe (1749–1832) admired *Śakuntalā*, and other poets were interested in India, e.g., Heinrich

Heine (1797–1856), Charles-Marie Leconte de Lisle (1818–1894) and especially Friedrich Rückert (1788–1866).

The first chairs in Europe were founded. This was a period of the flourishing of Arabic, Persian, Turkic, Chinese etc. studies, especially in France. Paris was also the accepted centre of the youthful field Indology, while the manuscript collections were in England. The classes of Eugène Burnouf (1801–1852) were crowded with students from all parts of Europe. Buddhist studies were started with the Sanskrit manuscript collection made by Brian Houghton Hodgson (1800–1894) in Nepal and divided by him between the libraries of Calcutta, London and Paris. History was cultivated by James Prinsep (1799–1840) in India and Christian Lassen (1800–1876) in Europe. Prinsep is remembered for his decipherment of the Brāhmī and Kharoṣṭhī scripts, Lassen for his four-volume *Indische Alterthumskunde*. Horace Hayman Wilson (1784/86–1860) studied Purāṇas and the history of North-West India.

Franz Bopp (1791–1867) and Rasmus Rask (1787–1832) laid the foundation of comparative Indo-European linguistics. August Wilhelm von Schlegel (1767–1845) applied the methods of classical philology to Sanskrit texts in his editions of the *Bhagavadgītā*, *Hitopadeśa* and the beginning of the *Rāmāyaṇa*. The whole epic was then edited and translated (into Italian) by Gaspare Gorresio (1807–1891). Much work was done with theatre (H. H. Wilson), law (G. C. Haughton) and narrative literature (Hermann Brockhaus, Theodor Benfey).

The focus was almost exclusively on classical Sanskrit. Modern languages were usually neglected, although a number of grammars and dictionaries were published in India. In Europe, Hindustani was taught in Paris by Joseph-Héliodore Garcin de Tassy (1794–1878) and in England at the East India College in Haileybury. Some Hindustani texts were published and translated by Duncan Forbes (1798–1868). In England there was also some interest in Tamil (Benjamin Guy Babington) and Telugu (Charles Philip Brown).

3. THE PERIOD OF INTENSIFICATION 1852–1914

After Burnouf's death, the centre of Western Indology moved to Germany, which provided professors even for English and Indian universities.[3] Albrecht Weber (1825–1901) in Berlin and Rudolf Roth (1821–1895) in Tübingen especially attracted students from many countries.

The linguistic study of Old and Middle Indian developed rapidly. We still use the grammars of William Dwight Whitney (1827–1894) and Jacob Wackernagel (1853–1938). Jacob Samuel Speyer (1849–1913) and Berthold Delbrück (1842–1922) wrote fundamental studies on syntax, Richard Pischel (1849–1908) on Prākrit. Vyākaraṇa studies were launched, although Whitney was strictly against this and criticized Pāṇini without understanding him. Otto Nikolaus von Böhtlingk (1815–1904) edited the *Aṣṭādhyāyī*, Franz Kielhorn (1840–1908) the *Mahābhāṣya*. In lexicography, Böhtlingk and Roth produced a solid foundation with the large St. Petersburg dictionary (1853–75), supplemented by the condensed, but also revised dictionary of Böhtlingk (1879–89). The big, one-volume dictionary of Monier Monier-Williams (1819–1899) started as a poor compilation, but the second edition (1899) was much better, probably thanks to his capable assistants. A third important lexical work was the "practical dictionary" of Vaman Shivram Apte (1858–1892).

This was the great period of Vedic studies. Beginnings had already been made by Colebrooke, Friedrich Rosen (1805–1837), Wilson and Burnouf. The careers of Weber and Roth started in the 1840s. Friedrich Max Müller (1823–1900) prepared his massive

---

[3] In the U.K., Friedrich Rosen, Reinhold Rost (1822–1896), Theodor Goldstücker (1821–1872), F. Max Müller, Theodor Aufrecht, Julius Eggeling (1842–1918) and others, in India, e.g., Georg Bühler, Franz Kielhorn, Eugen Hultzsch (1857–1927), Theodor Bloch (1867–1909), and Georg Thibaut.

edition of the *Ṛgveda* with the Padapāṭha and Sāyaṇa. While Wilson's translation still much depended on Sāyaṇa, the new generation tended to take the other extreme. The *Ṛgveda* was put in an Indo-European context and interpreted in the light of comparative linguistics and mythology. A corrective reaction came in 1889, when Karl Geldner (1852–1929) and Richard Pischel (1849–1908) re-established the *Ṛgveda* as an Indian text. In France, Abel Bergaigne (1838–1888) concentrated on Vedic religion. Much of the work of Hermann Oldenberg (1854–1920) dealt with the Veda, both religion and textual criticism. Arthur Coke Burnell (1840–1882) discovered in South India a number of new texts from manuscripts. Maurice Bloomfield (1855–1928) started with the *Atharvaveda* and provided an important tool in his *Vedic Concordance* (1906). Adolf Friedrich Stenzler (1807–1887) worked on domestic ritual and Alfred Hillebrandt (1853–1927) on religion. Leopold von Schroeder (1851–1920) was very industrious, though rather unenthusiastic, in editing the *Yajurveda* Saṁhitās. Arthur Anthony Macdonell (1854–1930) studied Vedic grammar and, together with Arthur Berriedale Keith (1879–1944), compiled the *Vedic Index of Names and Subjects* (1912).

Classical Sanskrit received less attention, but was not forgotten. Peter Peterson (1847–1899) in India worked on the Subhāṣita collections and Böhtlingk published his much used collection of *Indische Sprüche*. Sylvain Lévi (1863–1935) wrote his classic work on Indian theatre. Carl Cappeller (1840–1925) even wrote Sanskrit poetry himself. Johannes Hertel (1872–1955) and Richard Schmidt (1866–1939) concentrated on narrative literature (Schmidt also on the Kāmaśāstra, Hertel, with less success, on the Veda). A number of important scholars worked on Sanskrit epics: Both Adolf Holtzmanns (the uncle, 1810–1870, and the nephew, 1838–1914), Hermann Jacobi (1850–1937), Edward Washburn Hopkins (1857–1932), Moritz Winternitz (1863–1937) and Heinrich Lüders (1869–1943). In the early 20th century, Winternitz and Lüders launched a plan to prepare the critical edition of the *Mahābhārata*, eventually realized in India by the Bhandarkar Oriental Research Institute. In Denmark, Søren Sørensen (1849–1902) produced an index of the names in the *Mahābhārata*.

Both Indian and Western libraries acquired large collections of Indian manuscripts and an important line of work was the preparation of manuscript catalogues. Especially Weber and Aufrecht were active in Europe. The increasing knowledge of texts led to the first histories of literature (Weber, Max Müller, Winternitz). Georg Bühler (1837–1898) organized the search for manuscripts in India. Theodor Aufrecht (1822–1907) did good service collecting the "Catalogue of Catalogues".

History was rather neglected outside India (but German epigraphists in India like Bühler, Kielhorn and Hultzsch contributed), and art history even more. It is a frustrating task to read the silly, prejudiced opinions written about Indian art in the 19th and still in the beginning of the 20th century. Vincent Arthur Smith (1848–1920) is remembered as an example of an imperial historian. His opinions and conclusions are sometimes suspect, but he did some good work with source materials. One of the leading epigraphists of the period was John Faithful Fleet (1847–1917), while Robert Sewell (1845–1925) concentrated on South India and Emile Senart (1847–1928) on Aśoka. There were important epigraphists in India, but they, as well as historians, will be discussed in another part of the present volume.

The Archaeological Survey of India was founded in 1862, when Alexander Cunningham (1814–1893) was made the "Archaeological Surveyor". In the beginning, it was naively supposed that a few years' work by one man would be enough for a survey of the remains of India's past, but soon the Survey was put on a permanent basis. After Cunningham, it was directed by James Burgess (1832–1916).

This period also saw the beginnings of philosophical studies, although especially non-Indologists still loudly claimed that India had no philosophy at all. The pioneer in Europe, mainly concentrating on Vedānta, was Paul Deussen (1845–1919), although James Ballantyne (1813–1864) in India had already done some preliminary work. Another scholar of Vedānta was Georg Thibaut (1848–1914) in India. Rikhard Garbe (1857–1927) was the first to study Sāṁkhya, James Haughton Woods (1864–1935) Yoga.

Buddhism was peripheral to the majority of scholars, but there was the Pāli Text Society and the scholars around it (including some German, French, Dutch, Danish and Russian). The original task of the society was to publish the critical edition of the Pāli canon (in Latin script). This was completed in the 1920s, but then the Society had already started publishing the canonical commentaries, important post-canonical texts and translations of all these. Thomas William Rhys Davids (1843–1922) was dismissed from the Ceylon Civil Service, but he made a new career as a scholar of Pāli and Buddhism and founded the Pāli Text Society in 1881. After his death, it was led by his widow C. A. F. Rhys Davids (1858–1942). She started as an Abhidhamma specialist, but her later theories about the original "Aryan Buddhism" are among the less honourable chapters in the history of Western Indology. In mainland Europe, Hendrik Kern (1833–1917) and Emile Senart (1847–1928) were much interested in Buddhist studies, and H. Oldenberg wrote his famous book on the Buddha in 1881. In Denmark, Rask and N. L. Westergaard (1815–1878) were already interested in Pāli, which was then the main subject of Viggo Fausbøll (1821–1908) and Vilhelm Trenckner (1824–1891). In Paris, Léon Feer (1830–1902) combined material from all the main languages of Buddhism.

The second half of the 19th century also saw the beginnings of Jaina studies in the West. The pioneers were Albrecht Weber, Ernst Leumann (1859–1931) and Hermann Jacobi.

Beginnings of comparative New Indo-Aryan studies were started by A. F. R. Hoernle (1841–1918) and John Beames (1837–1902). Samuel Henry Kellog (1839–1899) compared Hindi and its close relatives. George Abraham Grierson (1851–1941) conducted the massive Linguistic Survey of India. Dinesh Chandra Sen (1866–1939) worked on Bengali. Comparative Dravidian linguistics was started by Robert Caldwell (1814–1891). Karl Graul (1814–1864) and George Uglow Pope (1820–1908) worked on the generally neglected Tamil. In India, U. V. Swāminātha Ayyar (1855–1942) collected and edited classical Tamil texts and finally edited the indispensable *Tamil Lexicon*. German missionaries also worked on Malayālam (Hermann Gundert) and Kannaḍa (Hermann Mögling and Ferdinand Kittel).

4. THE PERIOD OF SPECIALIZATION 1914–1978

Grammar: The great work of Wackernagel was slowly continued by his pupil Albert Debrunner (1884–1958), then by Karl Hoffmann (1915–1996) *et. alia*. Thomas Burrow (1909–1986) wrote on the formation and history of Sanskrit. Vyākaraṇa studies were pursued, e.g., by Bruno Liebich (1862–1939), Louis Renou (1896–1966) and Paul Thieme (1905–2001). The list of leading Vaiyākaraṇas also includes many Indians, e.g., Kashinath Vasudev Abhyankar (1890–1976). Etymology benefited a great deal from Manfred Mayrhofer (1926–2011) and his two dictionaries. In Pune, many Indian and foreign scholars and students in the 1950s already worked on the *Encyclopaedic Dictionary of Sanskrit on Historical Principles*, although the first fascicle came out only in 1976.

Veda: Karl Friedrich Geldner (1852–1929) translated the *Ṛgveda*. Willem Caland (1859–1932) edited ritual texts. Louis Renou and Jan Gonda (1905–1991) covered most aspects of the Veda in their studies. Thieme was one of the leading specialists on the *Ṛgveda*. In India, R. N. Dandekar (1909–2001) continued the Vedic bibliography started by Renou.

Epics: The most important achievement of this period was the publication of the critical editions: the *Mahābhārata* in Pune (1927/33–59), with Vishnu Sitaram Sukthankar (1887–1943) as the general editor, and the *Rāmāyaṇa* in Vadodara (1960–75) with Govindlal H. Bhatt (1901–1965) as the general editor.

Purāṇa: Willibald Kirfel (1885–1964) started the critical study with his reconstruction of the "Pañcalakṣaṇa". The first trained Indologist who gave attention to the Āgama literature was Friedrich O. Schrader (1876–1961); later on this became a speciality of the French Institute in Pondicherry with N. R. Bhat (1920–2009) and others.

For classical Sanskrit, too, focus was clearly in India. The massive *History of Dharmaśāstra* by Pandurang Vaman Kane (1880–1972) is one of the most important works of this period. Parashuram Krishna Gode (1891–1961) wrote on many aspects of classical literature and culture, while V. Raghavan (1908–1979), as a philologist, attracted a number of Western students. Raghavan also started the voluminous *New Catalogus Catalogorum*. In Europe, e.g., Sten Konow (1867–1948) and Arthur Berriedale Keith (1879–1944) wrote on theatre.

Philosophy: Ganganatha Jha (1871–1941) translated long texts. Fedor Ippolitovich Shcherbatskoj (Theodor Stcherbatsky, 1866–1942) and Stanisław Schayer (1899–1941) attracted attention as logicians. Otto Strauss (1881–1940) wrote perhaps the first really well-informed Western account of Indian philosophy. Erich Frauwallner (1898–1974) had a long and somewhat less reputable career, but his competence as a great specialist on Indian philosophy cannot be denied. In Paris, Olivier Lacombe (1904–2001), Suzanne Siauve (1919–1975) and others concentrated on the non-advaitic traditions of Vedānta. In India, the brightest stars include M. Hiriyanna, (1871–1950), S. Das Gupta (1885–1952), S. Radhakrishnan (1888–1975), T. M. P. Mahadevan (1911–1983) and Bimal Krishna Matilal (1935–1991).

Science: A thin tradition of the study of Indian astronomy with mathematics existed since the early Calcutta days (e.g., Colebrooke and at the end of the 19th century, Georg Thibaut). While Georg Rusby Kaye (1866–1929) seems rather prejudiced in his ideas, the remarkable achievements of David Pingree (1933–2005) started a new era. The study of Indian medicine was introduced in the 19th century by interested physicians (Franz Hessler and Gustave Liétard, but also Rudolf Roth). The collaboration of W. Kirfel and his student physician Luise Hilgenberg resulted in a fine translation of the *Aṣṭāṅgahṛdaya*. Jean Filliozat (1906–1982) started as an ophthalmologist, but soon switched to Indology. In East Germany, R. F. G. Müller (1882–1966), as a physician and Sanskritist, was a lone figure.

Buddhism: In the U.K., the Pāli Text Society continued its activities. The *Critical Pāli Dictionary*, originally based on the meticulous card index prepared by Trenckner, started appearing in 1924 under the editorship of Dines Andersen (1861–1940), and was continued by Helmer Smith (1882–1956). Sylvain Lévi (1863–1935), Louis de La Vallée Poussin (1869–1938) and Étienne Lamotte (1903–1983) worked on the Mahāyāna. Shcherbatskoj created the Russian school, then brutally stopped by the Stalin regime. Edward Conze (1904–1979) was a specialist on the Prajñāpāramitā literature. Giuseppe Tucci (1894–1984) remains outstanding in Tibetan studies. Franklin Edgerton (1885–1963) concentrated on language (Buddhist Hybrid Sanskrit). Just before the First World War the Central Asian fragments opened completely new possibilities for Buddhist studies. Among the early scholars studying them were La Vallée Poussin, Lévi, Lüders and Ernst Waldschmidt (1897–1985). The last-mentioned was also the first editor of the *Sanskrit-Wörterbuch der buddhistischen Texte aus den Turfanfunden*, continued by Heinz Bechert (1932–2005) and others.

Jainism: In Europe, an important *guruparaṁparā* leads from Walter Schubring (1881–1969) to Ludwig Alsdorf (1904–1978) and Colette Caillat (1921–2007). There were many active Jaina scholars in India starting with Vijaya Dharma Suri (1868–1922). Muni Punyavijaya (1895–1971) and his pupil Muni Jambuvijaya (1923–2009) were tireless editors of Jaina texts.

History was mainly studied in India and in England. Edward James Rapson (1861–1937) was a great specialist on Indian numismatics. From the long list of Indian historians, the names of

Hemchandra Raychaudhury (1892–1957), Ramesh Chandra Majumdar (1888–1980), K. A. Nilakanta Sastri (1892–1975) and Dinesh Chandra Sircar (1907–1985) come easily to mind. In England, then in Australia, A. L. Basham (1914–1986) was a noted cultural historian.

Archaeology: Even before the First World War there was a new start of the Archaeological Survey of India with John Marshall (1876–1958), who came fresh from Greek excavations and brought up-to-date methods with him. But the years in India eventually made them antiquated, and after his retirement, the Survey stagnated until Ernest Mackay (1880–1943) and R. E. M. Wheeler (1890–1976) revived it. Harappa and Mohenjodaro were discovered in the 1920s. Among Marshall's excavations, Taxila was also prominent. One of Marshall's merits is that he trained professional Indian staff for the A.S.I. Since Wheeler, the focus was on prehistory. H. D. Sankalia (1908–1989) founded his own school of prehistoric archaeology in Pune.

Art history: The great pioneer was Ananda K. Coomaraswamy (1877–1947), perhaps the first scholar to understand the aesthetics of Indian art. Heinrich Zimmer (1890–1943) has attracted both admiration and suspicion with his rather subjective interpretation of Indian art and thought. Perhaps more constructive was the work of Stella Kramrisch (1898–1993), Hermann Goetz (1898–1976) and Johanna Engelberta van Lohuizen-de Leeuw (1919–1983). From India we can name, e.g., Ordhendra Coomar Gangoly (1881–1974), Vasudev Saran Agrawala (1904–1966) and Calembur Sivaramamurti (1909–1983).

The scholarly emphasis was clearly on classical India and Sanskrit. However, there was a new beginning of Dravidian studies in the West. T. Burrow and Murray B. Emeneau (1904–2005) produced together the *Dravidian Etymological Dictionary*. Kamil Zvelebil (1927–2009) was a noted specialist on Tamil literature.

New Indo-Aryan linguistics: The work of G. A. Grierson was already mentioned. This was continued, e.g., by Jules Bloch (1880–

1953) and Alfred Master (1883–1978). Ralph Turner (1888–1983) provided an important tool with his *Comparative Dictionary of Indo-Aryan Languages*. In India, e.g., Suniti Kumar Chatterji (1890–1977), Sukumar Sen (1900–1992) and Siddheshwar Varma (1887–1985) were noted linguists. A separate school of Hindi studies developed in Russia with emphasis on lexical questions.

In the colonial period, anthropological research was still much bound to (partly racial) prejudices. An important task was the preparation of large encyclopedias of castes and tribes from various parts of India. Some Indian scholars such as Jivanji Jamshedji Modi (1854–1933) and Sarat Chandra Mitra (1863–1938) were noted anthropologists. Sociology with Louis Dumont (1911–1998) and anthropology with Verrier Elwin (1902–1964), David G. Mandelbaum (1911–1987) *et al.* contributed much to liberating the field from the colonial heritage.

5. PERIOD OF DISCOURSE 1978–

In 1978, Edward Said (1935–2003) published his famous criticism of Western Islamic studies, *Orientalism*. The Saidian criticism of Western scholarly traditions is often exaggerated, but must be taken seriously. In its Indological applications, the Saidian theory is sometimes turned upside down. In the heated discussion about Said's ideas, I would like to single out the balanced views of Wilhelm Halbfass (1940–2000).

The use of computers has made a change, the extent of which is still difficult to measure. A growing number of manuscripts, inscriptions, texts, books, journals, dictionaries and other materials is available on the web.

As all the contributions published in this volume deal with the earlier periods, I do not attempt any detailed analysis of the present situation and future here. We must, however, note the beginning of modern Indian studies in earnest: languages, literature, modern history, actual religion, sociology, and anthropology. The time of the dominance of Sanskrit philology and classical Indology is now past. All these fields have important tasks and a full right to exist on their own. However, the present cannot be fully understood without the past. Classical Indology still has an important task to do alongside and in collaboration with modern South Asian studies.

A Sanskrit Letter Written by Sylvain Lévi in 1924 to Hemarāja Śarmā (Cultural Nationalism and Internationalism in the First Half of the 20th Century: Famous Indologists Write to the Raj Guru of Nepal – no. 2)

ENRICA GARZILLI

1. INTRODUCTION

This paper will deal with the Sanskrit letter that Sylvain Lévi wrote on March 29, 1924 to his Nepalese *guru*, the Raj Guru of Nepal or Nayab Bada Ģuruju, His Holiness Hem Raj Sharma (or, as he signed his Sanskrit letters, Hemarāja Śarmā).[1] This document is part of a recently discovered corpus of official and private correspondence between Hem Raj and some of the most famous Indologists of the 20th century. The corpus includes fifteen Sanskrit,

[1] I dedicate this paper, as the other articles of the series, to the memory of Hem Raj. I should like to thank Hem Raj's eldest son, Kesari Raj Pandey, his wife Kiran, and their eldest son Prakash A. Raj for their help and encouragement in my work.

I should like to thank Dr. Roland Lardinois for inviting me to take part in the "Colloque International Sylvain Lévi (1863–1935): Histoire sociale et érudition orientaliste" held in Paris at the École Pratique des Hautes Études (Paris, France) on Oct. 7–10, 2003, where I read a shorter version of this paper.

I should like to thank Dr. Steve Farmer, who ameliorated the English of this paper.

I should like to thank my daughter, Dr. Andrea Rachele Fiore, for cheering my days.

one Nepali, and nine English letters written by Vidhuśekhara Bhaṭṭācārya, Carlo Formichi, Kesar Bahadur K. C., Sylvain Lévi, Srinivasa Murti, Rāhula Sānkṛityāyana, Hemarāja Śarmā, Baladeva Śarmā, Vishnu S. Suktankar, Gangadhar Tailang, Frederick W. Thomas, and Giuseppe Tucci.[2] The owner entrusted me with the publication of this correspondence. A book that includes copies of the letters along with an edition, transliteration and translation, historical introduction, exegetical apparatus, and biographies the authors (based in part on previously unpublished documents) is in preparation.

In this paper I will introduce the correspondence between Lévi and Hem Raj, sketch Hem Raj's life, and briefly discuss Lévi's love for Nepal and his relationship with Hem Raj. I will then present a facsimile of Lévi's original letter in Devanāgarī, a transliteration into Roman script (not diplomatic) along with an edition, an English translation and notes on *realia* discussed in the text.

There is little point in recapitulating here Sylvain Lévi's life and scientific work, which have already been written about by many scholars,[3] or Hem Raj's, of whom I have elsewhere offered the first short but comprehensive biography, along with some notes on little known aspects of Lévi's personality (Garzilli 2001). Therefore, here I will only offer a few previously undiscussed sides of Hem Raj's life and of his relationship with Lévi, as suggested in their correspondence.

---

[2] I gave more details on these letters in Garzilli 2000: 197–198. In these letters Hem Raj signs himself as Śarmā, while Baladeva Śarmā signs as such. On Giuseppe Tucci, see Garzilli 2012.

[3] See, e.g., *Hommage a Sylvain Lévi* (1964); *Mémorial Sylvain Lévi* (Renou 1937a); Bloch 1935; Foucher 1937; Maschino & Stchoupak 1937. A new perspective on Lévi is offered by his correspondence included in the book edited by Bongard-Levin, Lardinois and Vigasin (2002a), and in their communication (Bongard-Levin, Lardinois & Vigasin 2002b).

2. THE CORRESPONDENCE BETWEEN SYLVAIN LÉVI AND HEM RAJ SHARMA

The correspondence between Lévi and Hem Raj includes five letters, three of them written by Lévi to Hem Raj:

- The first, dated November 8, 1923, was written from Lévi's studio in his house in Paris V, at Rue Guy de la Brosse, no. 5.[4] We also have Hem Raj's one-page undated response to this letter, which mainly talks about the MSS that Lévi's asked Hem Raj to send him.
- The letter I am presenting in this article was written on March 29, 1924 from Paris.[5] To this we have Hem Raj's five-page undated response.
- The last letter we have was written by Lévi on September 4, 1924. Unfortunately, we do not have Hem Raj's response to this letter.

As I have pointed out elsewhere, a few letters or parts of them had been microfilmed by the Nepal-German Manuscript Preservation Project (Reel no. E 3017–E 3018) around 1977.[6] In the same year Prakash A. Raj, Hem Raj's eldest grandson, had given not only those letters to the NGMPP, but also the Nepali account of South India by Hem Raj, who went there on a pilgrimage with the Queen Mother in V.S. 1969.[7] Unfortunately, the latter document now appears to be lost.

The letter I am presenting here was given to me by the current owner in 1999, and has also been microfilmed by the NGMPP.

---

[4] This letter has been translated and studied by E. Garzilli (2001).

[5] A copy of this 1924 letter was published in *Pūrnimā* 21(3) (= no. 83): 60.

[6] See Garzilli 2001: 116.

[7] V.S. stands for Vikrama Saṃvat. I will often use this dating system (often spelled Bikram in Nepal), which is 56 or 57 years ahead of the Christian era, depending on how the start of the year is established using according the Nepali lunar calendar.

3. HEM RAJ SHARMA (1878–1953)

Hem Raj not only held a high public position as the deputy Royal Preceptor of the royal family and of Nepal (Skt *rājaguru* or Nep. *rāj gurujū*),[8] but he was also a scholar. He is credited with having initiated research work in Nepal in accordance with modern research methodology. His most important contributions are the Sanskrit edition and Hindi introduction on the *Kāśyapasaṃhitā*, based on his discoveries of a new manuscript, in which he tried to prove how Āyurveda has influenced Western medicine.[9] He also published a Sanskrit debate on the *Mahābhārata*.[10] His most important scholarly contribution was the first Nepali grammar, titled *Candrikā: Gorkhabhāṣa vyākaraṇa* (V.S. 1969).[11] The book was printed in Nepali by Hem Raj in his home in Dhoka Tole called Bharati Bhavan, the "House of Learning", in the heart of Kathmandu. The work first established grammatical rules for Nepali that are still considered the standard.[12]

Hem Raj was a friend of the great Nepali poet Motiram Bhatta (1866–1896), giving him some financial support, when the two were studying in Benares; Hem Raj was seventeen years old and

---

[8] Although *de facto* he was the Royal Preceptor.

[9] *Kāśyapasaṃhitā*, Bombay: Published by Tadavji T. Acharya, Kalbadevi Rd., V.S. 1995. The 2nd edition was published in 1953 (C.E.). Hara Prasad Shāstri had discovered a much shorter manuscript in Kathmandu in 1898. A chapter of the *Kāśyapasaṃhitā*, based on Hem Raj's book, has been translated by Dr. Dominik Wujastyk in Wujastyk 1998.

[10] Sharma 1935. On the paper, see also Pusalker 1955: 111 (I owe this reference to Prof. Albrecht Wezler).

[11] Around the same time Rammani Acharya Dikshit wrote a separate Nepali grammar titled *Gorkha vyākaraṇa bodha*, and between the two rivalry arose. In the chapter "Hemarāja in my view" of his book *Purāna samjhana* (Acharya Dikshit 2029: 51–57) Rammani Acharya said that his own grammar had no chance to become a standard grammar since Hem Raj was so close to the Ranas. Actually both families were close to the Ranas, and Rammani's family was very powerful as the advisor to the Prime Minister Chandra Shamsher Jung Bahadur Rana and the superintendent of the "Nepali Language Publications Committee", but Hem Raj had more prestige since he was the Raj Guru of both the Rana prime minister and the king.

[12] Cf. Pradhan 1999.

Motiram nineteen. Hem Raj later said that Motiram inspired his work on Nepali, since the poet spent most of his short life promoting Nepali language and literature and by establishing a printing press – as Hem Raj did some year later – which he used to publish Nepalese poems and other literary works.[13] Nevertheless, despite Motiram's work, Nepali grammatical rules were not established until many years later by Hem Raj.

Hem Raj was not only a pundit, but also a bibliophile and a collector of manuscripts and books. Hem Raj's love for books went back to when he was a boy. Around 1887, he received Rs. 10 from his father in Benares. His father wanted to see what the boy would do with the money. Hem Raj bought the *Raghuvaṁśa*, the *Aṣṭādhyāyi* and the *Amarakośa*.[14]

In a letter written by Motiram to Hem Raj in 1895, we read that Motiram gave Hem Raj his first collector-item books, accompanied by a short poem. He may have sent them since Hem Raj had already started his own library, which would soon become much larger than that of his friend's.[15]

As a bibliophile and collector Hem Raj's fame went well beyond Nepal and India. In his private library, which he maintained at home, he owned over 25,411 titles, 10,000 of which were manuscripts.[16] He printed and reprinted many rare books on his press on the ground floor of his house. Hem Raj lent manuscripts and books (and gave scholarly advices) to foreign scholars, including Lévi, as is apparent from extant correspondence and from the acknowledgements in the books of Lévi, Tucci, Formichi, Sankrityayan,

[13] Among the others, in 1887 Motiram discovered and printed the manuscript of the Nepali translation of the *Rāmāyaṇa* made by Bhanubhakta Acharya (1814–1868).

[14] Cf. Premraj Paudyal, cit. in Raj 1978: 111 and fn. 1.

[15] It should be considered that Hem Raj was much more affluent than his friend, and lived much longer. On the letter, see Raj 2030: 13.

[16] I am able to rectify the figures that I gave in Garzilli 2001: 119, thanks to the information given me by Mr. Dasharath Thapa, Chief of the National Library of Nepal.

and others.[17] Nevertheless, he could not meet foreign scholars at home, since no one was allowed to enter the house of such a sacred person until around the 1930s. Lévi wrote in 1925 that twice a week he had an academic meeting with Hem Raj at the Government Library. He could not visit Hem Raj's personal library because people would be scandalized to see a *mleccha* ('foreigner'), and as such impure, to step in the foyer of such a sacred person.[18]

The core of the collection of the Nepal Rashtriya Pustakalaya (Nepal National Library), which was established in January 1957 by government decree,[19] came from Hem Raj's personal library, which had been purchased at the cost of Indian Rs. 300,000 in the previous year.[20] The titles owned by Hem Raj were in Hindi (8,437), Sanskrit (4,536), Marathi (4,262), English (3,857), Bengali (3,394), Nepali (712), Prakrit (168), Urdu (21), Tibetan (12), and German (12), for a total of 25,411 titles. Some 10,000 manuscripts were also handed over to the National Archives, according to the decision of the Government, and the books in German were later transferred to the English Section.[21]

---

[17] Cf. Garzilli 2001: 120–123.

[18] Lévi 1925: xiii.

[19] The Library is a unit of the Ministry of Education, Government of Nepal. From the outset, the NNL had a collection of some 43,000 books and periodicals, including those brought in as a result of the amalgamation of the Central Secretariat Library. At present, NNL has more than 75,000 books, documents, and periodicals in different languages. It was first housed at Sikridhoka in Singha Durbar, then moved to the old Palatial Building called Harihar Bhavan, in Lalitpur, of the Rana Prime Minister. The building was the property of one of the sons of Chandra Shamsher. It occupies 19 feet of the first floor of the building. The collection of the Central Secretarial Library was also merged into its collection.

[20] Kesari who told me the exact figures of the transaction, did not know the exchange rate at the time of the sale. However, he told me that he went to the USA in 1961, and 1 US$ at that time was worth 7 rupees. Therefore, at the same exchange rate, the price of Hem Raj's library would be some $ 40,000, or some $ 200,000 using year 2000 adjusted to U.S. dollars.

[21] Information by the courtesy of Mr. Dasharath Thapa, who was at the time (September 18, 2001) the Chief Librarian.

Hem Raj was the first person in modern Nepal to be awarded the title of Vidvacchiromaṇi, or 'Crest-jewel of Scholars'.[22] This title was given to the "Nāyav Badā Gurujyū Hemrāj Paṇḍitjyū" by King Tribhuvan Bir Bikram Shah Dev (who reigned in 1911–1950 and 1951–1955) for outstanding work on Bidya (namely, *vidyā* 'scholarship') and Dharma, as it was written in the royal decree issued in 1993 V.S.[23] He was the only scholar to have held this prestigious title under the Rana administration.

Many scholars all over the world, including Lévi, appreciated Hem Raj's scholarship and went to him for manuscripts and scholarly suggestions.[24]

A nice description of the role and power held by Hem Raj is offered by the Italian Professor Carlo Formichi (1871–1943). Formichi was "the" Buddhologist and Indologist of Fascism, the Vice-President of the prestigious Reale Accademia d'Italia, which was established by Mussolini to sustain the Fascist *intelligentsia*, and to represent Italy abroad. Formichi was one of the most illustrious Italian scholars of the period, together with Giuseppe Tucci, his Sanskrit pupil and *protégé*. Formichi, who was also a close friend of Kalidas Nag (1892–1966) – who had been a student of Rabindranath Tagore, and in 1920 had moved to Paris, where he became a pupil of Lévi for three years – visited Nepal twice and became a friend and a pupil of Hem Raj.[25] In *Il Nepal* (1934) Formichi wrote of him:

> '... The Government [of Nepal] is despotic and one can say that the Mahārāja has full power. Nevertheless, he makes the most important decisions after

---

[22] A Sanskrit scholar named Kul Chandra Gautam was awarded this title eighteen years later. Babu Ram Acharya in 1953 was dubbed *Itihāsaśiromaṇi* ('Crest-jewel of Historians'), and Lekhnath Paudel was dubbed *Kaviśiromaṇi* ('Crest-jewel of Poets').

[23] The facsimile of the decree is found in Appendix 1 of Prakash A. Raj, *Vidvacchiromaṇi* (Raj 1978, unnumbered page after p. 80).

[24] Cf. Garzilli 2001: 120–122.

[25] Cf. Garzilli, forthcoming b. The paper was delivered as speech at the 12th World Sanskrit Conference held in Helsinki, Finland, on July 13–18, 2003.

consulting with a Great Council made of the king's relatives, of the generals, of a few more dignitaries called Kaji, Sirdar, Bhardar, and of the Rāj Guru or spiritual teacher of the Court. The latter is a figure rather unique and we can say venerable, since the Veda itself speaks about the *purohita* or court chaplain, who does not limit himself to giving spiritual advice to the king but, above all, political advice that is sometimes of a Machiavellian shrewdness and cunning. In Indra's sky he who truly governs is not Indra, but Bṛhaspati, his *guru*. Nowadays the spiritual and political teacher of the Mahārāja of Nepal happens to be the illustrious Hemarāj Śarmā, who is given the name of His Holiness. At the same time he is a saint, a wise man, and an erudite person, he knows all the elegances of Sanskrit, which he speaks fluently, and as Director of the Government Library, he is up-to-date on all the past and present publications in the vast field of Indian literature, on all the unedited codices that deserve or which do not deserve to come to light. Led by this famous sage, who is all dignity, intelligence and scholarship, I was able to discover five manuscripts still unedited and bring back a copy of them with me to Italy ... (Trans. E. Garzilli)[26]

Hem Raj was closely connected with the Ranas, the despotic rulers of Nepal for some 104 years, from 1846 until the revolution of 1951. Among them, he was especially close to the Prime Minister Chandra Shamsher Jung Bahadur Rana (who ruled from 1901 up to 1928), acting as his private adviser.[27] Since his main duty was

---

[26] "Il Governo è assoluto e può dirsi che il Mahârâja abbia pieni poteri. Prende egli, tuttavia, le più gravi deliberazioni dopo aver sentito il parere di un Gran Consiglio composto dai parenti del re, dei generali, d'altri pochi dignitari detti Kaji, Sirdar, Bhardar, e del Râj-Guru o maestro spirituale della Corte. Quest'ultimo è una figura quanto altra mai caratteristica e si può dire veneranda, perché il Veda stesso parla del *purohita* o cappellano di corte che non si limita a dare consigli spirituali al re ma soprattutto suggerimenti politici a volte d'una accortezza e scaltrezza machiavelliche. Nel cielo d'Indra chi veramente governa non è Indra, ma Bṛhaspati, il suo *guru*. Oggi maestro spirituale e politico del Mahârâja del Nepal si trova d'essere l'illustre Hemarâj Çarma, cui vien dato il nome di Sua Santità. Egli è al tempo stesso un santo, un savio e un erudito, conosce tutte le eleganze del Sanscrito, che parla correntemente, e come direttore della Biblioteca governativa, è a giorno di tutte le pubblicazioni del passato e del presente nel vasto campo della letteratura indiana, di tutti i codici inediti che meritano o non meritano di venire alla luce. Guidato da questo famoso saggio, tutto signorilità, dottrina e acume, riuscii a scovare cinque manoscritti ancora inediti e a portarne copie con me in Italia." (Formichi 1934: 29–30)

[27] In the same period, Rammani and Kashinath Dikshit were also appointed to equivalent posts (see Acharya Dikshit 2029: 211).

to give *dīkṣā mantra* to the royal family, he was called Raj Guru instead of Nayab Bada Gurujyu, although technically the Raj Guru was his elder brother Heramba Raj (who was deaf).

The post of Raj Guru was awarded to Hem Raj's family in 1846, in the time of his ancestor Bijaya Raj Pandit (1805–1878). Previously, in the first half of the 18th century, Gaurishwar, a member of the family, had been the Royal Preceptor to the King of Narabhupal Shah of Gorkha. In recent decades the post of Raj Guru is no longer hereditary, but as a hereditary post it lasted longer than the Rana regime. Under a regulation instituted in 1966, the post is open to all Brahmins who have studied Sanskrit, although Khagendra Raj, Hem Raj's nephew, was exempted from this. It was only in 1972 that someone outside the family was appointed Raj Guru.[28]

In November 1999, the eldest son of Hem Raj, Kesari Raj Pandey (b. 1926), was appointed Bada Guruju, after serving as Deputy Raj Guru for three years. He held the post until December 2002. For his service Kesari received from King Birendra Bir Bikram Shah (born on Dec. 28, 1945 and tragically killed on June 1, 2001) the royal order Lal Mohar, a special red seal certificate.

Hem Raj was the *de facto* Royal Preceptor of the royal family, the Ranas and, in a sense, of Nepal as a whole, and for this reason was referred to as His Holiness. This means that for almost half a century his opinion was asked whenever any religious ritual had to be performed by the Nepalese state and by the family of the king and the Ranas.

Hem Raj's role covered several functions, some of them specifically religious, and he combined intellectual as well as more

---

[28] Bishwa Raj Pandit (1883–1960), the youngest son of Lok Raj, Hem Raj's father, and known as Kanchha Gurujyu or 'Youngest Raj Guru', was the chief Royal Preceptor from 1956 to 1960 when his eldest brother Heramba Raj Pandit died. Khagendra Raj Pandit, the eldest son of Heramba Raj Pandit, was the Bada Gurujyu from 1964 to 1977; between 1977 and 1998 there were two Bada Gurujyus who did not belong to Hem Raj's family.

practical qualities. As the major *dharmaśāstra* expert of the country, as Royal Preceptor Hem Raj had dual religious and political/administrative responsibilities, which overlapped somewhat like those of the Archbishop of Canterbury in England.[29]

This is the background information on Hem Raj's position that Lévi gives us in *Le Népal*:

> The Brahmins of Gourkha arrived with the conquerors of Nepal: they are from the clan Kanyākubjīya, devoted to the śākta rites, and recognize the authority of the Tantras. Literate men there are rare, and astrology is the most cultivated science. They are divided into three categories, separated by marriage lines; the highest carries the title of *Upādhyāya*; they belong to the Yajurveda schools; they function as *gurus* (spiritual directors) and *purohitas* (house chaplains) to Brahmins and Rajputs. The first in dignity is the spiritual director of the king (Rājaguru) who knows all questions pertinent to caste ; part of any fines inflicted on such matters go to him; moreover, due to pious donations, he is the owner of vast fields which he leases out. His post, like all similar positions in Nepal, is renewable each year; but except in case of scandal or political revolution, he retains the office for life. (Trans. E. Garzilli)[30]

Here I will list and briefly discuss some of Hem Raj's responsibilities and activities. Fuller data will be given in my book in preparation *Sanskrit, English and Nepali Letters between K. Bahadur K. C., V. Bhattacarya, C. Formichi, S. Lévi, S. Murti, R̊. Sankritya-*

---

[29] On the overlapping of religion, politics and administrative duties, see Garzilli 1987 and esp. Garzilli 1990 and Garzilli 1997.

[30] "Les brahmanes de Gourkha ont accompagné les conquérants du Nepal : ils sont du clan Kanyâkubjîya, adonnés aux rites çâktas et reconnaissent l'autorité des Tantras. Les lettrés y sont rares, l'astrologie est la science la plus cultivée. Ils sont divisés en trois catégories séparées par la barrière du mariage ; la plus élevée porte le titre d'*Upâdhyâya* ; ils appartiennent aux écoles du Yajur Veda ; ils servent de *gurus* (directeurs spirituels) et de *purohitas* (chapelains domestiques) aux Brahmanes et aux Rajpoutes. Le premier en dignité est le directeur spirituel du Roi (Râja-guru) qui connaît de toutes les questions de caste ; une partie des amendes infligées à ce titre lui revient ; de plus il est, par les donations pieuses, propriétaire de vaste domaines qu'il afferme. Sa charge, comme toutes les fonctions au Népal, est renouvelable chaque année ; mais à moins de scandale ou de révolution politique, il en reste titulaire à vie." (Lévi 1905–08, I: 272)

Apparently Lévi did not know that Hem Raj's position was hereditary.

yan, B. Sharma, G. Tailang, G. Tucci, V. Sukthankar, F. W. Thomas and the Royal Preceptor of Nepal, Hem Raj Sharma in 1923–1953 (Garzilli, forthcoming a):

1. Legislative functions: The Council amended and issued laws, and as a member of the Prime Minister's court, the Bada Gurujyu had a strong influence over Council activities. In 1935–1936, under the Prime Minister Juddha Shamsher Rana, a decree was issued, in which Hem Raj was appointed as the legal advisor on Hindu matters, and he approved the Muluki Ain legal code of 1936.
2. *Jyotiṣī* ('astrologer') functions: Hem Raj organized the astrologers and chaired the *pañcāṅga* ('almanac') committee when it met to determine the dates of festivals and the times when *vratas* ('vows'), marriages, and specific rites could be performed under the Nepali lunar calendar.[31] There had previously been from five to seven separate calendars every year; under Hem Raj, calendars were unified. In 1941 V.S., the first printed calendar was issued by the committee. On February 22, 1961 V.S., Chandra Shamsher issued a decree that no one could print the official *pañcāṅga* without Hem Raj's approval;[32] the result was that by that time Hem Raj was officially in charge of unifying, updating and rectifying the calendar, and of printing the standard one. An "Annual calendar" was issued every year in 1963–2007 V.S., executed by Hem Raj with the help of other renowned scholars such as Bhuvanath Pandey,[33] who assisted him from 1963 V.S. to about 2000 V.S.

---

[31] As an example, the festival of Mahāśivarātri, 'Shiva's birthday', falls on the new moon day of the month of Falgun (February–March). According to the solar calendar, it was celebrated on February 21 in the year 2001, on March 12 in the year 2002, on March 1 in the year 2003, and on February 18 in the year 2004.

[32] See Pant 2019: 112f.

[33] The maternal great grandfather of Prof. Dinesh Raj Pant and Dr. Mahes Raj Pant, sons of the scholar Naya Raj Pant.

3. Administrative and executive functions: As the main authority of *dharmaśāstra* in the country, it was Hem Raj's responsibility to set fees and punishments in accordance with the sacred texts.
4. For some 50 years, up until 1951, he was the director of the Education Department for the all Sanskrit- and Nepali-based education. As such, he nominated teachers, decided on their salaries, and had the power to fire them at will. There were no Department Ministers at the time, and his post was the highest in Nepali education; for this reason, and because he was in touch with the highest authorities in the country, the post carried a lot of power. This was the main reason why pundits used to gather at the door of Hem Raj's house to greet him and pay homage to him. In 1947 Hem Raj settled the question with the student movement called Jayatu Saṃskritam ('Let Sanskrit Triumph!'). Its backers were young Brahmins who had special privileges – free room and board and pocket money – given by the government in order for them to be able to study Sanskrit. They wanted to enlarge their subjects to history and geography, subjects that were forbidden in the xenophobic Nepal of the time. A compromise was eventually reached.[34]
5. He organized Brahmins to perform rituals in festivals, and he himself performed special rituals and two *koṭīhoma*s ('ten million burnt offerings') as the main priest.[35] He learned to arrange the complex ritual in Varanasi at the age of 22, and in April 1904 he acted as the *ācārya* of the *koṭīhoma*. Chandra Shansher was so

[34] Cf. Garzilli 2001: 127 and fn. 37.

[35] In Nepal I asked pundits and believers, and they talked about *koṭīhoma*, *agnihotra* and *yajñacayana* as if they were the same rite. Actually, *agnihotra* is a Vedic solemn fire ritual, while *koṭīhoma* is a post-Vedic fire ritual. The two are clearly distinguished. – In *People's Review. A Political and Business Weekly* (Jan. 18 – Jan. 24, 2001) it was announced that Sadgurudev Balkrishnanda, Paramhansh Yog Sewa was scheduled to perform "Shiva Shakti Kotihom Mahayagnya" at Siddhapith Jalpadevi Temple, [...] Bhaktapur, from January 29 to February 18. On *agnihotra*, see Witzel 1986; 1992.

happy with his services that he gave him a compensation of 10 Rs. and a shawl, when the normal fee was Rs. 3–5 and never more than Rs. 6. The royal family and the Ranas organized the ritual, which was extremely expensive, about once every ten years. In 1940 or 1941, a big *koṭīhoma* was organized in Benares by the Queen, Chandra's first wife. All decisions regarding the religious occasion were made by Hem Raj, who served as the main priest. A short account of the *koṭīhoma* of 1904 is given by Hem Raj himself in a two-page autobiography, which he wrote in his diary on January 1, 1909.[36]

6. He advised the king on various ritual matters, such as the proper actions to take following inauspicious occurrences, as when a vulture was found sitting on the top floor of the Royal Palace, on the number of mourning days for a distant relative of the king, on the best date for the coronation ceremony of the king, and so on.
7. He calculated the exact time of birth of Crown Prince Tribhuvan according to the *pañcāṅga.* He was also in the group of close relatives in attendance at Tribhuvan's birth and presided over the ceremony involving offerings to the sun and moon.[37]
8. He was responsible for performing *nāmakaraṇa*, the ceremony of naming a child after birth, of the future king Tribhuvan Bir Bikram Shah,[38] and chose the auspicious date of the ceremony (July 7, 1907) and the child's secret name.
9. He was the king's official in charge of donating grain, gold and sweets to Brahmins on festivals and auspicious occasions. This ceremony was performed at the royal palace and various pal-

---

[36] The first translation of Hem Raj's autobiography is offered in Garzilli 2001: 129–133. The short account of the *koṭīhoma* is found on p. 132.

[37] From Hem Raj diary of July 17, 1907. The historian Gyan Mani Nepal in 2057 V.S. published under the sponsorship of Mahendra Sanskrit University in Kathmandu *Paṃ. Hemarāja Śarmā: unakā kṛti ra samīkṣā*, which is the diary kept by Hem Raj between 1906 and 1954 (Nepal 2057).

[38] Tribhuvan's calculated flight to New Delhi in 1950 was the one event that started the Nepalese revolution, which overthrew the Ranas.

aces of the Ranas that the Brahmins were required to attend. In 1969 V.S., Chandra Shamsher gave Hem Raj the authority to appoint which Brahmins would be sent to special occasions such as funeral ceremonies, weddings, etc. His official designation in this role was Dānadakṣa. The document says that if Hem Raj recommended giving *dāna* ('honorarium') to Brahmins who were not eligible, he would be the one responsible. This position provided a considerable amount of income for Brahmins, which meant that Hem Raj wielded a great deal of power through his patronage.

10. He was in charge of advising the Ranas and the king's family on the proper rites to be performed on various occasions, such as the coronation ritual. As the most important and sacred of the Brahmins, Hem Raj personally performed rituals for the royal family.[39]
11. He also performed special rites for the Shahs and Ranas. A fuzzy picture exists that shows Hem Raj wearing what may be his honorific headdress called in Nepali *śrīpec*, praying in front of a huge carcass of a rhino with a person standing inside it. The caption above reads:

> Another imposing scene which sometime[s] occurs in Sikar Party is the observation of a certain appealing religious service derived from the custom of ancestral worship [...] Here, in the picture, we see a big Rhino rent form top to the toe and a gentleman related to Rana family is standing inside the carcass of the beast facing the Royal Guru standing outside in white achkan with a book in hand from which he chants the lore from the Hindu scripture relating to ancestral worship. The sum and substance of this is to give Tarpana from the blood stream flowing from the veins of the rhino recently killed, uttering the names of ancestors. This helps the departed souls to absolve from all sorts of trouble in the land of Hades. (Bhandary, n.d.: 111)

---

[39] There are many pictures, including Hem Raj, in the photo book *The Coronation Book of Their Majesties of Nepal*, published in Kathmandu by Adya Charan Raj Bhandary when King Mahendra Bir Bikram Shah and Queen Ratna Rajya Laksmi Devi Shah were crowned (most probably just after the coronation in 1955), such as those showing Hem Raj, wearing his *śrīpec*, walking near the Crown Prince Mahendra for his wedding procession (Bhandary, n.d.: 48, 49 and 113).

12. Since he was initiated as a Tantric, in 1957 V.S., he was the *dīkṣā guru* of King Tribhuvan, giving him initiation according to the Kālī worship,[40] and of the last Rana Prime Minister Mohan Shamsher, who ruled from 1948 to 1951. He was also the *gāyatrī guru* to Padma Shamsher Rana, who ruled before Mohan in 1945–1948. He also gave *gāyatrī mantra* to several Rana generals.[41]
13. He was supposed to attend to foreign scholars who arrived in the country either to study or to travel to Tibet, and he often helped them in their search for manuscripts and rare books.

Hem Raj was very active in carrying out all the above functions, and acted efficiently on other special occasions. On November 10, 1906 he welcomed, together with the royal family, Colonel Lord Kitchener who arrived in Kathmandu.[42] In 1906, he supervised the arrangements in the Karsa Camp of Chitwan for the hunting party of the Prince of Wales George Frederick Ernest Albert, who later became George V, and Edward, who later became Edward VIII.[43] Hem Raj was also in charge of welcoming them.

During World War I Hem Raj had been given the responsibility of supplying food for British army personnel and was in charge of the War Office. For this service he was awarded the order called Nepal Tara or "Most Refulgent Order of the Star of Nepal". This order is conferred for military service during war and peace.

---

[40] *Dīkṣā mantra* is used to worship Durgā during the 10-day festival in honor of goddess. Animals are killed and offered in sacrifice to the goddess: water buffaloes, goats, chickens, ducks and sheep. They symbolize different negative emotions, which human beings should overcome: anger, lust, timidity, apathy and stupidity, respectively. The size and the importance of the animal to be sacrificed vary according to the importance of the family. Hem Raj family sacrifices a goat.

[41] *Dīkṣā guru* and *gāyatrī guru* must be two different persons. They can also be mother and father.

[42] Cf. Hem Raj diary (Nepal 2057) dated November 10, 1906.

[43] We can see the photo of the camp including George V, Hem Raj, Kaiser Shamsher Rana and Juddha Shamsher Rana in Raj 1994: 41, and in the initial unnumbered pages of *The Coronation Book*.

Hem Raj also played an important part at the time of the great earthquake of January 15, 1934. He established the first fire brigade in Nepal, which he named after Juddha Shamsher Rana, who was Prime Minister in 1932–1945. He also calculated for the government how much could be recovered and how much could be lost from the loans given to those afflicted from the earthquake. His calculation made Juddha Shamsher decide to exempt people from repaying. For the good reputation that Juddha achieved by this act – not only in Nepal, but in foreign countries as well, which widely appreciated the Nepalese government – Hem Raj was "privately" given Rs. 10,000 as a gift from Juddha Shamsher.[44]

4. SYLVAIN LÉVI (1863–1935) IN NEPAL

Lévi was much loved in Nepal, which he considered his second homeland. In the Kaiser Shamsher Library his painted profile is hung between that of Hara Prasad Shastri and that of Giuseppe Tucci.

As Lévi wrote on March 14, 1925:

> I had the good luck to visit India twice, with a gap of twenty-five years in between. A gap sufficient to measure the prodigious strides made by the so-called unchangeable Orient.
>
> Besides the observations which the spectacle of everyday life suggests, I had the chance to bring back real material treasures, especially from Nepal, a country which I love like a small motherland, where the enlightened protection of the Maharaja has made my task easier.
>
> This country so rigidly closed to foreigners has welcomed me twice. I am its historian, its historiographer in person, and since it is the unique repository of ancient manuscripts, I was able to discover texts which had always been believed to be irremediably lost ... (transl. E. Garzilli)[45]

---

[44] A facsimile of the original letter, in which the "disciple" Juddha thanked Hem Raj and presented him the gift, is published in Raj 1978: 81–82.

[45] "J'ai eu la bonne fortune de visiter deux fois,l'Inde, à vingt-cinq années de distance. Assez d'intervalle pour mesurer le chemin prodigieux parcouru par le soi-disant immuable Orient. Outre les observations que suggère le spectacle de la vie quotidienne, j'ai eu la chance d'en rapporter de véritables trésors de

Lévi goes on to tell of the discovery of two important Buddhist manuscripts of the *Viṃśatikā* and the *Triṃśikā*, both of which he received from Hem Raj, as our letters show. Lévi went three times to India and Nepal: the first time was in January–March 1898. Afterwards he went on with the study of the old period of Indian literature.[46] His second long trip dates to 1921–22. In November 1921 he left Paris for Sri Lanka, then crossed over to and up through India to take part in the inauguration of Śāntiniketan on December 22, and proceeded on to Dacca, Calcutta, Benares and Nepal, where he resided four months. Then he crossed India again, stopping in many places, including Mysore and Bombay, went on to Colombo and Indo-China, and from there moved on to Tokyo. Wherever he halted, he not only searched for manuscripts, but also gave classes and delivered lectures. He returned to Paris in June 1923.[47] He possibly visited Nepal again for a few days in 1928.[48]

Besides his scientific report on the trip of 1922–23 (Lévi 1923), he wrote some social and geographic annotations in *La Géographie* 41 (1924), where is also published his lecture for the *Société de Géographie* on Tagore and Śāntiniketan, and on Nepal and its government.

There were several reasons for Levi's love for Nepal. He was very well welcomed in Nepal, as was every serious scholar who wanted to visit it for reasons of study. Lévi appreciated Nepal's climate, which being much more temperate than that of India was

---

matériaux, en particulier du Népal, un pays que j'aime comme une petite patrie, où la protection éclairée du Maharaja a facilité ma tâche. Ce pays si rigoureusement fermé aux étrangers m'a accueilli deux fois. J'en suis l'historien, l'historiographe même et comme il est l'unique *conservatoire* des anciens manuscrits, j'ai pu y découvrir des textes qu'on avait toujours cru irrémédiablement perdus ..." (In Lefèvre 1925: 116)

[46] See Lévi 1898 and all the Vedic works between 1890 and 1900. For a comprehensive bibliography, see fn. 3 above and Renou 1937b.

[47] On this long tour, see the diary of his wife: D. Lévi, *Dans l'Inde (de Ceylan au Népal)* (1925).

[48] Two colleagues at the "Colloque International Sylvain Lévi" told me that Lévi went to Nepal two times only.

more pleasant and also preserved the delicate manuscripts written on *tālapatra* ('palm leaves'). Moreover, Lévi also praised the fact that a country so closed to foreigners was so open to scientists.[49]

In spite of the general hostility of the tyrannical Rana rulers towards foreigners, all of them, and especially Bir Shamsher Rana (Prime Minister from 1885 until his death in 1901), were eager to deal with Lévi, among all the foreign scholars who visited Nepal. Chandra Shamsher asked a Bengali teacher to translate into English Lévi's book *Le Népal*, which Lévi had published in 1905–08.[50] All this happened despite the fact that the British tried to discourage any contact between Nepal and foreign scholars, and despite the fact that Chandra was especially favorable to the British (he was also the first fluent English speaker among the Ranas). Later, Chandra gave "a nice collection of Nepalese art" as a gift to the Institut de la Civilisation Indienne à la Sorbonne, where Lévi was teaching Sanskrit.[51]

In Kesari Raj Pandey's house, a small picture in a big wooden frame is hung in his living room, below a picture of Hem Raj, his third wife and their three children. It is a Christmas and New Year's card dated 1923–24 written to Hem Raj by General Kaiser

[49] See this letter; the introduction to the Lévi 1925: xii, fn. 12; Lévi 1905–08, I: fn. 18, pp. 23, 43–45, 51 *et passim*; his interview in Lefèvre 1925.

[50] The scholar, politician and human rights activist Dr. Rishikesh Shaha, according to what he told me on Feb. 7, 1999, holds the copyright on the English translation. *Le Népal* is dedicated to the Maharajas "Bir Sham Sher Jang, Deb Sham Sher Jang, and Chander Sham Sher Jang" for having supported and encouraged Lévi's research. Chandra's picture is found on the page before the introduction to the same book. Chandra Shamsher is also thanked in the introduction of the Lévi 1925, for having allowed him to visit Nepal twice. The second time Lévi lived there for four months (March 24 – July 24) and was welcomed with hospitality "fasteuse autant que cordiale" ['both stately and cordial'] that allowed him to carry out research under the best conditions.

[51] "une belle collection d'art népalais" (in a letter by Lévi to Sergej F. and Elena G. Ol'denburg dated Jan. 20, 1929). See Bongard-Levin, Lardinois & Vigasin 2002a: 162.

Shamsher Rana, who owned the second biggest library in Nepal.[52] The caption at the bottom reads:

> Professor Sylvain Lévi, the eminent French Orientalist and Epic Historian of Nepal, in the MSS Library, Kathmandu with the Manyavan [sic] Gururaj Hem Raj Panditjyu.

The picture was clearly taken in the Government Libray, since it shows a smiling Lévi and Hem Raj, holding a manuscript, surrounded by the pundits working there under Hem Raj's direction. Nevertheless, as I have already said, Hem Raj lent MSS to Lévi taken from his personal library.

5. ON LÉVI AND HEM RAJ

I want to conclude with a few words on the relationship between Lévi and Hem Raj, as it appears from their letters.

All the correspondence we have between Hem Raj and Lévi is marked by respect and affection. Lévi considered Hem Raj not only as the best of scholars, but also as his friend and *guru*.

This was due not only to the fact that Lévi asked Hem Raj for manuscripts and information about them, and depended on Hem Raj to get Chandra's permission for him to visit the country, but also because the Indological knowledge of Hem Raj, who was a high-caste Brahmin educated as a pundit and the chief of all Nepali Brahmins, was undoubtedly more extensive than that of Lévi himself.

On the second page of a three page letter dated September 4, 1924, which will be published in my edition of Hem Raj's correspondence, Lévi wrote:

> *api bhavantamīye tasmin pustakālaye punar bhaveyaṃ, śiṣyaś ceva bhavantaṃ gurum upasareyam.*

---

[52] Kaiser Shamsher Jung Bahadur Rana (the third son of Chandra Shamsher) gave 600 palm-leaf manuscripts to the Royal Library. The MSS were photographed in 1976 by Prof. Michael Witzel for the NGMPP.

Might I also be in this library of Your Holiness again, and like a pupil might approach Your Holiness, the *guru*!

6. ABOUT THIS LETTER

Lévi wrote this letter in Paris on March 29, 1924. Except for the signature at the bottom, which is in Roman script, the letter is written in a clear Devanāgarī on two sides of a sheet of French light blue paper measuring 25 x 19.30 cm. Unfortunately, the left edge of the sheet, facing the first side, is slightly spoiled.

In this letter Lévi asks Hem Raj for a copy of the *Viṃśatikā-bhāṣya* of Vasubhandu, since he had earlier received the *Triṃśikā-bhāṣya*. It was his plan to publish a French translation, based as well on Tibetan and Chinese versions of the work. He also asks in the letter for Hem Raj's permission to return to Nepal, although he probably never visited there again after the two trips in January–March 1898 and in 1921–22 (it is possible that he may have also spent a few days there in 1928).

In this letter Lèvi also asks for two Buddhist works by Ārya-deva, the *Bauddhadharmaślokasaṃgraha* and the *Pratipattisāra-śataka*. Āryadeva was, together with his teacher Nāgārjuna, one of the originators of the Mādhyamika school. Āryadeva's most famous work is the *Catuḥśataka*. According to Nakamura, we only have six works which were certainly written by Āryadeva, and some of them only exist in Tibetan or Chinese translations, while four more texts have been wrongly ascribed to him.[53] Neither the *Bauddhadharmaślokasaṃgraha* nor the *Pratipattisāraśataka* are listed among these ten known or spurious works.

---

[53] According to Nakamura (1987: 244–245), Āryadeva's genuine works are: 1. *Śataśāstra* (in Chinese); 2. *Catuḥśataka*; 3. *Akṣaraśataka* (in Chinese and Tibetan); 4. *Mahāpurṣaśāstra* (in Chinese); 5. *Cittaviśuddhiprakaraṇa*; 6. a polemic work having only the Chinese title, which means *Explanation of Nirvāṇa by [twenty] Heretical and Hīnayāna Teachers*. Four more works are spuriously ascribed to Āryadeva: 1. *Jñānasārasamuccaya* (in Tibetan); 2. *Skhalitapramathanayuktihetusiddhi*; 3. *Maḍhyamakabhramaghāta*; 4. *Āryaprajñāpāramitā-mahāparipṛcchā*.

Nevertheless, in the *New Catalogus Catalogorum*, the *Pratipattisāradaśaka*, which might refer to the *Pratipattisāraśataka*, is listed among Āryadeva's writings.[54] The *Pratipattisāraśataka* in fact exists in its Tibetan version.[55] It is a tantric work that seems to be related to the *Hevajratantra*. There appears to be a Newari version of the text extant as well.[56] The text in Newari script is cataloged by the NGMPP, reel B-29/27. Nothing is found in the *New Catalogus Catalogorum* on the *Bauddhadharmaślokasaṃgraha*, which we know was not a title of a section of the *Catuḥśataka*. Nevertheless, the text is cataloged by the NGMPP reel B-24/21.

I am presenting here the first translation of this letter. To make full sense of it, and to understand the full range of the language, form, structure, and sense of the text, it is necessary to study all five of the letters exchanged by Hem Raj and Lévi. We should also take into account that, although the main value of this correspondence lies in the historical information it provides on texts, the language of the letters at times reflects matters understood in detail only by the authors. Authors refer to historical situations known and experienced by them personally; they are historically determined. For example, Nepal at the time was a xenophobic country. Nepalese people, with the exception of the Ranas and the king's family, could not cross the border of the country, except in the case of a few affluent families who could send their sons to study in India. As a Brahmin, and the head of all Brahmins, Hem Raj was not supposed to write books in Nepali but only in Sanskrit, and of course he could not cross the ocean. He helped foreign scholars

[54] *New Catalogus Catalogorum*, II, p. 168, s.v. Āryadeva.

[55] *Pratipattisāraśataka, go bar byed pa snying po brgya pa*, Sde-dge, Tohoku catalog 2334 (*rgyud 'grel* ZHI 278b1–283a2), Peking 4695 (*rgyud 'grel*, PHU 152a8–157b6) (vol. 82). (I thank Dr. Paul Hackett for this bibliographic information.) Tsukamoto *et al.* 1989: 375–376 informs that the Sanskrit MS is kept in the Bir Library in Kathmandu. (I thank Dr. Jonathan Silk for this bibliographic information.)

[56] See Sonam & Sonam Rinchen 1994: 335, fn. 20.

even though he was not supposed to meet or touch them;[57] he also supported foreign scholarship and collected also foreign books although no Nepalese at the time were allowed to read any foreign book, or except in rare cases (such as in the case of Brahmins) any books at all; this is why all foreign scholars resorted to him. In short, to know the *realia* of our letters we must know the historical situation of the time and the language of the authors.[58]

Hem Raj was not only a scholar, but a bibliophile and book collector. As such, his fame went well beyond Nepal and India. Nevertheless, his personal library, located in between two wings of his palace in Dhoka Tole, was closed to the Nepalese people and to foreigners.[59] This reflected the political situation at that time, and explains why in this letter Lévi promises him to give him as a gift in return, once he had obtained the MSS he wanted, all the books Hem Raj desired, since it was difficult even for Hem Raj to get his hands on them. As we know, the Ranas did not allow people in the country, not even Royal Preceptors, to read foreign books.[60] Hem

---

[57] On this issue, on Jan. 24, 1999 Kesari told me that he did not believe that his father let foreigners in at home. Surely they could not visit the whole house, and perhaps not even the library. This agrees with what Lévi wrote in the Introduction to the Lévi 1925, fn. 14. Kesari also told me that "people say that once Hem Raj shook the hand of a white person and after that immediately washed his own".

[58] On this, see Garzilli 1996a, and especially my Introduction (pp. i–xv) and my paper, Garzilli 1996b.

[59] After his death, in 1956, his library was sold by his wife and their two sons to the king for Rs. 300,000. Kesari Raj Pandey told me the exact figures of the transaction, but did not know the exchange rate applicable at the time of the sale. However, he told me that he went to the USA in 1961, and 1 US$ was exchanged with 7 Rs. Therefore, at the same exchange rate, the price of Hem Raj's library would be some US$ 40,000, which would be equivalent to some 200,000 US$ in year 2000.

[60] Dvij Raj Pandit became Royal Preceptor after the death of his brother Nagendra (whose elder son was Hem Raj's father Lok Raj) and held the post from 1878 to 1895. He had three sons, Chandra Raj Pandit, Bhim Raj Pandit and Kubalay Raj. The latter was the Royal Preceptor from 1895 to 1910, when he was forced to resign. He lived in exile in Bombay, making a fortune by investing in the Indian stock market. He was in fact studying English with a tutor, while the study of English was strictly forbidden to the Raj Guru family. The then

Raj was used to formality, and to being treated in an extremely respectful way. This is essential to understanding certain peculiarities in the language of the letter, including the normal use of the third plural person whenever he is being addressed. Lévi asked for Hem Raj's help to go to Nepal to study, since he needed the permission of Chandra Shamsher, and Hem Raj was probably the person whom Chandra trusted most.

In short, from these few examples is clear that we must know not only the *realia* of the letters, but also the situation of the time and the relationships between our authors in order to understand their correspondence.

Both the manuscripts of the *Viṃśatikā* and the *Triṃśikā* mentioned in this letter were given to Lévi by Hem Raj, to whom the book *Vijñaptimātratāsiddhi* is dedicated.[61] The *Vijñaptimātratāsiddhi* includes the *Viṃśatikā* with a short commentary of Vasubandhu and the *Triṃśikā* with a commentary of Sthiramati.[62]

Prime Minister Chandra Shamsher Rana, who followed Bir Shamsher Rana (who was Prime Minister in 1885–1901), and Dev Shamsher Rana (whose prime minister-ship in 1901 lasted only 114 days since he was dismissed in a coup d'état by his brother Chandra) did not like Kubalay Raj. One of the reasons for that was that Kubalay had studied English and this, according to Chandra, was immoral. Another reason was his supposed curiosity about Chandra's English books. In fact, while on duty, Kubalay used to pick them up from Chandra's study racks. These books were marked by Chandra with red ink and a complaint was made against Kubalay that he used to look at the red marked portions in Chandra's absence. He was accused of being too curious and this was his big sin, in a country where libraries, as well as literacy, and cultural and political information, were forbidden to public. Kubalay was unable to tolerate Chandra's pressure and left Nepal forever, living the rest of his life in Bombay (see Asoj 2030, cited in Raj 1978: 18, fn. 1.

[61] Lévi 1925, Introduction (pp. x and xvi).

[62] On the "idealism of Vasubandhu" as taught in the *Viṃśatikā* and the *Triṃśikā*, see a forgotten paper by one of the most important philosophers belonging to the Bengali *intelligentsia* of the first half of the 20th century, Das Gupta 1928. Das Gupta was a friend of Kalidas Nag and of the Italian Indologist and Tibetanologist Giuseppe Tucci, who made use of him to make propaganda abroad to the Fascist Regime. Cf. Garzilli 2012.

This is Lévi's description of Hem Raj and his discovery of the *Viṃśatikā* and the *Triṃśikā* in the introduction to his book *Vijñaptimātratāsiddhi*:

> The Government Library is placed under the control of an admirable savant who performs the high functions of Rāj Guru "spiritual director of the kingdom", "His Holiness" (as he is called) Hemāraj Śarmā. Born from a family originally from Kangra, educated in the schools of Benares, he has a brilliant mastery of Sanskrit; versed by profession in theology, familjar with all the subtleties and details of the science of grammar, he combines his sharp awareness of the real world and public affairs with the erudition of a pundit. I will sketch in another place the portrait of this strong personality; but here I want to express my gratitude for the help, which he has never ceased to provide me and which has never slackened since my departure from Nepal. I owe to him the discovery of my two texts. (p. xii)
>
> [...] The Rāj Guru, who after my departure did not cease to look for ancient manuscripts and to call attention to significant works, announced to me, among others things, the following discovery in a (p. xiii) letter dated February 24, 1924 … (p. xiv) (trans. E. Garzilli)[63]

[63] La Bibliothèque du Gouvernement est placée sous le contrôle d'un savant admirable qui exerce les hautes fonctions de Rāj-Guru 'directeur spirituel du royaume', 'Sa Sainteté' (comme on l'appelle) Hemrāj Śarmā. Issu d'une famille originaire du Kangra, formé aux écoles de Bénarès, il possède une maîtrise éblouissant du sanscrit; versé par profession dans la théologie, familier avec toutes les finesses et les subtilités de la science grammaticale, il joint à l'érudition d'un pandit le sens aigu des réalités et des affaires publiques. J'aurai à tracer ailleurs le portrait de cette personnalité vigoureuse; mais ici je dois lui exprimer ma reconnaissance pour le concours qu'il n'a jamais cessé de me prêter et qui ne s'est point ralenti depuis mon départ du Népal. C'est a lui que je dois la découverte de mes deux textes.

[...] Le Rāj-Guru qui n'avait pas cessé depuis mon départ de poursuivre la recherche des anciens manuscrits et de me signaler les trouvailles de valeur, par une (p. xiii) lettre datée du 24 février 1924, m'annonçait entre autres la découverte suivante ... (Lévi 1925 : xiii–xiv)

7. COPY OF THE ORIGINAL LETTER

Recto

पारिसनगरात्, २९ मार्च १९२४

श्रीः

हे सुहृच्छ्रेष्ठ ! विद्वद्वर्य !

भवदीयं लेखं पश्यता मयामृतमिव पीतं, भूयो ऽपि पठता। अक्षराणां हि रूपं मनोहरं चक्षुषोर् आमोदम् आधत्ते। वाक्यानाम् अर्थो चेतःप्रीणीकरोति। स चार्थो ऽत्यन्तं प्रीतिवर्धनः। न हि केवलं गतस्य दूरदेशं सुहृदः स्मरणं ध्रियते किं तु तदुद्देशेनपुस्तकानि बहुशः प्र- भवता कृताः। तेषां चाविर्भूतानि फलानि कौतूहलं विस्मयम् आनन्दं प्रेम संदीपयन्ति।

प्रोषिते हि मयि लब्धा ये ग्रन्थास् ते प्रायो ऽपि श्रुतपूर्वनामधेया विनष्टमूलका इव बभूवुः। तेषामन्तरे प्रथमकार्यक्रमेण विंशतिकाभाष्यम्। त्रिंशिकाभाष्यं प्राणं भवतः प्रसादात् प्राप्तम्। अद्यतनस्य अनुवादौ। प्रकरणेषु बहुसंपन्नेष्वपि त्रिंशिका निस्तरा विंशिकादि पृष्ठतश्च ग्रन्थान्तरे विंशिका। इति बौद्धाचार्यपरंपरया देशितम्। उभयोरपि प्रकरणयोर् अनुवादौ रचितौ द्विधा चीनभाषायां च भोटभाषायां च। तदनुवादसंप्रयोगेन मूलस्यापो- ऽविशुद्धस्य वा यदि वा किंचिद् त्रुटितस्य मुक्तं ऽपि विशदीभवति। तस्माद् एष मे ऽभिप्रायः श्री३ महाराजस्यानुज्ञया यदि भवान् पुस्तकस्य प्रतिरूपकं संपादयितुम् अर्हति यथा त्रिंशिकाभाष्यस्य तथा विंशिकाभाष्यस्यापि संस्कृतमूलं प्रकाशयिष्यामि भोटानुवादसहितं चीनभाषानुवादसंयुक्तं च।

कर्मविभङ्गग्रन्थमालायाः तथैव प्रार्थना क्रियते। भवता हि लिखितं पूर्वं प्राप्त-

२८

Verso

महाकर्मविभङ्गग्रन्थः प्राप्तो ऽस्मिन् संवदति " इति।

पत्रकारादीनां सर्वेषाम् अन्येषां पुस्तकानां दर्शनं बाढम् अभीप्सते। विशेषतस्तु तदन्तरे द्वयोरेव प्रकीर्णतालपत्रावलिविषये संगृहीतयोः ५ (II–III) संख्याङ्कितयोर् आर्यदेवविरचितयोः एकस्य नाम बौद्धधर्मश्लोकसंग्रह इति। इतरस्य तु प्रतिपत्तिसारशतकम्। प्रतिरूपककरणं पुनर् दीर्घकालिकं [illegible] भवेद् धनव्ययपीडाकरं विपुलव्ययान्वितं च। तत्र क उपायः ?। भवान् प्रमाणम्। अपि विधेद् आनुकूल्येन शक्यं भवेद् भवद्देशागमनं प्रियतदर्शनं च तालीपुस्तकसंसंनिकटे च प्रियालापयपि ग्रन्थानां पर्यालोचनम्!

यानि पूर्वं पुस्तकापणिकैर् विक्रेयपुस्तकानां सूचीपत्राणि प्रकाशितान्यभवन् तान्याधुनिकानि तानि न प्रकाश्यन्ते। अपरं च दीनाराणां प्रतिदेशम् अनित्यार्घत्वात् मूल्यं निकारम् अभिरत उपैति। यानि तु तादृशानि मुद्रितपूर्वाणि लभ्यन्ते लप्स्यन्ते वा तान्य् अभिलष्य संचित्य च एकत्र प्रेषयिष्यामि। इयं मे प्रतिज्ञा।

सर्वस्य कुटुम्बस्य कुशलं वर्तते। एवं च भवतः सकुटुम्बस्य भूयादित्याशंसा।

भवदीयः

29

8. TRANSLITERATION

[1]

parisa-nagarāt, 29 marca 1924

śrīḥ

he suhṛc-chreṣṭa! *vidvad-agra!*

bhavadīyaṃ lekhaṃ paśyatā mayāmṛtam iva pītaṃ, bhūyo 'pi paṭatā. akṣarāṇāṃ hi rūpaṃ manoharaṃ cakṣuṣīr āmodaṃ ādhatte, vākānāṃ arthaṃ cottānīkaroti. sa cārtho 'ty antaṃ prīti-vardhanaḥ. na hi kevalaṃ gatasya dara-deśaṃ suhṛdaḥ smaraṇaṃ dhriyate; kiṃ tu tad icchā-saṃpūraṇārthaṃ bahudāḥ prayatnā bhavatā kṛtāḥ. teṣāṃ cāvir bhūtāni phalāni kautūhalaṃ vismayam ānandaṃ prema saṃpoṣayanti.

proṣite hi mayi labdhā ye granthās te prāyo 'pi śruta-pūrvanām adheyā vinaṣṭa-mūlakā iva babhūvuḥ. teṣām antare prathama-kalpikam[64] *eva viṃśaṭikābhāṣyam. triṃśikābhāṣyaṃ prāg bhavataḥ prasādāt prāptam. bhadantasya vasubandhoḥ prakaraṇeṣu bahu-saṃmateṣv api triṃśikā niruttarā viśiṣyate pṛṣṭhataś ca svacchāntare*[65] *viṃśikā iti bauddhācārya-paraṃparayā deśitam. ubhayor api prakaraṇayor anuvādo racito dvidhā, cīna-bhāṣāyāṃ ca bhoṭa-bhāṣāyaṃ ca, tad-anuvāda-saṃprayogeṇa mūlasyārtho 'viśuddhasya vā yadi vā kiṃcit truṭitasya sukaraṃ viśadī bhavati. tasmād eṣa me 'bhiprāyaḥ śrī3 mahā-rājasyānujñayā yadi bhavāt pustakasya pratirūpakaṃ saṃpādayitum arhati yathā triṃśikā-bhāṣyasya tathā viṃśikā-bhāṣyasyāpi saṃskṛta-mūlaṃ prakāśa-yiṣyāmi bhoṭānuvāda-sahitaṃ phranca-bhāṣānuvāda-saṃyuktaṃ ca.*

karma-vibhaṅga-grantham āsādya tathaiva-prārthanā kriyate. bhavatā hi likhitaṃ pūrva-prāpta-[2] *mahā-karma-vibhaṅga-granthaḥ prāyo 'smin saṃvadati iti.*

---

[64] Read *kalpitam* instead of *kalpikam*.

[65] Read *svalpāntare* instead of *svacchāntare*.

pañcakārādīnāṃ[66] *sarveṣāṃ anyeṣāṃ pustakānāṃ darśanaṃ bāḍham, abhīṣyate viśeṣatas tu tad antare dvayor eva prakīrṇa-tāla-patrāvali-paryāye saṃgṛhītayīḥ 5 (ii–iii)*[67] *saṃkhyāṅkitayor āryadeva-viracitayo[r] ekasya nāma bauddha-dharma- śloka-saṃgraha iti, itarasya tu pratipatti-sāra-śatakam; pratirūpaka-karaṇaṃ punar dīrgha-kālikaṃ bhavet hasta-citta-pīḍākaraṃ vipula-vyayātvitaṃ ca. tatra ka upāyaḥ? bhavān pramānaṃ. api vidher ānukūlyena śakyaṃ bhaved bhavad-deśa-gamanaṃ priya-jana-darśanaṃ ca rājñī-puṣkari[n] saṃnikaṭe ca priyāṇām api granthānāṃ paryālocanam.*

yāni pūrvaṃ pustakā-paṇikair vikreya pustakānāṃ sūcī-patrāṇi prakāśitāny abhavan(n) ādhunik[ā]lān na prakāśyante. aparaṃ ca dīnārāṇaṃ pratideśam

anityārghatvan mūlyaṃ vikāram avirata[m] upaiti; yāni tu tādṛśāni mudrita-pūrvāṇi labhyante lapsyante vā tāny anviṣya saṃcitya ca paścā[t] preṣayiṣāmi. iyaṃ me pratijñā.

sarvasya kuṭumbasya kuśalaṃ vartate. evaṃ ca bhavataḥ sa-kuṭumbasya bhūyād ity āśasā.

bhavadīyaḥ

Sylvain Levi

---

66 Read *pañcakramādīnāṃ* instead of *pañcakārādīnāṃ*.

67 In Roman numbering in the text.

8. TRANSLATION

[1]

From the city of Paris, March 29, 1924

Venerable

O best of friends! Most eminent of scholars![68]

I have seen your letter, drunk it like ambrosia, [and] I read it once more.

In fact the charming shape of [your] characters brings joy to [my] eyes, and the meaning of [your] words makes them open wide and (that meaning) greatly increases [that] joy. In fact, not only the memory of [your] friend,[69] gone to a distant country, is kept, but Your Holiness has made generous efforts in order to fulfill his[70] wishes! And their[71] visible fruits increase [my] curiosity, amazement, joy, affection.

---

[68] I have translated the honorific titles applied to Hem Raj, which Lévi uses in the third person plural as a sign of respect, according to the most probable use in Nepal at the beginning of the century. Cf. Garzilli 2001: 148, fn. 131. In this letter *bhavat* is translated as "Your Holiness", as Lévi acknowledges Hem Raj in the Introduction to the *Vijñaptimātratāsiddhi*. Honorific titles for Śrī3 Mahārāja3 (meaning 'The Three-time-venerable Maharaja') are translated as "His Highness" or "Prime Minister", and for the king as "His Majesty". For the use of all these words, see Sen & Mishra 1951: 48 (document 20) and 116 (letter to the Raj Guru of Nepal by the Indian king of Udayapattana, Śardāra Siṃha Deva, where the Raj Guru is always addressed with *śrīmat* and *śrī*, which are translated as "Your Holiness").

I have put in square brackets what I added to a better understanding of the text, and in parenthesis what I thought redundant. Punctuation is freely rendered, although I tried as much as possible to adhere to the original text.

I should like to thank the excellent Sanskritist Roberto Donatoni, who has been so patient as to read my translation of Lévi's letter and make precious suggestions.

[69] I.e., Lévi himself.

[70] = Lévi's.

[71] I.e., the fruits of those efforts.

In fact in my absence [you] have found those books, whose titles have been commonly heard before, [but] were as if [their] originals had disappeared. Among them the foremost composition is indeed the *Viṃśatikābhāṣya*. I have earlier obtained the *Triṃśikābhāṣya* by the favor of Your Holiness. Many also agreed that of the commentaries of the revered[72] Vasubandhu, the *Triṃśikā* has no superior,[73] and the *Viṃśatikā* comes close behind. This has been shown by the lineage of Buddhist teachers. And the translation of both commentaries has been composed in two parts, in Chinese and also in Tibetan, and by uniting the translation (of the meaning) of the [two] original[s], either unedited or fragmentary, it becomes easy to make [it] clear. Because of that, this is my plan: if, with the permission of the Maharaja3[74], Your Holiness is allowed to make produce copy of the book[75], just as [was done] with the *Triṃśikābhāṣya*, in such a way also of the *Viṃśatikābhāṣya*, I will display [in my book] the original Sanskrit together with the Tibetan translation, combined with the translation into French as well.[76]

Having obtained the book *Karmavibhaṅga*,[77] thus a prayer is made. In fact it is written by Your Holiness that the book **[2]**

---

[72] *Bhadanta* is a term of respect applied to a Buddhist.

[73] Literally, the *Triṃśikā* is distinguished [as having] no superior.

[74] Chandra Shamsher.

[75] I.e., the MS of the *Viṃśatikābhāṣya*.

[76] Vasubandhu (ca. 4th century CE), one of the great Yogācārins' teachers, wrote these two classical treatises on idealism. The discovery of the Sanskrit originals of the *Viṃśatikā* with the author's commentary, and the *Triṃśikā* with the commentary of Sthiramati, is attributed to S. Lévi. He edited them from Sanskrit for the first time (*Vijñāpatimatratāsiddhi*, cit.). The *Viṃśatikā* with the author's commentary has been translated into French from the Tibetan by Louis de La Vallée Poussin (1912). In this letter looks as if Lévi attributed both commentaries to the *Viṃśatikā* and the *Triṃśikā* to Vasubandhu.

[77] The *Karmavibhaṅga* or *Mahākarmavibhaṅga* is a book different from the *Karmavibhaṅgasūtra*. An enlarged version of the *Majjhimanikāya* no. 135 (one of the collections of the *Suttapiṭaka* of the Pāli Canon that was compiled in the period shortly before Aśoka) called *Cūlakammavibhaṅga*, which also exists in the Chinese *Madhyamāgama* and in two other recensions, is the *Mahākarmavibhaṅga*, discovered by S. Lévi in a Nepalese manuscript, which most probably

Mahākarmavibhaṅga, which previously arrived, largely coincides with this.

I strongly look for inspecting all the other books of Pañcakrama[78] and so on, but especially, among them, the two collected indeed in the synonym collection of mixed palm leaves that carries the number 5 (II–III)[79], composed by Āryadeva – one called the *Bauddhadharmaślokasaṃgraha*, but the other *Pratipattisāraśataka*. To make a copy again takes a long time, it would afflicting mind and hands, and would be very expensive. What is [our] means of salvation (*upāyaḥ*) in this case? The authority (*upāyaḥ*) [on it] is Your Holiness.[80] Also, in conformity with the law,[81] it could be possible to go to the country of Your Holiness and to bask in the vision of [Your] Dear Person and to browse the beloved books [kept] in proximity of the Pound of the Queen.[82]

Those indices [that] were printed to be sold again through booksellers,[83] (almost) recently are not being published. Moreover exchange rates vary in different areas, [and] price[s] are continuously changing. But I am obtaining or [soon] will those that have already been printed; afterwards, after collecting [them], I will send [them to you] those desired. This I promise you.

---

was given to him by Hem Raj, as this letter suggests. See *Annual Bibliography of Indian Archeology for the Year 1929*, pp. 1ff. (See Winternitz 1972: 618).

[78] I read *Pañcakrama* instead of *Pañcakāra* (in the text). The *Pañcakrama* is a work attributed to Nagarjuna, which was translated by La Vallée Poussin (1896).

[79] Perhaps this is Hemarāja's numbering since after ca. 1970 his collection is marked no. 5 in the Archives.

[80] Lévi is apparently playing with technical Tantric language here, since *upāyaḥ* ('means of salvation') and *pramānam* (literally, 'means of knowledge') are often used by Abhinavagupta, whose *Tantrasāra* Hem Raj read with Giuseppe Tucci, and other famous Tantric teachers.

[81] It was forbidden to foreigners to visit or transit Nepal without the permission of the Prime Minister.

[82] The Pond of the Queen or *Rājñīpuṣkari* is now called *Rāṇipokharī* or Pond of the Female of the Rāṇi family. The Queen of Nepal (as well as the Prime Minister) usually belongs to the Rāṇi family. The pond is located near the Royal Library (and present Royal Palace), where Lévi and Hem Raj used to meet.

[83] *Paṇika*, the word used by Lévi, literally means 'beggar'.

All in [my] family are well. And indeed I hope that [this] might be [true] as well of the family of Your Holiness!

Yours,

Sylvain Lévi

REFERENCES

ACHARYA DIKSHIT, Rammani, n.d. *Gorkha vyākakaraṇa bodha*. Kathmandu [V.S. 196?]

—— 2029. *Purāṇa samjhana*. Kathmandu: Nalinidevi Acharya Dikshit (V.S. 2029).

Annual Bibliography of Indian Archeology for the Year 1929. Leiden: Kern Institute, 1931.

ASOJ, Sāun Bhadau 2030. Nayarājajyūko ciṭṭhī. *Nepālī* V.S. 2030.

BHANDARY, Adya Charan Raj, n.d. *The Coronation Book of Their Majesties of Nepal*. Kathmandu [1955?].

BLOCH, Jules 1935. Obituary of Lévi. *L'univers Israél*, Nov. 9, 1935.

BONGARD-LEVIN, Grigorij M., Roland LARDINOIS & Aleksej VIGASIN (eds.) 2002a. *Correspondances orientalistes entre Paris et Saint-Pétersbourg (1887–1935)*. (Mémoires de l'Académie des Inscriptions et Belles-Lettres, 26.) Paris: Boccard.

BONGARD-LEVIN, Grigorij M., Roland LARDINOIS & Aleksej VIGASIN 2002b. Deux indianistes dans la cité. Portraits croises de Sylvain Lévi (1863–1935) et de Sergej F. Ol'denburg (1863–1934). *Académie des Inscriptions et Belles-Lettres: Comptes rendus des séances de l'année 2002*, Avril–Juin: 707–725.

DAS GUPTA, Surendra Nath 1928. Philosophy of Vasubandhu in Viṃśatikā and Triṃśikā. *The Indian Historical Quarterly* 4(1): 36–43.

FORMICHI, Carlo 1934. *Il Nepal. Conferenza tenuta all'"Augusteo" di Roma il 26 febbraio 1934-XII*. Roma: Reale Accademia d'Italia, 1934-XII. (Republished in: *India Pensiero e Azione* [Biblioteca di scienze moderne, 135]: 321–337. Milano: Fratelli Bocca Editori, 1944).

FOUCHER, Alfred 1937. Lettre sur Sylvain Lévi. In: *Sylvain Lévi et son œuvre*, (Bulletin de la Maison franco-japonaise, 8.2–4 [1936]): 4.

GARZILLI, Enrica 1987. Lo *strīdharma* nei *dharmaśāstra*. *Annali della Facoltà di Lettere e Filosofia della Università degli Studi di Perugia* 25 (nuova serie 11 [1987–88]): 11–26. Perugia: Sezione Studi Classici.

—— 1990. The *strīdharma* in the *dharmaśāstras*: The difference between *svadharma* and *strīdharma*, and the *strīsvabhāva*. *Annali della Facoltà di Lettere e Filosofia della Università degli Studi di Perugia* 28 (nuova serie 14): 149–165. Perugia: Sezione Studi Classici.

—— (ed.) 1996a. *Translating, Translations, Translators. From India to the West* (Harvard Oriental Series, Opera Minora, 1.) Cambridge, Mass: Dept. of Sanskrit and Indian Studies, Harvard University.

—— 1996b. One birth from the encounter between text and translator, and the non-other: The translation of the *Spandasaṃdoha* of Kṣemarāja. In: E. Garzilli (ed.), *Translating, Translations, Translators: From India to the West* (Harvard Oriental Series, Opera Minora, 1): 11–23. Cambridge, Mass.: Dept. of Sanskrit and Indian Studies, Harvard University.

—— 1997. *Strīdhana*: To have and to have not. In: E. Garzilli (ed.), *Journal of South Asia Women Studies: Collected Issues – 1995–1997*: 31–49. Milan: Asiatica Association.

—— 2000. Brief Communication. *Indo-Iranian Journal* 43: 197–198.

—— 2001. A Sanskrit letter written by Sylvain Lévi in 1923 to Hemarāja Śarmā along with some hitherto unknown biographical notes (Cultural nationalism and internationalism in the first half of the 20th century: Famous Indologists write to the Raj Guru of Nepal – no. 1). In: A. Wezler (ed.), *Commemorative Volume for 30 Years of the Nepal-German Manuscript Preservation Project*. (*Journal of the Nepal Research Centre* 12 [Kathmandu]): 115–149.

—— 2012. *L'esploratore del Duce. Le avventure di Giuseppe Tucci e la politica italiana in Oriente da Mussolini a Andreotti (Con il carteggio di Giulio Andreotti)*, I. [The Explorer of The Duce. The Adventures of Giuseppe Tucci and the Italian Politics in the East. Including the Correspondence with Giulio Andreotti]. Roma: Asiatica Association.

—— forthcoming a. *Sanskrit, English and Nepali Letters between K. Bahadur K. C., V. Bhattacarya, C. Formichi, S. Lévi, S. Murti, R. Sankrityayan, B. Sharma, G. Tailang, G. Tucci, V. Suktankar, F. W. Thomas and the Royal Preceptor of Nepal, Hemraj Sharma in 1923–1953.* (Book in preparation.)

—— forthcoming b. A Sanskrit letter written by Carlo Formichi in 1933 to Hemarāja Śarmā along with his comprehensive biography (Cultural nationalism and internationalism in the first half of the 20th century: Famous Indologists write to the Raj Guru of Nepal – no. 3). (In preparation.)

Hommage à Sylvain Lévi pour le centenaire de sa naissance (1963). Conférences par Luciano Petech, Étienne Lamotte, Paul-Émile Dumont [à l'Institut de civilisation indienne]. Paris: Éditions E. de Boccard, 1964.

LA VALLÉE POUSSIN, Louis de (trans.) 1896. *Pañcakrama: études et textes tantriques*, (Recueil de travaux publiés par la faculté de philosophie et lettres, 16.) Gand: H. Engelcke – Louvain: J.-B. Istas.

—— 1912. Viṁśakakārikāprakaraṇa: traité des vingt ślokas, avec le commentaire de l'auteur. *Le Muséon* 1912: 53–90.

LEFÈVRE, Frédéric 1925. *Une heure avec* ... Troisième série: MM. Ferdinand Ossendowski, Henri Brémond, A. Meillet [etc.]. (Les documents bleus, 25.) Paris: Librairie Gallimard.

LÉVI, D. 1925. *Dans l'Inde (de Ceylan au Népal)*. Paris: F. Rieder et cie.

LÉVI, Sylvain 1898. *La Doctrine du sacrifice dans les Brâhmanas*. (Bibliothèque de l'École des hautes études, Sciences religieuses, 11.) Paris: E. Leroux.

—— 1905–08. *Le Népal. Étude historique d'un royaume hindou*, I–III. (Annalès du Musée Guimet: Bibliothèque d'études, 17–19.) Paris: Ernest Leroux.

—— 1923. Communication. *Journal Asiatique* 203: 359.

—— 1924. L'Asie nouvelle. *La Géographie – Bulletin de la société de géographie* 41.

—— 1925. *Vijñaptimātratāsiddhi. Deux traités de Vasubandhu: Viṁśatikā et Triṁśikā*. Paris: Librarie Ancienne Honoré.

MASCHINO, Marcel & Nadine STCHOUPAK 1937. Rétrospective: l'œuvre complet de Sylvain Levi [bibliography by M. Maschino] + Index [by N. Stchoupak]. In: *Bibliographie bouddhique* VII–VIII (Mai 1934–36). Paris : P. Geuthner.

NAKAMURA, Hajime 1987. *Indian Buddhism. A Survey with Bibliographical Notes*. Delhi: Motilal Banarsidass.

NEPAL, Gyan Mani 2057. *Paṃ. Hemarāja Śarmā: unakā kṛti ra samīkṣā*. Kathmandu: Mahendra Sanskrit University (V.S. 2057).

New Catalogus Catalogorum. An Alphabetical Register of Sanskrit and Allied Works and Authors. Madras: University of Madras 1949–.

PANT, Naya Raj 2019. Upodghāta. In: D. Vajrācārya *et al.* (eds.), *Itihāsa-saṃśodhanako pramāna-prameya*. Lalitpur: Jadagambā prakāśana (V.S. 2019).

People's Review. A Political and Business Weekly. Jan. 18 – Jan. 24, 2001.

PRADHAN, Mira 1999. *Candrikā vyākaranako bhāṣāvaijñānik adhyayan*. Kathmandu: Vidvacchiromaṇi Hemarāja Puraskār Guthī.

Pratipattisāraśataka [of Āryadeva], *go bar byed pa snying po brgya pa*, Sde-dge, Tohoku catalog 2334 (*rgyud 'grel* ZHI 278b1–283a2), Peking 4695 (*rgyud 'grel*, PHU 152a8–157b6 (vol. 82).

Pūrṇimā 21(3) (= no. 83). Kathmandu: Samśodhana Maṇḍala, V.S. 2048.

PUSALKER, Achut Dattatraya 1955. *Studies in the Epics and Purāṇas*. Chaupatty, Bombay: Bharatiya Vidya Bhavan.

RAJ, Prakash A. 1978. *Vidvacchiromaṇi Hemarāj Śarmā (jīvanī)*. Kathmandu: Raj.

—— 1994. *Portraits & Photographs from Nepal*. Kathmandu: Hillside Press.

—— 2030. Motīrāmko ciṭṭhī. *Gorkhapatra* V.S. 2030, Asoj (Sept.–Oct.): 13.

RENOU, Louis (ed.) 1937a. *Mémorial Sylvain Lévi*. Paris: Paul Hartmann.

—— 1937b. Sylvain Lévi et son œuvre scientifique. In: L. Renou (ed.), *Mémorial Sylvain Lévi*: xi–li. Paris: Paul Hartmann.

SEN, Surendranath & Umesha MISHRA 1951. *Sanskrit Documents. Being Sanskrit Letters and Other Documents Preserved in the Oriental Collection at the National Archives of India*. Allahabad: (on behalf of the National Archives of India by the) Ganganatha Jha Research Institute.

SHARMA, Hem Raj 1935. Some reflections on the Mahābhārata. *ABORI* 16(3–4): 212–231.

—— (ed.) 1995. *Kāśyapasaṃhitā*. Bombay: Tadavji T. Acharya, Kalbadevi Rd. (V.S. 1995). (2nd ed.: *Kāśyapasaṃhitā: Vṛddhajīvakīyaṃ tantraṃ vā*. Vārāṇasī: Caukhambhā Saṃskṛta Saṃsthāna, 1953.)

—— 1969. *Candrikā: Gorkhabhāṣa-vyākaraṇa*. Kathmandu, V.S. 1969.

SONAM, Ruth & Geshe SONAM RINCHEN 1994. *Yogic Deeds of Bodhisattvas*. Ithaca: Snow Lion Publications.

TSUKAMOTO, K., Y. MATSUNAGA & H. ISODA 1989. Bongo Butten no Kenkyū, IV: Mikkyō Kyoten Hen [A Descriptive Bibliography of the Sanskrit Buddhist Literature: The Buddhist Tantra]. Kyoto: Heirakuji-Shoten.

WINTERNITZ, Moriz 1972. *A History of Indian Literature*, II. 2nd edition [1st ed. 1927]. New Delhi: Munshiram Manoharlal.

WITZEL, Michael 1986. Agnihotra-Rituale in Nepal. In: B. Kölver & S. Lienhard (eds.), *Formen kulturellen Wandels und andere Beitrage zur Erforschung des Himalaya*: 157–187. St. Augustin: VGH Wissenschafts-verlag.

—— 1992. Meaningful ritual: Structure, development and interpretation of the Tantric agnihotra ritual of Nepal. In: A. W. van den Hoek, D. H. A. Kolff & M. S. Oort (eds.), *Ritual, State and History in South Asia. Essays in Honour of J. C. Heesterman*: 774–827. Leiden: Brill.

WUJASTYK, Dominik 1998. *The Roots of Āyurveda. Selections from Sanskrit Medical Writings*. New Delhi: Penguin.

The Beginnings of Indology and Modern Historiography in India

KLAUS KARTTUNEN

1. BACKGROUND

There is no real shortage of brief histories, or even larger studies of the development of Indology, but the majority of them tend to give a somewhat one-sided picture. Thus, for instance, the work and career of its early British pioneers in Calcutta has been described very fully, and even when dealing with the 19th century, the histories tend to concentrate on the work done by Europeans. While I have myself done much work on the history of Western Indology, I intend here to consider the other side of the picture, the role of Indians themselves in the study of their own past.[1]

My title shows another aspect somewhat ignored in existing studies. The majority of classical Indologists are nowadays mainly concerned with religion and philosophy (and the rest with language and literature), but in the pioneering years of our field, history was rightly seen to be of foremost importance, next to the linguistic studies. Without history, everything in the past is just an unorganized mass.[2] We must remember that it was the work of early

---

[1] The first version of this article was read in the symposion *The reception of Western Values and Ideas in Asia*, held in Stockholm, 29–30 May, 1996. A much revised version was prepared and given as a lecture at the University of Bologna in March 2002. Margot Whiting has kindly checked my English.

[2] Too much and often quite useless speculation has been written about the supposed opposites of the Indian cyclical and the Western linear ideas of history.

Indologists in history that provided us with the chronological frame, in accordance with which we can arrange our studies of ancient India. The way of achieving at least somewhat reliable results in chronology was not an easy one. It went from the enthusiastically early dates of the pioneers to the over-criticism and exaggeratedly late dates in the second half of the 19th century.

It is an often repeated claim in Indological literature that history as a subject of literature and study was more or less completely missing in ancient India. Strictly speaking, this is not the whole truth. There are cases such as the Pāli chronicles, the Kashmir verse chronicles, the Vaṁśāvalīs of Orissa and Nepal, the panegyric Kāvya and many dynastic chronicles.[3] Nevertheless, it is true that these do not quite represent the same kind of tradition of historical scholarship as we find among the Greeks, Arabs and Chinese. These three have often been contrasted to the Indians and especially in earlier literature, this has been interpreted as a serious lack in Indian civilization and several unfavourable explanations were offered. Nowadays it is instead thought that a tradition of historical writing is by no means necessary for a civilization and it has been reasonably pointed out that we should try to explain its existence rather than its absence.[4] While the above-mentioned peoples tried to learn statecraft from history, Indians early developed statecraft into an independent science with a remarkable degree of generalization and theory unknown among their neighbours.[5]

The relative lack of history did also not mean any lack of chronological sense. It is here enough to point to the traditions of genealogy and legendary history as laid down in the epics and

---

The cyclical idea in India belongs to religion – and even here we have a clear historical tradition of doxography with *guruparaṁparās* – and cases of linear history will be soon pointed out.

[3] For a full survey of this literature, see Warder 1972, further Philips 1961.

[4] See Bechert 1969; Wezler 1993: 318ff.; from a different angle Thapar 1972.

[5] I have not forgotten Plato, Aristotle, Nizām al-Mulk, Machiavelli and Chinese legalists, but I think the palm as theoreticians still goes to ancient Indians.

Purāṇas. And although there were often no annals – and the knowledge of earlier history was completely shrouded in legends – the different eras were continuously used through many centuries and always calculated correctly.

However, while the relative ahistoricity of ancient India is certainly no vice, it is an important factor in the history of Indian historiography. Islamic rule in India imported the tradition of Arabic historiography, which soon grew much more important than the local chronicles in Sanskrit and modern Indian languages. There soon appeared important historical works in Arabic and Persian, but they always concentrated on the Muslim period and more or less ignored earlier times. Therefore, it also happened that the early Western historiography of India, in the few cases it was not content with its own colonial past, concentrated on Islamic times and was hardly aware of what had been before it.[6]

The historiography of ancient India, in its first beginnings in the late 18th century, had thus to start from almost nought, and it took a long time to build up something really coherent. As there was no reliable previous tradition on which to base further studies,[7] new methods were developed and the research was very closely connected with primary sources such as epigraphy and numismatics. We shall return to the details later on.

Classical Indology in the narrow sense, especially in its traditional form, is a philological study and this means that here the situation was completely different from history. Both in India and in the West, philology can boast exceptionally long traditions. The Western methods were developed in classical philology, originating in the Hellenistic school of grammarians in Alexandria in the

---

[6] Good examples are François Bernier in the 17th, Robert Orme in the 18th and Henry Miers Elliot in the 19th century. It is of no use to list here pure colonial histories; their range extends from Castanheda in the 16th to Mill in the early 19th century and beyond.

[7] Even now, the attempt to reconcile the historical legends of the Purāṇas with real history offers great problems, and it was impossible to build history solely from them. See L. Rocher 1986: 115ff.

third century BC, and already achieved high standards with the humanist scholars of the Renaissance.[8] The Indian tradition is still earlier, starting with Yāska (if not before him in the Brāhmaṇas) and other scholars of Vedic exegesis. Its further history is laid down in the long tradition of grammatical literature, lexicography, exegetical tracts and commentaries. The number of original Sanskrit works without any commentaries is meagre, indeed, and, in addition to explaining, the commentators often had an important role in fixing recensions of the texts they commented upon.

While the study of Indian history was started by the British using methods imported from Europe, philology – Indology – started as a teamwork between Indian pandits and Western scholars.[9] This is something that was – and even now is – often passed over in silence, as the results were generally, though not always, published under the name of the Western scholar alone. Nevertheless, until the middle of the 19th century, at least, almost every Western scholar of Indology working in India had a pandit with whom to collaborate. Though not often mentioned on title pages of books or articles, many of these pandits are also known by name and reputation.

In most cases, this relationship seems to have been fruitful and respectful. A case such as that of the over-credulous Wilford, who was fed by his pandit inauthentic records of the kind he was eagerly seeking, was clearly an exception.[10] In Europe, the unavailability of pandits was a serious disadvantage in the beginnings of Indology. There was for this some compensation derived from the much better knowledge of Western philological tradition and

---

[8] I am fully conscious of their shortcomings, too, but this is no place to discuss them.

[9] On the role of these pandits, see also Dodson 2007: 43ff.

[10] Colonel Francis Wilford (1771–1822) found the whole geography of Europe and Africa in these Pseudo-Purāṇic records. Hundreds of pages of the early numbers of the *Asiatick Researches* are filled with his ramblings, which, in addition to being unreliable source material, were even then methodically highly questionable.

methods than was found among the civil servants and officers working in India.[11]

2. ORIENTALISM AND LAW STUDIES

I have always found it difficult to see early Indology as Orientalism in the Saidian sense.[12] In the beginning, a scholar such as Sir William Jones was so deeply involved in an attempt to learn and understand, and to build up something corresponding to Graeco-Roman philology with Indian material, that it is difficult to explain him as a Saidian Orientalist. There was the preference for the classical period, true, but this was one of the weakest among Said's arguments. Such a preference was not just means of subjugation, but part of the Western intellectual framework of the period, well seen in contemporary Western philology and historiography (concentrating on classical antiquity) and many other fields of scholarship unconcerned with the East. We must also remember that on a political level, early Indology, though sometimes supported by the colonial elite, rather represented an opposition, which was then crushed in the 1830s. After that, there was a long period when the majority of Western Indologists came from countries with no political or economic interest in India.

However, the Saidian interpretation can at least be used in the case of the most practical side of early Indology, legal studies, which I shall discuss below. A still better parallel to the Saidian Orientalist can perhaps be found among early missionary scholars such as Carey and Ward, but in the purest sense, he is represented by a Western historian, such as James Mill, not interested in Indology and Indian civilization at all. A truly Saidian phase in

[11] In the 18th century, boys were often sent to India at the age of 14 or 15 to start their service from the bottom. A man such as Sir William Jones, who already was a scholar (of Greek and Arabic) of considerable repute when he came to India, was a rare exception.

[12] See Said 1978. In the case of early Indology, Dodson 2007: 52ff. is more useful reading.

Indology, if at all, we meet only in the post-1857 Victorian period. But even then, Indian scholars, though despised by some, had a much more important role in Indology than, for instance, Arab scholars in the development of contemporary Western Arabic studies.

A paper like this could not be written without mentioning Said. Now that I have, I can turn to a more interesting topic, the relationship between the Indian philological tradition of the pandits and Western scholarship. Such a relationship was not without antecedents in India. I can briefly refer to the work of translating Buddhist classics into Chinese and Tibetan and the long tradition of East Asian Siddham scholarship. A great number of Indian scholars going abroad and Chinese and Tibetan ones studying in India were involved in this work. Later on, Indian astronomy, mathematics, medicine and other sciences aroused the interest of Arab scholars and started the tradition of intellectual exchange culminating in al-Bīrūnī. The intellectual activity of Dārā Shikoh and a few other Mughal nobles led to a learned collaboration resulting in voluminous translations of Sanskrit literature into Persian. This translating work did not stop in the Mughal 17th century; it continued, and new Persian versions were still made in British Bengal in the second half of the 18th century. It seems to me that the role of these translations in early Indology has been somewhat neglected,[13] though with two major exceptions: the *Vivādārṇavasetu* translated by Halhed in his *Code of Gentoo Laws* (see below) and the Persian *Oupnekhat* translated by Anquetil-Duperron and read with so much enthusiasm by Schopenhauer. However, there were many other such translations and their manuscripts were purchased and studied by early scholars such as Halhed, Shore and Jones. This was the first contribution that traditional Indian scholarship gave to the beginnings of modern Indology.

---

[13] See, however, R. Rocher 1983, *passim* (see index s.v. Persian); Aliev 1986; Modi 1925. A number of such translations can be found listed in Hadi 1995.

Another method was direct collaboration and consulting. It was a myth of 18th-century Orientalism, which has somehow lingered and been carried on even into modern books, that the Brahmins categorically refused to teach their sacred language to foreigners.[14] There were perhaps some zealots, who refused, but there were more of those who had no time for such a thing – if somebody comes to me asking me privately to teach him or her Sanskrit, I would probably refuse – while those who were really interested in learning were, after all, a small fraction of the British working in India. Thus, it was not always easy for the student and master to find each other, but still the serious students usually found teachers and we do not hear of persecutions against the teachers afterwards. On the contrary, some of them seem to have been much respected as pandits and scholars. Even before the British period, some missionary scholars, such as Heinrich Roth, Johannes Ernst Hanxleden and Paulinus a Sancto Bartholomaeo, found teachers, and then Wilkins and Jones soon became rather famous for their knowledge of Sanskrit.

This brings us to the subject of law. According to the famous principle of the rising colonial empire, the Indians were to be ruled according to their own laws, i.e., the Muslims according to Islamic law and the Hindus according to Dharmaśāstra. The result was not always very happy[15] and the procedure contained difficulties we cannot take up here. In any case, the system offered employment to a great number of specialists of both legal traditions and, as it soon came out that some of these were ready to exploit the system for their own benefit, it soon became a major reason for the colonial government to acquire some direct information from the primary sources of the two legal traditions. The need to understand Islamic law thus motivated an early flourishing of Persian and Arabic

[14] Cf. Mukherji 1985: 43ff.

[15] An example of the problems involved is that the principle first led to a kind of sanction of suttee in some cases.

studies in Calcutta,[16] but here we are mainly interested in the Dharmaśāstra.

The first attempt to clear up things was the commission set up by Warren Hastings and consisting of eleven pandit lawyers who compiled the Sanskrit digest called the *Vivādārṇavasetu*. This was then translated into Persian by a munshi working for the East India Company and from Persian into English by Nathaniel Brassey Halhed.[17] The book was of great importance for the beginnings of Indology, but as a juridical handbook, it turned out something of a failure. There were soon new attempts at such a digest, now working directly from Sanskrit into English. One was headed by Jones himself and employed such scholars as Rādhākānta Śarmā Sarvoru Tewari and Jagannātha Tarkapañcānana.[18]

The work started by Jones, who also, with the help of his pandits, had translated the *Mānavadharmaśāstra* for the first time into English, was continued by others. This has been described in detail by historians of Indian law, like Duncan Derrett and Ludo Rocher. Here I would like to emphasize that the work included new Sanskrit works compiled by pandits for the benefit of European scholars. After the *Vivādārṇavasetu*, we can name the *Vivādasārārṇava* by Sarvoru Tewari[19] and the *Vivādabhaṅgārṇava* by Jagannātha Tarkapañcānana (together with several assistants).[20] Moreover, this

[16] It must be noted that the Arabic and Persian munshis collaborated with British students much in the same way as Sanskrit pandits and many of them were employed as teachers at the new College of Fort William in Calcutta. See Fück 1955: 135ff.

[17] See R. Rocher 1983: 48ff.; Dodson 2007: 48ff.

[18] See Mukherji 1985: 51f.

[19] Sarvoru Candra (or Śarmā) Tripāṭhī (Tewari) of Bihar. On him, see R. Rocher 1989: 630f. He was pandit to the Patna council, and from 1788 a member of Jones' legal committee, representing the Bihar legal traditions. The work was written in 1789 (Kane 1975: 1104). From 1794 he and Rādhākānta Śarmā were pandits of the Sadar Divali Adalat in Calcutta. Both were still there in 1802. (R. Rocher 1989: 632f.)

[20] Tarkapañcānana: Traditional dates for this famous Bengali Brahmin scholar of Triveni, 1695–1806, seem rather exaggerated, but this does not diminish his importance as a scholar and teacher. In another source (by Jones), his year of

activity was by no means restricted to legal studies. Much of Jones' knowledge of Hindu traditions and the Purāṇas came from Rādhā-kānta Śarmā's *Purāṇārthaprakāśa.*[21] In the first half of the 19th century, Rāja Rādhākānta Deva,[22] assisted by a number of pandits, compiled his large Sanskrit encyclopaedia, the *Śabdakalpadruma*, which even now can be consulted with much benefit.[23]

In fact, there are some precedents even for the system of pandits assisting Western scholars. In the 17th century, Abraham Roger, Heinrich Roth and Hendrik Adriaan van Rheede tot Drakenstein all had their assisting pandits,[24] and in the 18th century, in French

---

birth is given as 1704. See Kane 1975: 978ff.; Mukherji 1985: 52ff.; R. Rocher 1989: 631.

[21] Rādhākānta Śarmā Tarkavāgīśa, Jones' Radhacaunt (1703?–1803). According to Ludo Rocher (1986: 215f.), this pupil of Tarkapañcānana compiled the text at the request of Hastings in 1784. It was soon translated into Persian by Zūrāvār Singh and from Persian into English by Halhed (anonymously published in London in 1809, see R. Rocher 1983: 193). Jones got a copy of the Persian version in 1787 from John Shore and soon afterwards the original from the author, which he used for his "Essay on the Chronology of the Hindus" (*Asiatick Researches* 2 [1790, repr. 1799], pp. 111–147). See further Mukherji 1985: 50f.; R. Rocher 1989: 627.

[22] Deva (Deb; 1784–1867) was one of the founders of the Calcutta Hindu College and a pioneer of women's education. See Sen Gupta 1975 and the life sketch included in the *Śabdakalpadruma*.

[23] Though it is often true that the industry of Indian scholars was not appreciated to its full extent, we can point to the case of Deva to show that neither was it fully neglected. At the time of his death, he was not only a member of the Asiatic Society of Bengal, but also of the Société Asiatique (Paris), of the American Oriental Society and of the Academies of Berlin, St. Petersburg and Vienna.

[24] Roger (1609–1649) was a Dutch clergyman serving in South India and author of the posthumously published account which, *inter alia*, contains the Dutch translation of two of Bhartṛhari's Śatakas made with the help of a pandit. See also Sweetman 2003: 89ff. Roth (1610–1668) was a German Jesuit who studied Sanskrit in Agra and wrote a Sanskrit grammar in Latin. Van Rheede (1635–1691) was a Dutch colonial officer who compiled a great work about the plants of Kerala, also giving their Sanskrit and Malayalam names. This *Hortus Indicus Malabaricus* (I–XII, 1678ff.) is a rare work and I have never actually seen it (but it is now available as scanned in internet; see, e.g., https://archive.org/stream/HortusMalabaricus or http://leesmaar.nl/malabaricus/index. htm. According to Eichhorn (1807: 205), his Keralan assistant was called Itti-Aciuden (Itti-Acyutan).

Pondichéry Maridās Pillai was not only an assistant to several scholars but was himself known as a notable scholar.[25]

There were further pandits involved in the beginnings of British Indology. In Vārāṇasī, the Kashmirian Pandit Kāśīnātha[26] was the teacher of Charles Wilkins and acquainted with Jones. His protegé was Goverdhan Kaul[27] of Kashmir, who later assisted Jones in Indian chronology. Jones' first Sanskrit teacher had been Pandit Rāmlochan,[28] a learned physician, who taught at Nadia. Rādhākānta Śarmā (above), before Jones, assisted Warren Hastings and John Shore (later Lord Teignmouth), while Pandit Rādhācaraṇa[29] was behind the astronomical studies of Samuel Davis. In the early 19th century, Umākānta Tarkālaṅkāra[30] and Mṛtyuñjaya Vidyālaṅkāra[31] were willing to assist the Baptist missionaries of Serampore (Śrīrāmapura), and the help of Kamalakānta Vidyālaṅkāra[32] was in-

---

[25] Pillai or "Poullé" (1720?–1796) helped Le Gentil to study Indian astronomy and translated into French the Tamil *Bhāgavatapurāṇa*, published in 1788 in Paris. He kept a famous diary in Tamil.

[26] Kāśīnāth (Cashynath), like so often, there is very little information available about the lives of these early pandits.

[27] Govardhan Kaul. Kāśīnāth sent him to Calcutta to apply for the post of a pandit to the Supreme Court (Mukherji 1985: 46). He was nominated in 1786 and worked there until 1794 (R. Rocher 1989: 628, 632).

[28] Rāmlocan was a non-Brahmin Sanskrit scholar from Nadia. See Kejariwal 1988: 47; Mukherji 1985: 48f. It may be noted here that Rādhākānta, at the request of Jones, recommended the *Śakuntalā* as the best among the ancient plays and that the famous translation was then made by Jones with the help of Ramlochan. See Kejariwal 1988: 59; R. Rocher 1989: 629.

[29] Rādhācaraṇa of Varanasi was also connected with Jones (Mukherji 1985: 54).

[30] Tarkālaṅkāra hailed from the Nadia district of Bengal and came as pandit to Calcutta. His grandson was the famous philosopher Krishnachandra Bhattacharyya (1875/6–1949). See Bagchi 1967.

[31] M. Vidyālaṅkāra (Bidyalankar; 1762–1819) came from Orissa and was the Head Pandit ("Pundit") of the College of Fort William. He is also known as a pioneer of Bengali prose. See Kopf 1969: 112ff., 205ff.; Sen 1954: 746ff.

[32] K. Vidyālaṅkāra was the Sanskrit Librarian of the Asiatic Society and died in old age in 1843. According to H. W. Torrens (short obituary notice in JASB 12[2] [1843], pp. 1013f.), his "critical ingenuity and wonderful acumen ... supplied in our lamented friend, James Prinsep, the want of philological accuracy."

dispensable to James Prinsep in his famous epigraphical work. Rāmacandra Vidyābhūṣaṇa taught at Bishop's College, a Christian school in Calcutta, and collaborated with William Hodge Mill composing the Christian "Purāṇa" *Śrīkhṛṣṭasaṁgīta*, also known as *Khṛṣṭugītā*.[33]

3. INDOLOGY IN CALCUTTA

With the mention of epigraphy, we have returned to history. As an auxiliary discipline of history, epigraphy originated in the West in the 15th century, at the beginning concentrating on Greek and Latin inscriptions. In the 18th century, Semitic epigraphy was added to these – not to speak of the fantastic speculations devoted to Egyptian hieroglyphs and Mesopotamian cuneiform writing – but the first interest in Indian epigraphy only came with the beginnings of Indology, in the early years of the Asiatic Society. Several inscriptions were copied in different parts of India and sent to Calcutta, where Wilkins and Jones handed them over to pandits for interpretation. Here their help was especially needed: a command of Sanskrit that enables one to read the *Bhagavadgītā* and the *Hitopadeśa*, especially when a teacher is always available to explain the more difficult passages, is not sufficient in epigraphy. Palaeographical problems add here to the difficulty.[34]

The first epigraphical articles were published in the early numbers of the *Asiatick Researches*. Among the authors, Charles Wilkins is most often mentioned, but it is important to note that both Rāmlochan and Rādhākānta Śarmā became as independent scholars.[35] This was, however, an exception. These late 18th-century

[33] On Vidyābhūṣaṇa, see Young 1979: 219ff.

[34] See also Kejariwal 1988 and Salomon 1998: 199ff.

[35] A historical copper plate grant from Salsette was presented by Ramlochan in 1787 and published in the first volume of the *Asiatick Researches* (1788 [1798], pp. 357–367; see Kejariwal 1988: 50f.). In the next year, Rādhākānta presented his interpretation of the Firuz Shah Kotla Cāhamāna inscription (also published in the same volume, pp. 379–382; see Kejariwal 1988: 56f.). Cf. Salomon 1998: 202.

pandits did not know English and were not allowed to present their studies in the meetings of the Asiatic Society. There was a custom – which also affected many British non-members – that a study was only allowed to be presented by a member, and when it was published, the name of the presenting member, who perhaps contributed a few lines of introduction and a couple of footnotes, is given in the place where the modern reader is accustomed to find the real author. The volumes of the *Asiatick Researches* and the early numbers of the JASB offer numerous examples.

Later, too, epigraphy seems to have attracted Indian scholars. Although the glory of the decipherment of Brāhmī and Kharoṣṭhī goes to Prinsep, the history of Indian epigraphy already contains a great number of Indian names in the 19th century. We must here especially refer to the Bombay Asiatic Society, which comprised such famous names as Bhāu Dāji[36] and Bhagwanlāl Indraji.[37] They were both much appreciated as eminent epigraphists in India as well as in Europe.

In the early formative period in the 18th century, Indology had mainly concentrated on presenting information about ancient India in articles and translations. At the turn of the century the work of editing the original texts also began, and this has ever since been a field very much in hands of Indian scholars. In Calcutta, Colebrooke encouraged the munshis and pandits to edit Arabic, Persian and Sanskrit classics and many were published at public cost. Others appeared from Serampore Baptist Press and through the private printing houses, which soon multiplied in Calcutta. The number of these early Calcutta editions is remarkable,[38] and although there were still no critical editions, not even according to the standards of time, they had an important role in making classi-

[36] Daji (1821–1874), a Sarasvati Gond Brahmin from Goa, physician and epigraphist in Bombay. See Windisch 1921: 6f., and JASB 38 (1963, a memorial volume).

[37] Indraji (1839–1888), a Gujarati Brahmin from Junagadh. See Windisch 1921: 9ff., and JASB 55–59 (1981–84 [1986], a memorial volume).

[38] They were long ago listed by Gildemeister 1847.

cal Indian literature known and available, both in India and in the West.

Two major projects must be mentioned here. A committee of pandits compiled an extensive Sanskrit–English dictionary from lexicographical sources, which was edited by Horace Hayman Wilson and has been known ever since as "Wilson's Dictionary". It is surprising how much of modern Sanskrit lexicography goes back to this work. This is particularly true with the much used dictionaries of Monier Williams and Apte.[39]

The second project, the last of the pre-Macaulay period, resulted in the first printed edition of the entire *Mahābhārata*, which was published in four large volumes in Calcutta in the 1830s and is commonly known as the "Calcutta edition".

The new policy of education using English as a medium designed by Macaulay brought an abrupt change to this activity. In 1835, public funds were withdrawn from publications in Indian and Islamic languages and it was even demanded that the existing books were "to be sold as waste paper". But outside the narrow circle of politicians, the importance of text editions for scholarship, however, was not completely forgotten. Some were published in Europe, mainly in France and Germany, and many more in India by private Indian publishers. In 1848, the Asiatic Society in Calcutta again took the lead, founding the famous *Bibliotheca Indica* series, with Eduard Roer as the general editor.[40] But although Roer, Ballantyne,[41] Cowell and other Western Indologists were active, the major part of the work was again done by Indian scholars. In the

[39] In Monier Williams, many words are derived from Wilson and marked with "W" (thus referring to the lexicographical authority of the Bengal pandits), while Apte sometimes silently copies Wilson's explanations.

[40] In its early years, the series also contained many volumes of Arabic and Persian texts, but a change of policy in 1856 restricted it to Indian classics (mainly Sanskrit, but still some Persian included). A summary of the editing activities of the Society is found in Mitra 1885: 55ff. The German Roer (1805–1866) worked about twenty years as a teacher in Bengal.

[41] On James Robert Ballantyne (1813–1864) and his work at Benares Sanskrit College, see Dodson 2007: 94ff.

1880s, Rājendralāl Mitra[42] counted their contributions: Bhārata-candra Śiromaṇi[43] had edited 16 fascicles for the series and Jaya-nārāyaṇa Tarkapañcānana[44] and Maheśacandra Nyāyaratna[45] 19 fascicles each, while the prolific Pandit Satyavrata Sāmāśramī[46] had 44 and Mitra himself no less than 83 fascicles to his credit (Mitra 1885: 66).

When the Asiatic Society was founded in 1784, Jones had left open the question of whether Indian scholars should be accepted as members. To his credit, it must be said that, although it is not made quite clear, Jones himself seems to have been rather inclined to allow them, but in the end they were not accepted and the ban lasted until 1829.[47] Among the first Indian members accepted was Rāmkamal Sen,[48] a friend of Wilson and Prinsep, who then became the "Native Secretary" of the Society. At this time, however, there was already an attempt at independent Indian scholarship, appearing in the wake of the Bengal Renaissance. I have already mentioned Rāja Rādhākānta Deva and his great Sanskrit encyclopaedia. Rāja Rāmmohan Rāy,[49] though more a philosopher and religious reformer than a scholar, was a prolific author, who carried on an

---

[42] Mitra (1824–1891) was a lawyer and the librarian of the Asiatic Society in Calcutta. On him, see, e.g., Singh 2004: 322ff.

[43] Śiromaṇi, Pandit in Calcutta, died before 1879.

[44] Tarkapañcānana (Joynarayan Tarkapanchanan; 1806–1872), Pandit and Professor at Sanskrit College in Calcutta.

[45] Nyāyaratna (1836–1906), Pandit, Mahāmahopādhyāya, Professor at – and from 1882 Principal of – the Sanskrit College in Calcutta. He was a philosopher and Nyāya scholar, who attended the 9th International Congress of Orientalists in London in 1892.

[46] Sāmāśramī (1846–1911), a Vedic scholar born in Patna and educated in Varanasi. He lived many years in Calcutta and, in addition to his Bibliotheca Indica editions (not only Vedic texts), published many Vedic texts in his own printing press in Bengali script. See Vidyabhusana 1911.

[47] See Kejariwal 1988: 152f.; from Mitra (1885: 8) we learn that the credit of opening the Society to Indians goes to H. H. Wilson.

[48] Ram Comul Sen (1783–1844), a Bengali scholar and the grandfather of Keshab Chandra Sen. See Kopf 1969: 116ff.; Ray 1985.

[49] Rāy (Ram Mohun Roy; 1774–1833). There is no end to the literature about him.

important dialogue about the interpretation of Indian religious traditions, often leading to controversy either with traditional Hindus or Christian missionaries. After the Persian *Oupnekhat*, his publications were the first to open the Upaniṣads for Western scholars both in original text and English translation. Among the lesser names, we can cite Nīlaratna Hāldār,[50] Maharaja Kalikrishna Bahadur,[51] Tāranātha Tarkavācaspati,[52] Premacandra Tarkavāgīśa,[53] and Īśvaracandra Śarmā Vidyāsāgara.[54]

4. MAHARASHTRA

Many historians of Indology would have been more or less content with this, but there remains in fact an important question: When all this was happening in Calcutta, what was taking place in other parts of India? The simple answer is: More or less the same, but a few decades later and perhaps to a somewhat lesser degree. Nevertheless, this is certainly worth pursuing little further.

---

[50] Hāldār (Baboo Neelruttun Huldar): *Bohoodurson [Bahudarśan], or Various Spectacles, Being a Choice Collection of Proverbs and Morals in the English, Latin, Bengalee, Sanskrit, Persian, and Arabic Languages*. Serampore 1826. 2nd ed. 1830.

[51] Kalee Krishen Bahadur (1809–1874): *Miscellaneous Moral Maxims, Collected from Various Authors and Drawn up Alphabetically*. 38 p. in 12°. Serampore 1830; *The Neeti Sunkhulun or Collection of the Sanscrit Slokas of Enlightened Moonies*, in Bengali characters with a transl. 91 p. Serampore 1831; *The Vidvun-Moda-Taranginee or Fountain of Pleasure to the Learned*. 52 p. Serampore 1832. 2nd ed. with the text, Calcutta 1834.

[52] Tāranātha Tarkavācaspati Bhaṭṭācārya (1812–1885) was Professor of Grammar and Philosophy at Calcutta Sanskrit College and known as a lexicographer and editor.

[53] Tarkavāgīśa (Prem Chand Tarkabargis; 1806–1867) was Professor of Alaṅkāra at Calcutta Sanskrit College and much appreciated as a teacher. He published many text editions and for a while assisted Prinsep in his epigraphical studies.

[54] Vidyāsāgara (Bidyasagar; 1820–1891) was the Principal of Calcutta Sanskrit College from 1851. He published editions of Sanskrit texts, their Bengali translations, and independent works in Bengali. See Sen 1954: 830f.; Zbavitel 1976: 218f.

The second centre of British India was Bombay (now Mumbai).[55] In the 18th century, we hear hardly anything concerning Indology from Bombay – with the exception of some travellers visiting Elephanta Island – but in the first half of the 19th century, things went on more or less on the same lines as in Calcutta. A Bombay Literary Society was founded in 1804, with its own journal, and later (1827) it became affiliated with the Royal Asiatic Society (of London) and was known as the Bombay Branch of it; it is now the Bombay Asiatic Society. British scholars such as Vans Kennedy and Lancelot Wilkinson had their assistant pandits and in the 1830s Molesworth, supported by Government money, employed a team of pandits for his great Marathi dictionary.[56] I have already mentioned that the interests of the Bombay Society were much turned to history and epigraphy and soon there were also Indian scholars doing work on historical studies. In the very first volume, we encounter two epigraphical articles by Bāl Gaṅgādhar Śāstrī Jambhekar,[57] who also assisted George LeGrand Jacob in epigraphical studies. In the second half of the 19th century, the Bombay Society could boast of the first Indian scholar of really international standard. This was, of course, Rāmkṛṣṇa Gopāl Bhāṇḍārkar,[58] who widely surpassed Rājendralāl Mitra of Calcutta.

When we think about Maharashtra in the second half of the 19th century, we must not forget that several German Indologists were employed in important positions in the Bombay Educational Service. Most of them eagerly continued their chosen study, with much important help from and collaboration with local pandits and

---

[55] For the history of early Indian studies in Bombay, see also Windisch 1921.

[56] These pandits are listed and briefly presented by Sh. Gogate at the end of the biographical sketch of Molesworth appended to the new edition of the *Marathi–English Dictionary* (Poona 1975), pp. xv–xviii.

[57] Ball Gungadhar Shastree (1812–1846). The articles are in nos. 5 and 6, published in April and October 1843. The second volume also contains two contributions by him.

[58] Bhāṇḍārkar (1837–1925) was Professor of Sanskrit in Bombay and Pune. See, e.g., Windisch 1921: 11ff.; Dandekar 1976.

scholars. Martin Haug in Pune was the first to observe and describe Vedic Śrauta rituals. Georg Bühler organized the search for Sanskrit manuscripts extending as far as Kashmir, employing many Indian scholars and bringing to light a great number of half-forgotten Sanskrit and Prākrit works. Franz Kielhorn was active as an epigraphist and grammarian, always in close association with pandits.[59]

Before we move to the south, it must be noted that a kind of combination of the traditional pandit scholarship and modern Indology soon developed in many places. In a way, it can well be claimed that the pandits needed little more than the art of printing to develop a tradition of modern Sanskrit scholarship of their own. Combining the traditional commentarial method and modern textual criticism with the collating of manuscripts, and using Sanskrit as a medium, has continued until the present. Important and often high quality editions were published by the Nirṇaya Sāgara Press in Bombay, while Sri Venkateshwar Press concentrated on making the Purāṇas available in printed form. This is perhaps the best place to mention that at the end of the 19th century and the beginning of the 20th, new important centres of Indian studies developed in places such as Pune (with Ānandāśrama), Allahabad, Mysore, Madras, Kumbakonam and Trivandrum.

Alongside this pure Sanskrit scholarship of traditional pandits, there were also new developments. Rāmmohan Rāy was actually the first Indian scholar to use English for propagating his views. In the pre-1835 period, it was still feasible to use Indian languages (or Persian), but when English was accepted as the language of higher education, it soon also became that of modern scholarship even in Indology and a growing number of Indian scholars used it in their work. Bhandarkar and Mitra are perhaps the best examples. Government Service was a natural breeding ground for this new kind of scholarship. To take just two examples, the most famous

[59] Haug (1827–1876) was in India from 1859–66, Bühler (1837–1898) from 1863–80, and Kielhorn (1840–1908) from 1866–81.

Sanskrit lexicographer of the second half of the 19th century, Vāman Śivrām Āpṭe[60] in Pune, was a teacher, while the grammarian Ānandarām Baruvā[61] was a civil servant and lawyer.

The factors affecting scholarship and sometimes even deciding its contents often came from outside. Thus the ideology of nationalism was imported from the West and had nothing to do with Sanskrit learning and Indology, but it soon took root in India and this was also reflected in Indological studies. For a nationalist, a glorious past was indispensable and early Indology had in fact already revealed one to start with. We must here also take into account the general vein of the post-mutiny Victorian historiography of India, which often roughly belittled the Indian past – and this happened not only in the United Kingdom.[62] In this situation, the formation of a tradition of national historiography attempting to glorify the Indian past in every respect was completely natural, if not even necessary, as an answer. If names are needed, Romesh Chunder Dutt[63] in Calcutta was a pioneer, and Bāl Gaṅgādhar Tilak[64] in Maharashtra a kind of culmination, although we have still not seen the end of this development. Furthermore, even with all its exaggerations and biased claims, it seems to have been necessary and even useful. In addition to Tilak, the nationalist movement in Maharashtra also gave rise to Viśvanātha Kāśīnātha Rājawade,[65] the father of Maratha history.

---

[60] Apte (1858–1892) was Professor of Sanskrit and Principal of Fergusson College in Pune.

[61] Anundoram Borooah (1850–1889).

[62] Note Albrecht Weber's attempts to derive almost every original idea and important tradition of ancient India from Western influence. For a somewhat overstated account of the roots of nationalist history, see R. C. Majumdar in Philips 1961: 416ff.

[63] Rāmeśa Candra Datta (1848–1909) was one of the very first Indian members of the Indian Civil Service in 1871–97.

[64] Tilak (1856–1920), called Lokamanya, the famous nationalist politician. As a scholar, he became known for his theory of the 'Arctic Home of the Aryans', first proposed in 1893.

[65] Rājwade (1863–1927), a nationalist historian, who used many years locating, editing, and publishing primary sources for the history of the Marathas.

In the second half of the 19th century, there is no end to important names in Indological studies. We can note editors such as Pandit Durgāprasād,[66] Śivadatta,[67] Nārāyaṇ Bālkṛṣṇa Godabole and Kāśīnāth Pāṇḍuraṅg Parab,[68] lawyers such as Viśvanāth Nārāyaṇ Mandlik,[69] Trailokya Nāth Mitra[70] and Kāśīnāth Trimbak Telang,[71] historians such as Gaurīśaṅkar Hīrācand Ojhā.[72] The pioneers of Indian archaeological scholars were growing among the "native assistants" of the Archaeological Survey of India,[73] although the full-fledged scholars appeared only in the 1920s. Hurree Babu's anthropological interests had their counterpart in real life, too.[74]

The flourishing of studies did not only affect Hindus and Muslims. Though I am deliberately leaving out the development of Islamic studies in India – this is rather beyond my competence and in any case would need separate treatment – I would like here to mention some culturally important minorities, who, being outside

---

[66] Durgāprasād was one of the "pandits attached to the court of the Maharaja of Jeypore", i.e, Jaipur.

[67] Pandit Śivadatta was the Head Pandit of the Sanskrit Department at Lahore Oriental College.

[68] While the names Godbole and Parab are familiar enough, it seems difficult to find any information about them.

[69] Mandlik (1833–1889), a lawyer in Bombay, also taught at the University of Bombay. See Windisch 1921: 7.

[70] Mitra (1844–1895), a lawyer and judge in Calcutta, also taught at the University of Calcutta.

[71] Telang (1850–1893), a Sarasvati Gond Brahman from Thana, became a judge of the High Court of Bombay and President of the Bombay Asiatic Society. He prepared several editions and translated the *Gītā* and two related texts for The Sacred Books of the East series (vol. 8, 1882). See Windisch 1921: 34.

[72] Ojhā (1863–1947) was a Rajput and worked as Curator in the Victoria Hall Museum in Udaipur and in the Rajputana Museum in Ajmer. He was an important pioneer of scholarly writing in Hindi.

[73] E.g., Babu Poorno Chunder Mukharji (d. 1903), see Singh 2004: 316ff.

[74] It should be mentioned here that Hurree Babu also had a real model. This was the Tibetologist Sarat Chandra Dās (1849–1917), and a comparison between the reality and the fiction allows us a good glimpse of the condescending attitude of the British towards Bengali intellectuals. See Hopkirk 1996: 223ff.

all orthodox traditions of the two major religions of the country, soon took scholarship as one way to further their position and self-consciousness. The Armenian Johannes Avdall[75] wrote articles about Armenian history for the JASB as early as the 1830s, and at the turn of the century, Mesrovb Jacob Seth[76] made a full study of the history of Armenians in India. The Parsis had been studied as an object (more or less in the Saidian sense) by Henry Lord, A. H. Anquetil-Duperron, and John Wilson.[77] The misunderstanding and condemnatory publications of the missionary John Wilson became in fact a major stimulus for the offended Parsis to attain a scholarly level in the study of their own tradition.[78] Indo-Portuguese such as Joseph Gerson da Cunha[79] in Bombay and José Nicolão da Fonseca[80] in Goa were active scholars of Indo-Portuguese history.

---

75 Hovhannes Avdaleanc (1803–1870). In 1827, he translated from Armenian the *History of Armenia from B.C. 2247 to A.D. 1780*, written by the Mekhitarist Father M. Chamchian (Čamčean) and furnished it with an appendix bringing the history up-to-date. We may also note here that Mesrop Taghitiantz (1803–1858) lived in India from 1826–30 and later (1841) published a history of Pre-Muslim India in Armenian (Thorossian 1951: 255).

76 Seth (1871–1939) came from New Julfa near Isfahan and lived in Calcutta.

77 Henry Lord (1553–16??): *A Display of Two Forraigne Sects in the East Indies, viz.: the Sect of the Banians, the Ancient Natives of India, and the Sect of the Parsees, the Ancient Inhabitants of Persia*, I–II (London 1630); Abraham-Hyacinthe Anquetil-Duperron (1731–1805): *Le Zend-Avesta*, I–III (Paris 1762–69); John Wilson (1804–1875): *The Parsi Religion Unfolded, Refuted and Contrasted with Christianity*. Bombay 1843. See Sweetman 2003: 64ff. (Lord) and 148ff. (Anquetil-Duperron).

78 As this belongs rather to the history of Iranian studies, I list here only some of the most prominent representatives: Tehmuras Dinshaw Anklesaria (1842–1902) and his son Behramgore Tehmuras Anklesaria (1873–1944), Edalji Kersaspji Antia (1842–1913), Shapurji Kavasji Hodivala (1870–1931), Kavasji Edalji Kanga (1839–1904), Jivanji Jamshedji Modi (1854–1933), Cursetji Erachji Pavry (1859–after 1933), and Darab Peshotan Sanjana (1857–1931). Detailed information about their careers and works is scattered and often difficult to find; for a sort of summary, see Katrak 1974.

79 Joseph Gerson da Cunha (1842–1900). See Windisch 1921: 7ff.

80 Fonseca (1837–1886) was physician and for ten years the President of the Sociedade dos Amigos das Letras in Goa.

The Jainas, too, came forth as scholars, headed by Vijaya Dharma Sūri[81] and others.

5. SOUTH INDIA

Ignorance of South Indian matters has been often confessed by Indologists, among Westerners and North Indians alike. It is true that the South is always slightly (sometimes even much) different, and it has been a marked tendency of Indology to ignore the South. Nevertheless, it is quite clear that much of the Sanskrit scholarship lost in the North has been preserved in the South. Even texts originally written in the North are sometimes only preserved in Southern manuscripts. But the South also has a great importance on its own. I do not pretend to be a specialist on things Southern – though at least I have been there a few times and even have some experience of fieldwork – but a few remarks are necessary here.

If we leave out early missionary scholars such as Ziegenbalg and Beschi, the start was not unlike that in Calcutta and Bombay. The local British started a society with its own *Madras Journal of Literature and Science*. It is, unfortunately, very rare, and I have not yet been able to go through the early issues (and I assure you, going through old periodicals is an important part of the fun in this kind of study). As far as Sanskrit was concerned, there is not much new to be recorded here. There were at least as many Sanskrit pandits in the South as in the North and they were used as assistants by British scholars just like in the North. Occasionally, some of them also came to the North, such as Cavally Venkata Ramaswami,[82] who was Head Translator and Pandit at the Literary and Antiquarian Department in Calcutta as early as the 1820s and made South Indian literature known in his English publications. As

[81] V. D. Sūri (1868–1922) was a famous Jaina religious figure and scholar who collaborated with many Western scholars.

[82] K. Veṅkata Rāmasvāmi (1765–1840).

a special case, we must note Ram Raz[83] who wrote the first – and for a long time the only – published account of Indian architecture in English (1834). I have already referred to the manuscript libraries of Mysore, Madras and Trivandrum and to their important role in editing rare Sanskrit works in the second half of the 19th century. There are also other, local, editions published in Grantha letters, which the majority of Indologists cannot even read.

What is really peculiar to the South, however, are the important literary traditions in Dravidian languages, especially in Tamil, which can boast of an antiquity of at least two millennia.[84] But if it is true that a great part of Sanskrit learning and science had been forgotten in the North, the same was even more true with the Tamil classics in the South. The maxims of the *Tirukkuṟaḷ*, the hymns of the Vaiṣṇava and Śaiva saints, and the medieval theological literature were familiar to Tamil pandits, but other great classics, such as the Caṅkam (Sangam) anthologies, the grammar *Tolkāppiyam*, the two epics *Cilappatikāram* and *Maṇimēkalai*, only existed in a few manuscripts and were unknown to the majority of them.

The few Western scholars of Dravidian languages made good use of the same kind of collaboration as was common with Sanskrit. As early as the beginning of the 19th century Benjamin Guy Babington (1794–1865) was capable of translating the *Tirukkuṟaḷ* with the help of his Tamil Pandit. M. Rāmānuja Kavirāyar[85] assisted the missionaries Rhenius, Winslow and Pope in their work on Tamil as Ravipati Gurumūrti Śāstrī[86] did for Charles Philip Brown in his Telugu studies. Traditional pandits wrote and published grammars of Dravidian languages wholly under the influence of the Pāṇinian tradition with a result that was as incapable of

---

[83] Rām Rāz (d. 1834) was the Head English Master at the College of Fort St. George in Madras. On him, see Singh 2004: 308ff.

[84] I remain unconvinced at the recent attempt to postpone the dates of Tamil classics by several centuries.

[85] M. Irāmāṉuja Kavirāyar (1785/90–1852/53) was originally a sepoy soldier, then much appreciated Tamil teacher and book printer.

[86] Śāstrī (1770–1837), a Telugu prose author and grammarian.

doing justice to the peculiar nature of Dravidian languages as were the early practical manuals written by missionaries and the British.

Nevertheless, I would like to pick out one name because of his rather original approach, though still wholly in accordance with traditional Sanskrit scholarship. Śrīraṅgapaṭṇada Kṛṣṇamācārya,[87] a lawyer by profession, wrote a Kannaḍa grammar published in 1838. In this work, he made the interesting attempt to explain the relationship between Dravidian languages based on the model of traditional Indo-Aryan grammar, but not starting with Sanskrit. For him, classical Tamil was the Prakṛti, like Sanskrit in Indo-Aryan, while Kannaḍa, Telugu and Malayālam were the Prākrits, defined in their relationship to Tamil and by using the terms *tatsama*, *tadbhava*, and *deśya*.

The last part of this survey is the rediscovery of the classical Tamil literature.[88] For those mainly concerned with Northern India, it is easy to fail to see its importance for Indian Indology. Part of its historical significance lies in the fact that this was done without any participation or prompting from Western scholars. On the contrary, when it happened, it was hardly noted by them at all. All the results were published in Tamil and a tradition of modern Tamil scholarship was soon established. The few Western scholars seriously interested in Tamil have always understood and openly expressed that they are just outsider students and not in any way in leading positions.

The great name here is U. V. Swāminātha Ayyar.[89] Beginning in 1880, he organized, together with Dāmodara Piḷḷai[90] and a few

[87] Krishnamacharya (dates unknown), lawyer in Madras. See Sreekantaiya 1968.

[88] A good summary is given by Zvelebil 1975: 5ff..

[89] U. Vē. Cuvāmināta Aiyar (1855–1942) was a Śaiva Brahmin from Tañjavur district who taught as Professor of Tamil at colleges in Kumbakonam and Madras. See, e.g., Zvelebil 1992: 184ff.

[90] Ci. Vai. Tāmōtaram Piḷḷai (1832–1901) came from Sri Lanka. In 1858, he was one of the two first students to receive a B.A. at Madras University and worked then as Professor of Tamil and as a lawyer. He found and edited several important Tamil classics. See Zvelebil 1992: 174ff.

others, an extensive search for Tamil manuscripts and edited all the great classics found. Many of these editions are still reprinted and used. Another result of this activity was the compilation of the massive *Tamil Lexicon* under the general editorship of Swaminātha Ayyar himself in the early decades of the 20th century.

To conclude my notes about South India, I would like to mention V. Kanakasabhai Piḷḷai[91] as the first one to attempt to cull historical information out of these newly found Tamil classics and P. Sundaram Piḷḷai[92] as the pioneer of South Indian archaeology.

REFERENCES

ALIEV, Gazanfar Ju. 1986. Die Rolle persischer Übersetzungen der Sanskritschriftdenkmäler in der indo-moslemischen kulturellen Synthese. In: *Sanskrit and World Culture* (Schriften zur Geschichte und Kultur des alten Orients, 18): 83–85. Berlin: Akademie-Verlag.

BAGCHI, K. 1967. Krishnachandra Bhattacharyya: A Philosopher of Indian Renaissance. *Visvabharati Quarterly* 32 (1966–67): 37–49.

BECHERT, Heinz 1969. *Zum Ursprung der Geschichtschreibung im indischen Kulturbereich.* (Nachrichten der Akademie der Wissenschaften in Göttingen 1969[2]). Göttingen: Vandenhoeck & Ruprecht.

DANDEKAR, R. N. (ed.) 1976. *Ramakrishna Gopal Bhandarkar as an Indologist.* Poona: Bhandarkar Oriental Research Institute.

DODSON, Michael S. 2007. *Orientalism, Empire, and National Culture. India 1770–1880.* (Cambridge Imperial and Post-Colonial Studies Series.) Basingstoke: Palgrave Macmillan.

EICHHORN, Johann Gottfried 1807. *Geschichte der Litteratur. Von ihrem Anfang bis auf die neuesten Zeiten*, V.1. (Geschichte der neuern [sic] Sprachenkunde, 1.) Göttingen: Vandenhoek und Ruprecht.

FÜCK, Johann 1955. *Die arabischen Studien in Europa. Bis in dem Anfang des 20. Jahrhunderts.* Leipzig: Otto Harrassowitz.

GILDEMEISTER, Johannes 1847. *Bibliothecae Sanskritae sive recensus librorum sanskritorum hucusque typis vel lapide exscriptorum critici specimen.* Bonnae ad Rhenum: H. B. Koenig.

[91] V. Kaṉakacapai Piḷḷai (1855–1906), a lawyer and postal employee. His *Tamils Eighteen Hundred Years Ago* (Madras 1904) was originally a series of articles in *Madras Review* 1895–1901.

[92] P. Cuntaram Piḷḷai (1855–1897) was Professor of Philosophy in Trivandrum.

HADI, Nabi 1995. *Dictionary of Indo-Persian Literature.* New Delhi: Indira Gandhi National Centre for the Arts.

HOPKIRK, Peter 1996. *Quest for Kim. In Search of Kipling's Great Game.* Oxford: Oxford University Press .

KANE, Pandurang Vaman 1975. *History of Dharmaśāstra,* I.2. 2nd rev. ed. (Government Oriental Series, Class B, 6.) Poona: Bhandarkar Oriental Research Institute.

KATRAK, Jamshid Cawasji 1974. Gujarati literature on Iranology. In: *Commémoration Cyrus. Hommage universel.* (Acta Iranica, 1.1): 360–378. Leiden: E.J. Brill.

KEJARIWAL, O. P. 1988. *The Asiatic Society of Bengal and the Discovery of India's Past.* Delhi: Oxford University Press.

KOPF, David 1969. *British Orientalism and the Bengal Renaissance.* Berkeley: University of California Press.

MITRA, Rajendralal 1885. History of the Society. Part I in: A. F: Rudolf Hoernle & P. N. Bose (eds.), *Centenary Review of the Asiatic Society of Bengal, 1784–1884.* Calcutta: Asiatic Society.

MODI, Jivanji Jamshedji 1925. King Akbar and the Persian translations of Sanskrit books. *ABORI* 6: 83–107.

MUKHERJI, Abhijit 1985. European Jones and Asiatic Pandits, *JASB* (4th Series) 27(1): 43–58.

PHILIPS, C. H. (ed.) 1961. *Historians of India, Pakistan and Ceylon.* London: Oxford University Press.

RAY, P. K. 1985. Ramkamal Sen and the Asiatic Society. *JASB* (4th Series) 27(3): 79–107.

ROCHER, Ludo 1986. *The Purāṇas.* (A History of Indian Literature, II.3.) Wiesbaden: O. Harrassowitz.

ROCHER, Rosane 1983. *Orientalism, Poetry and the Millennium. The Checkered Life of Nathaniel Brassey Halhed 1751–1830.* Delhi: Motilal Banarsidass.

—— 1989. The career of Rādhākānta Tarkavāgīśa. An eighteenth-century pandit in British employ. *JAOS* 109: 627–633.

SAID, Edward W. 1978. *Orientalism.* New York: Pantheon Books. (Paperback edition: Harmondsworth: Penguin, 1985.)

SALOMON, Richard 1998. *Indian Epigraphy. A Guide to the Study of Inscriptions in Sanskrit, Prakrit, and the Other Indo-Aryan Languages.* New York: Oxford University Press.

SEN, Dinesh Chandra 1954. *History of Bengali Language and Literature.* 2nd edition. Calcutta: University of Calcutta.

SEN GUPTA, S. 1975. Radhakanta Deva, the educator: Popular and female education. *JASB* (4th Series) 17: 60–87.

SINGH, Upinder 2004. *The Discovery of Ancient India*. New Delhi: Permanent Black.

SREEKANTAIYA, T. N. 1968. Krishnamacharya's "Hosagannaḍa Nuḍigannaḍi": A Modern Kannada grammar of the early nineteenth century. In: Bh. Krishnamurti (ed.), *Studies in Indian Linguistics (Professor M. B. Emeneau Ṣaṣṭipūrti Volume)*: 322–331. Poona: Deccan College.

SWEETMAN, Will 2003. *Mapping Hinduism. 'Hinduism' and the study of Indian religions 1600–1776*. (Neue Hallesche Berichte, 4.) Halle: Franckesche Stiftungen.

THAPAR, Romila 1972. The tradition of historical writing in early India. *Indian Church History Review* 6(1): 1–22.

THOROSSIAN, H. 1951. *Histoire de la littérature arménienne. Des origines à nos jours*. Paris: H. Thorossian.

VIDYABHUSANA, Satis Chandra 1911. Acharyya Satya Vrata Samasrami (A.D. 1846–1911). *JASB* 7 (Proceedings): cxiiif.

WARDER, Anthony Kennedy 1972. *An Introduction to Indian Historiography*. Bombay: Popular Prakashan.

WEZLER, A. 1993. Towards a reconstruction of Indian cultural history: Observations and reflections on 18th and 19th century Indology. *Studien zur Indologie und Iranistik* 18: 305–329.

WINDISCH, Ernst 1921. *Philologie und Altertumskunde in Indien. Drei nachgelassene Kapitel des III. Teils der Geschichte der Sanskrit-Philologie und indischen Altertumskunde*. (Abhandlungen für die Kunde des Morgenlandes, 15.3). Leipzig: F. A. Brockhaus.

YOUNG, Richard Fox 1979. Church Sanskrit: An approach of Christian scholars to Hinduism in the nineteenth century. *WZKS* 23: 205–231.

ZBAVITEL, Dušan 1976. *Bengali Literature*. (A History of Indian Literature, IX.3.) Wiesbaden: O. Harrassowitz.

ZVELEBIL, Kamil V. 1975. *Tamil Literature*. (Handbuch der Orientalistik, I.I.1.) Leiden: E.J. Brill.

—— 1992. *Companion Studies to the History of Tamil Literature*. (Handbuch der Orientalistik, II, Ergänzungsband 5.) Leiden: E.J. Brill.

How Sanskrit Came to Sweden
The History of Swedish Indology until c. 1950[1]

KLAUS KARTTUNEN

1. BACKGROUND

The history of Indology as an independent branch of scholarship in the West is little more than 200 years old. Until the end of the 18th century, the main sources on India available to Europeans were the Greek and Latin accounts, the misinterpreted Biblical accounts of Ophir and other mysterious lands that were erroneously connected with India, and early accounts of missionaries and travellers. In the 18th century a few missionaries, such as the French Jesuits and

[1] In 1996 there was a meeting of Scandinavian Indologists in Göthenburg. As my own contribution to the meeting consisted of the presentation of a still unfinished project not suitable for publishing at that time, I promised the convener of the meeting, Professor Folke Josephsson to contribute instead an account of the history of Sanskrit studies in Sweden. For various reasons, however, I was not capable of completing it in time and the draft remained on my desk (and hard disc). When it turned out to be possible to arrange a special session on the history of Indology during the 12th International Sanskritt Conference, I started working on it again, and the results are here. Jarl Charpentier, whose profound scholarship I have always admired, has already told the major part of this history in Charpentier 1924 (see also Segerstedt 1976 and Simonsson 1976), but I think it is time to tell the story of early Swedish Indology in English, and I have occasionally been able to add something. Fortunately, we have rather many – though by no means all – of the relevant publications in Helsinki. Professor Gunilla Gren-Eklund has kindly given some additional material. An asterisk (*) denotes books and articles I have not seen myself. Julie Uusinarkaus has kindly checked my English.

Paulinus a Sancto Bartholomaeo, began studying of Sanskrit and Indian culture, mainly in South India. The next phase was soon introduced by Charles Wilkins, Sir William Jones and other Britons in Calcutta and many of their works and translations were soon republished and translated in Europe. This was the beginning of the serious study of Sanskrit by Westerners. In Europe, early knowledge of Sanskrit soon led to the development of comparative linguistics, pioneered by such scholars as Friedrich Schlegel, Franz Bopp and Rasmus Rask.

Before the establishment of Sanskrit studies, the picture of India in early Swedish literature was quite vague, simply a reflection of what was stated in Central European sources. In Old Swedish literature of the 14th and 15th centuries, there are Swedish versions of such popular texts as the Alexander Romance (*Siälinna thröst* and the poem *Konung Alexander*), the legend of Barlaam och Joasaph (*Barlaam och Josaphat*), the Letter of Prester John (*Joan prest af India land*) and the story of the Seven Wise Masters (*Sju vise mästare*, in three versions).

In the 18th century, the ships of the Swedish East India Company sailed to China, but every attempt to acquire a share in Indian trade was frustrated by stronger competitors.[2] The first Swedish traveller with some first-hand knowledge of India was probably **Georg Carl von Döbeln** (1758–1820), who visited South India in the French military service in 1783 and described his experiences in his diary.[3] The translations of Sanskrit works published at the end of the century in English and soon translated further into other European languages were perhaps first read in their original English, German and French,[4] but the first Swedish version, the

---

[2] For the history of the Swedish East India Company, see e.g. Frängsmyr 1976 and Olán 1923.

[3] See Aalto 1991 and briefly Karttunen 2003. Parts of the diary were published in Döbeln & Strindberg 1856. The diary includes a small glossary of useful words and phrases, analysed by Aalto.

[4] According to Charpentier (1924: 57), the **Stockholmsposten* n. 180 in 1791 contained a review of Forster's German *Śakuntalā*.

**Bhagavadgītā*, appeared anonymously in the journal *Klio* only in the 1810s.[5]

Even in the 18th century there existed a sort of comparative "linguistics" in Sweden, combined with the nationalistic "Gothic" fantasies.[6] Both European languages and Persian were thus derived from Gothic, which was explained as an early form of Swedish.[7] Methodically, this was completely wrong, but because of loan-words and recognisable common Indo-European words, some actual comparisons were right.

2. THE BEGINNINGS

Besides information culled from foreign books, a certain idea of Sanskrit was presented by **Fabian Wilhelm af Ekenstam** (1786–1868; until 1810 Ekenman). In 1810–11 he published at the University of Lund a small dissertation of five pages, entitled **Dissertatio academica de Lingua Sanscrit.* According to Charpentier, his main sources, in addition to Sir William Jones, were Paulinus a Sancto Bartholomaeo, Anquetil-Duperron and Francis Wilford. Even then, they were not necessarily the best possible guides, but at least Ekenstam had already adopted Jones' theory of a common parent language (*e lingua quadam primitiva seu originali*). However, Ekenstam's knowledge of Sanskrit was meagre. He confused it with Tamil, which he knew from Ziegenbalg, and then proceeded to compare them both to Chinese. The little booklet never had any influence, but must be noted as the first dissertation on Sanskrit

---

[5] Charpentier 1924: 57. Apparently Charpentier had himself not seen it. He supposes that it was founded on Wilkins' English version, which seems obvious, though perhaps the direct origin was Majer's German rendering of Wilkins. Perhaps it was only a selection.

[6] A famous example is the *Dissertatio philologico-historica de convenientia linguae persicae cum gothica* defended in 1827 by Olaus Odhelius with Olof Celsius as praeses in Uppsala. Probably Celsius, the famous philologist, was also its author. The booklet has been analysed by Droixhe 1994.

[7] This went so far that many Swedish forms were given instead of Gothic, e.g. *dotter* pro *dauhtar* and *bättre* pro *batiza* (Droixhe 1994 lists more examples).

published in Sweden. After this the author seems no longer to have had any scholarly aims. He became a schoolteacher and priest. He was a Moravian (Herrnhutian) Christian, later a Swedenborgian. In 1832 he was described as "en innerligt god, livlig och naiv människa".[8]

To the prehistory of Indology also belongs **Jakob Ekelund** (1790–1840), a priest and a schoolteacher of history, who translated the *Śakuntalā* into Swedish from Jones' English and Forster's German version.[9] According to Charpentier, the result was not good even as a literary work. As an introduction to it he wrote an account of Indian life, mythology etc. which is said to be full of errors not found in the writings of Jones. Ekelund was also known as a prolific translator of European literature and as an author of textbooks of history and other school subjects.[10]

We can also briefly mention the historian and classical philologist **Vilhelm Fredrik Palmblad** (1788–1852), from 1835 Professor of Greek at Uppsala. Without knowing Sanskrit himself, he keenly followed Indological literature and presented some of its productions in Swedish in the articles he wrote for the journal *Svea*.[11]

3. UPPSALA

The old university of Uppsala was first established in 1476/77 and, reopened after a period of stagnation in 1595, was always the leading university of the country. Just as in other Nordic universities

---

[8] Charpentier 1924: 58; Elgenstierna 1926: 516.

[9] **Sakontala. Ett Indiskt dramatiskt Poem af Kalidas (efter Jones och Forster).* 48+171 p. Stockholm 1821.

[10] On Ekelund, see Charpentier 1924: 57. His Master's thesis dealt with Germans in Latin literature (*De Arminio, duce Cheruscorum*, 1815).

[11] On Palmblad, see Charpentier 1924: 57; an autobiography in *Biographiskt Lexicon* 11 (1843): 17–35. According to UAM 1841, he wrote the articles *"Om Hinduernas fornhäfder" in *Svea* 2, *"Om Tibet" in *Svea* 4, *"Om Hinduernas Dramatiska Poesi" in *Svea* 13 (founded on Wilson's *Select Specimens*), and further a dissertation **De Buddha et Wodan*, I–IV, Uppsala 1822).

(Copenhagen and Helsinki),[12] the teaching of Sanskrit was started at Uppsala University in the 1830s, here by **Otto Fredrik Tullberg** (1802–1853).

Tullberg was originally a priest and Semitic scholar, from 1832 Docent of Hebrew and Aramaic at Uppsala. During a journey to Germany, Italy, France and England (1835–37), he studied, among other subjects, Sanskrit under Kosegarten, Bopp, Stenzler and Burnouf. In London he started the manuscript collation for his forthcoming edition of the *Mālavikāgnimitra.* Back in Uppsala he started teaching Sanskrit, although only two students were interested. In 1840–41 he was abroad again, this time visiting Lassen in Bonn and Wilson in Oxford. During his travels he purchased a number of Sanskrit books for the Uppsala university library.

In 1843–53 Tullberg was the Professor of Oriental Languages at Uppsala University. Although he was now in charge of the Semitic languages as well, he also continued with his Sanskrit studies. His main interest, however, seems now to have been Syriac. In any case, his only published contribution to Indology remained the first volume (containing the text) of a critical edition of the *Mālavikāgnimitra* (*Malavika et Agnimitra, Drama Indicum Kâlidâsae adscriptum.* 9+108 p. Bonn 1840). The promised Latin translation and critical notes never appeared.[13] His small collection of manuscripts is kept in the Uppsala university library, and according to Zetterstéen's (1908) report, it consists of Syriac (numbers 1–7), Hebrew (8–9) and Sanskrit (10.1–5 & 11.1–13) texts.[14]

---

[12] On Copenhagen, see Pauly 1992 and Zysk, in this volume; on Helsinki, Aalto 1971 and Karttunen 1997 & 2003.

[13] He also planned an edition of the *Pañcatantra*, but abandoned this plan in favour of Kosegarten. On Tullberg, see Charpentier 1924: 58–62, and Å. Nilsson in SMK, VIII (1955): 57f. His elder brother, Hampus Christofer Tullberg (1796–1876), was a Semitic scholar teaching at Lund.

[14] They are all in Tullberg's handwriting and mostly written during his study travels. They contain copies of texts, translations, grammatical notes and glossaries. One easily notes an interest in narrative literature: Tullberg had copied several texts. There is further an incomplete Swedish translation of the *Mālavikāgnimitra* (which breaks off in Act 3) and an English translation of the *Ṛtusaṁhāra*, probably by Wilson (published in Zetterstéen 1910).

Tullberg did not really start a tradition, and he had only a few students interested in Indian literature. Among them was at least **Carl Fredrik Bergstedt** (1817–1890), Docent of Greek at Uppsala from 1843. Although mainly a classicist, he had also attended the lectures of Westergaard, Lassen and Burnouf during his travels and collected material for a study on Vedānta. In the 1840s he published a series of popular translations, which were deemed rather good by Charpentier.[15] A small dissertation about Vedānta[16] concluded his scholarly career, which he then abandoned in order to become a journalist. Later he was also active in politics and sat in the first chamber as a "democratic conservative" in 1867–75. His dissertation in 1850 seems to be the first instance that the Devanāgarī script was printed in Sweden.[17]

After Tullberg there was a long period when Sanskrit was apparently not taught at all at Uppsala. The only spark of light in this period seems to be an anonymously published modest dissertation containing a small specimen of the Nala story (the first chapter) in Sanskrit and Latin.[18] It hailed from **Lars Edman** (1824–1921), who started his career as an Oriental scholar and perhaps had learnt Sanskrit from Tullberg. From 1864 he taught at Uppsala as Associate Professor (adjunkt) of German and English, but his whole literary

---

[15] *Sâvitrî, en episod ur den Indiska Epopéen Mahâ-bhârata.* 10+44 p. Uppsala 1844; **Metriska öfversättningar från Sanskrit.* 127 p. Uppsala 1845; **Vikrama och Urvasî eller Hjelten och nymfen, ett Indiskt skådespel of Kâlidâsa.* 111 p. Stockholm 1846; further: "Sagan om syndafloden hos de gamla hinduerna", *Frey* 1840: 201–212 (translated from the *Mahābhārata*); "En fornindisk fabel (Jägaren och dufvan)", *Frey* 1840: 477–482 (from the *Pañcatantra*).

[16] **De cognitione animi commentatio Vedantica.* 25 p. Uppsala 1850 (an edition of the *Jñānabodhinī* of Pseudo-Śankara). We can also note a few articles on comparative linguistics: *"Något om den comparativa philologien och dess inflytande på de orientalistiska språkstudierna", *Läsning för bildning ock nöje* 1848: 722–745; *"Om de nyaste upptäckterna i Asiens fornkunskap, särdeles med afseende på den så kallade kilskriften", *Frey* 1850: 449–491; *"Hvad är språkvetenskap", *Nordisk Tidskrift* 1881: 243–281, 584–586.

[17] On Bergstedt see V. Svanberg in SBL, III (1922): 681–688 (with photo); Charpentier 1924: 62–64.

[18] **Śrīmahābhārate nalopākhyānam / Nalus Mahábhárati episodium.* Liber primus. 8 p. Uppsala 1868.

output is contained in no more than five titles. Charpentier supposes that the Nala fascicle was perhaps used by him as a text in his teaching of elementary Sanskrit.[19]

The situation was changed only in the 1870s by Erdman. **Axel Erdman** (1843–1926) was mainly a scholar of the English language, but he had studied Sanskrit in 1872–73 under Gildemeister at Bonn and then taught the language at Uppsala in 1873–74, 1877 and 1880–91. In 1877–91 he was also the official examiner of Sanskrit at the university. In 1892 he became an extraordinary Professor "i nyeuropeisk lingvistik, sp. germanska språk" and later (1904) the Professor of English. He was one of the pioneers of modern linguistics in Sweden and wrote much on English and linguistics, but Indology was only involved in the articles he wrote for the encyclopaedia *Nordisk Familjebok* (especially "Indiens språk och litteratur", vol. VII [1884]: 549–568).[20]

Erdman's student in Sanskrit was **Olof August Danielsson** (1852–1933), who continued his studies under Windisch and Lindner at Leipzig in 1881–82. There he also prepared his only contribution to Sanskrit studies, which, however, was deemed rather important.[21] From 1879 he worked at Uppsala University as a Docent of Classical Languages, in 1883–84 also as acting extraordinary Professor of Comparative Linguistics and from 1891 as the Professor of Greek Language and Literature. He was a neogrammarian linguist mostly interested in ancient Italic languages and never contributed more to Sanskrit studies.[22]

---

[19] On Edman, see UUM 1916. The other four titles listed there are his dissertation on Hebrew, a small study on Chaucer's language and two studies on German grammar.

[20] Also in the new edition, revised by K. F. Johansson, vol. XII (1910): 534–552. On Erdman, see Charpentier 1924: 64; E. Ekwall in SBL, XIV (1953): 34–38. His writings are listed in UUM 1926.

[21] "Die Einleitung des Mahābhāshya übersetzt", ZDMG 37 (1883): 20–53.

[22] On Danielsson, see Charpentier 1924: 64f.; Nachmansson in SBL, X (1931): 238–244; Charpentier, *Indogermanisches Jahrbuch* 18 (1934): 327–332; publications in UUM 1926.

It seems that we must also name **Herman** Napoleon **Almqvist** (1839–1904), even though he was mainly an Arabic scholar. He had been Docent of Arabic from 1867, but in 1880 he was made an extraordinary Professor of Comparative Linguistics (jämförande språkforskning) and probably had to teach Sanskrit, too. In Sanskrit he was a student of Brockhaus, but his main occupation in Leipzig had been to delve deeper into Arabic philology under Fleischer, and his only contribution on Sanskrit remained the brief article "Om det sanskritiska aham" (UUÅ 1879, 18 pages), which is, in fact, a published lecture. Even this is more an attempt of a comparative study of personal pronouns than a study of Sanskrit. It seems that he soon left Sanskrit and comparative Indo-European linguistics to Erdman in order to concentrate on Arabic and Semitic studies (including comparative Semitic), and in 1892 he became the Professor of Semitic Languages. As an Arabist he was a famous scholar, strict critic and a very demanding teacher.[23]

Another scholar formally not related to Sanskrit or Indo-European studies was **Per Persson** (1857–1929), from 1895 Professor of Latin at Uppsala. In his published work, starting with his dissertation (**Studia etymologica*, 1886), he mainly dealt with questions of etymology and morphology, always taking the whole field of Indo-European studies, including Sanskrit, into account.[24]

The list of Indological dissertations at Uppsala during the 19th century is brief enough. In addition to those already mentioned we must name **Oskar Frithiof Hedström**'s (1846–1904?) dissertation **Om Sakuntala, ett indiskt drama* (21 p. Uppsala 1875). Hedström was a priest, schoolteacher and translator, but apparently did not further pursue his interest in Sanskrit.[25]

The chair of Sanskrit and Comparative Indo-European linguistics (Sanskrit med jämförande indoeuropeisk språkforskning) at

---

[23] On Almqvist, see *Nordisk Familjebok*, I; *Svensk Upplagsbok*, I (photo); Zetterstéen 1924: 11–22.

[24] On Persson, see UUM 1926.

[25] On Hedström, see Ljungberg 1880; photo in Dahl & Uggla, *Lärarekåren*. Stockholm 1898–1909. Both reproduced in *Scandinavian Biographical Archives*.

Uppsala University was finally established in 1908. This new chair was entrusted to **Karl Ferdinand Johansson** (1860–1926), who had already been in charge of its teaching for many years. He seems to have been Erdman's and Danielsson's student (in Germany only in 1889 and 1891) and, although his doctoral dissertation in 1886 had dealt with Greek philology, he soon became the first professional Sanskrit scholar at Uppsala University. He was a Docent of Indo-European Linguistics from 1886 and an extraordinary Professor from 1893 (acting already in 1889, 1890 and 1892–93).[26] Like his German teachers, Johansson was a linguist (Indo-European, Sanskrit and Middle Indic) and a Vedic scholar. As he died before the age of retirement, he was in charge of Sanskrit studies until his death, when he was succeeded by his famous student Jarl Charpentier, a Docent of Sanskrit and Comparative Indo-European Linguistics since 1908.

Jarl Hellen Robert Toussaint **Charpentier** (1884–1935), professor at Uppsala in 1926–35, was a multifaceted and very productive scholar with a good education, fine linguistic proficiency and an excellent memory. His interests ranged from the Vedas to the Jains, from the Avesta to Middle Indo-Aryan languages, from ety-

---

[26] As the published bibliography of Johansson's considerable scholarly work is easily available, I list here only a few major works: **Der Dialekt der sog. Shāhbāzgarhī-Redaktion der vierzehn Edikte des Königs Aśoka*, I–II. Leiden & Uppsala 1893; "Eine analoge neubildung der verbalflexion im altindischen und balt.-slavischen", *Zeitschrift für vergleichende Sprachforschung* 32 (1893): 434–513; "Die bildung des dativus sing. der *a*-stämme im Arischen", *Bibliotheca Buddhica* 20 (1894): 81–102; **Bidrag till Rigvedas tolkning*. 38 p. Stockholm 1897; **Solfågeln i Indien*. 80 p. (UUÅ.) Uppsala 1910; **Über die altindische Göttin Dhiṣaṇā. Beiträge zum Fruchtbarkeitskultus in Indien*. 170 p. (Kungliga humanistiska Vetenskaps-Samfundet, Skrifter 20.1.) Uppsala 1919; **Etymologisches und Wortgeschichtliches*. 87 p. (UUÅ 1927.1.) Among his translations: **Indiska sagor*. 1. *Jātaka*. 273 p. Stockholm 1907; "Ur Veda", in N. Söderblom (ed.), *Främmande Religions-Urkunder*, II: 5–215. Stockholm 1907; and other extracts from Indian literature in Sanskrit, Pāli and Prakrit, *ibid*. pp. 217–619. On Johansson, see Charpentier 1924: 68–70 & *Indogermanisches Jahrbuch* 12 (1928): 324–329; Wikander in SBL, XX (1975): 262f.; UUM 1926, with bibliography. *Festskrift tillegnad K. F. Johansson* (Gothenburg 1910) contains no personalia and only one contribution (by Charpentier) deals with Indology.

mology to Greek accounts of India, and from epigraphy to Portuguese accounts. He had good relations with British colleagues and visited England every summer.[27] His career was dramatically cut short by an accident when he was just over 50.

Charpentier's successor **Helmer Smith** (1882–1956), professor in 1936–47, had been in 1921–35 Docent of Indology at Lund. Helmer Smith was, as a student of Dines Andersen in Copenhagen, mainly a Pāli scholar, also familiar with Sinhalese. He was a skilled linguist who also knew Slavic, Finno-Ugrian and Semitic languages, and a specialist of metrics, a sharp critic and a meticulous scholar. He never took a Ph.D. and published little of his wide learning.[28] After the war, Pentti Aalto, the future Professor of Sanskrit and Comparative Linguistics at the University of Helsinki (my teacher), was among his students.

---

[27] As Charpentier is by far the most important scholar among those presently discussed by me and as his literary production is remarkably large, I give a bibliography of his works as an appendix. On him, see further the obituary notices by H. S. Nyberg, MO 29 (1935): 191f.; E. J. Rapson, JRAS 1936: 177–179; *BSOS 8 (1935–37): 282f.; and UUM 1926.

[28] The main works by Smith are the following: Edited with D. Andersen: *Sutta-nipāta*. London: Pali Text Society, 1913; *The Pāli Dhātupāṭha and the Dhātumañjūsā*. (Det Kgl. Danske Videnskabernes Selskab, Historisk-filologiske meddelelser, 4.6.) Copenhagen 1921; *Critical Pāli Dictionary*. fasc. I.1ff. Copenhagen 1924–; "Epilegomena" to vol. 1 of the *Critical Pāli Dictionary*. 99 p. Copenhagen 1948. Edited alone: *Khuddaka-Pāṭha with Paramatthajotikā*. London: Pali Text Society, 1915; *Sutta-nipāta Commentary. Being Paramatthajotikā II*, I–III. (Pali Text Society text series, 128–130.) London 1916–18; *Dhammapada Commentary*, I.1. Rev. ed. London: Pali Text Society, 1925; *Aggavaṁsa, Saddanīti*, I–V. Lund 1928–. Further, "W. Geiger et le vocabulaire singalais classique", JA 238 (1950): 177–223; Les deux prosodies du vers bouddhique", *Humanistiska Vetenskapssamfundets i Lund Årsberättelse* 1949–50: 1–43; "Retractationes rhytmicae", *Studia Orientalia* 16(5) (1951), 37 p.; *Inventaire rythmique des Pūrva-Mīmāṁsā-sūtra*, 141 p. (UUÅ 1953.8.) Uppsala 1953; "En marge du vocabulaire sanskrit des bouddhistes", *Orientalia Suecana* 2 (1953): 119–128 & 3 (1954): 31-35 & 4 (1955): 109–113. On Smith see LUM 1924–25; UUM 1936; Björn Collinder, *Svenska Dagblad* 11.1.1956 & *Kungl. vitterhets historie och antikvitets akademiens årsbok* 1956: 55–59, with photo; H. Hendriksen, *Critical Pali Dictionary*, II (1960), pp. v–viii; Peiris, *Buddhism*, pp. 226–229; S. W[i]k[ande]r in SMK, VII (1954): 110f.

The next professor, **Hans Hendriksen** (1913–1989), a Dane, remained in Uppsala only a few years (1947–51) and then returned to Copenhagen as the successor of Poul Tuxen. He had written his doctoral dissertation on Pāli[29] and a study on Hittite before he conducted fieldwork among the Himachalis North-East and East of Simla in 1952–53 (and again in 1964). After him **Stig Wikander** (1908–1983), best known for his dissertation, *Der arische Männerbund* (1938), was a professor at Uppsala University in 1953–74.[30] He came from Lund, having been a Docent of Iranian Languages there.[31]

Of the docents connected with the chair, we must first mention **Kasten Rönnow** (1897–1943), from 1928 Docent of Indology at Uppsala (and acting Professor during the absence and after the death of Charpentier). He was mainly a Vedic scholar. Two other docents, Arbman and Lindqvist, will be discussed later in the context of comparative religion.[32]

---

[29] *Syntax of the Infinite Verb-Forms of Pāli.* 169 p. Copenhagen 1944. In 1944 a doctoral dissertation on Pāli was still considered news. Two days later *Berlingske Tidende*, the leading newspaper of Copenhagen, published a poem and a cartoon on the theme. They were republished by Pauly (1992: 559).

[30] After Wikander the chair has been occupied by Nils Simonsson in 1975–85, Gunilla Gren-Eklund in 1986–2003 and William L. Smith in 2004–09.

[31] By Wikander: diss. *Der arische Männerbund.* 12+111 p. Lund 1938; *Vāyu*, I: *Texten.* Uppsala 1941; *Feuerpriesten in Kleinasien und Iran.* (Humanistiska Vetenskapssamfundets i Lund, Skrifter 40.) Lund 1946; "Études sur les mystères de Mithras. 1. Introduction", *Veteskapssocieteten i Lund Årsskrift* 1951: 5–46; "Sur les fonds communs indo-iraniens des épopées de la Perse et de l'Inde", *La Nouvelle Clio* 1–2 (1949–50): 310–329; *Recueil de textes kourmandji.* 108 p. (UUÅ 1959.10.) Uppsala 1959; articles on Iranian, Armenian, and Indology, especially on the *Mahābhārata*, e.g. "Tansarnāmeh och Mahābhārata", AO 30 (1966): 213–217; "Nakula et Sahadeva", *Orientalia Suecana* 6 (1957): 66–96; "Från Bråvalla till Kurukshetra", *Arkiv för Nordisk filologi* 75 (1959): 183–193; "A Central Asian Loanword in Arthaśāstra" in *Pratidānam* (= Festschrift Kuiper), pp. 270–274. The Hague 1968. On Wikander, see *Bio-bibliographie de 134 savants.* (Acta Iranica, 20), pp. 548f. Leiden 1979; UUM 1951–1960, with bibliography; *Vem är Vem & Vem är det.*

[32] By *Rönnow*: diss. *Trita Āptya*, I. 28+181+2 p. (UUÅ 1927.5); "Zur Erklärung des Pravargya, des Agnicayana und der Sautrāmaṇī", MO 23 (1929): 113–173; "Viśvarūpa", BSOS 6(2) (1931): 469–480; "Die Verse der Sarparājñī, Rigveda 10, 189", MO 25 (1931): 269–288; "Some remarks on Śvetadvīpa", BSOS

4. LUND

The old University of Lund was established in 1667 to take care of higher education in the newly acquired southern parts of Sweden. From the very beginning Oriental studies were part of the curriculum, but at first this only meant Hebrew and perhaps Syriac and Arabic. The teaching of Sanskrit came here rather late. In 1862, there had been a small dissertation by **Ernst** Gustaf Ferdinand **Olbers** (1837–1919) presenting a Swedish translation and commentary of Cantos 9 and 10 of the Nala episode.[33] We do not know whether the language was also taught at Lund; in any case Olbers seems to be an autodidact in what little Sanskrit he had. Olbers became a schoolteacher and later a minister, but apparently did not further pursue his Sanskrit studies.[34]

When Olbers published his dissertation, Tegnér was already a student at Lund, but apparently not yet interested in Sanskrit. Later on it was he who seems to have started the teaching of Sanskrit at Lund. **Esaias** Henrik Vilhelm **Tegnér** (1843–1928), a nephew of the famous poet, was in 1872–79 Associate Professor in Comparative Linguistics (adjunkt i jämförande språkkunskap). Even later, as the Professor of Oriental Languages at the University of Lund (1879–1908), he also taught Persian and Sanskrit in the 1880s, but soon Semitic and also Swedish took the majority of his attention. He was long an active member of the Swedish Bible translation committee and in retirement the editor-in-chief of the great Swedish dictionary project of the Swedish Academy.[35]

---

5 (1929): 253–284; "Kirāta. A study of some Ancient Indian tribes", MO 30 (1936): 90–170; "Ved. *kratu*-. Eine wortgeschichtliche Untersuchung", MO 26–27 (1932–33): 1–90; "Ved. barháṇā", BSOS 9(1) (1937): 55–68; "Ved. *krívi*", AO 16 (1938): 161–180. On Rönnow, see UUM 1936 & 1937–1950, with bibliography.

[33] *Nionde och tionde sångerna af Nala och Damayanti, från Sanskrit öfversatte och kommenterade.* 26 p. Lund 1862.

[34] On Olbers, see Herrlin in Carlquist 1951: 71–76.

[35] On Tegnér, see LUM 1924–25 (with bibliography) and Zetterstéen 1924: 30–33. The festschrift *Studier tillegnade Esaias Tegnér den 13 januari 1918* (Lund 1918) contains a photo, but no biographical information or bibliography.

When August **Hjalmar Edgren** (1840–1903) in 1880 became Docent of Sanskrit at Lund, he had already had a chequered career. As a young officer of the Swedish army, he had gone to the USA in order to get baptism by fire in the Civil War. After several years' further service in Sweden, he left the army and returned to the States, where he then studied linguistics under Whitney at Yale. After obtaining his Ph.D. in 1874, he taught French and in 1878–79 acted as Whitney's deputy. His activity at Lund remained brief; in 1884 he accepted a chair of Sanskrit and Modern Languages at Nebraska University in Lincoln. After some years, however, he was again back in Sweden, and we shall meet him soon in Gothenburg. During his time in Lund he published an elementary Sanskrit grammar in Swedish, later also translated into English,[36] and continued his activity as a translator of Sanskrit classics that had already started in New Haven.[37] He was probably the first Swedish Indologist of international standards,[38] but the main part of his activity occurred in the United States.[39] In addition, he wrote poetry and translated Longfellow and Tennyson into Swedish.

There seems to be only one among his publications related to Indology: the unfinished and only privately distributed linguistic study *De ariska språkens palataler.* 40 p. Lund 1878.

[36] *Sanskritspråkets formlära jämte kort öfversigt af Prākritdialekten.* 246 p. Lund 1883; English version: **A Compendious Sanskrit Grammar.* London 1885. It included the three first chapters of Nala (pp. 203–220) and a Sanskrit–Swedish glossary (pp. 221–238).

[37] Translated into Swedish: Kālidāsa: *Schakuntala, eller den förlorade ringen.* 181 p. Stockholm 1875; **Molnbudet (Meghadūta).* 45 p. Malmö 1875; **Mâlavikâ, ett indiskt skådespel.* Malmö 1877; further **Nalasagan.* 1880.

[38] Among his scholarly publications we can mention *"Statistical and discursive notes on Vrddhi-derivatives in Sanskrit", (LUÅ, 17) (1880–81); "On the verbal roots of the Sanskrit language and of the Sanskrit grammarians", JAOS 11 (1885): 1–55; "Palatal and labial vowels (i, î, u, û) and their corresponding semivowels (y, v)", JAOS 11 (1885): 67–88; *"Of the propriety of retaining the eighth verb-class in Sanskrit", *Lincoln University Studies* 1(1) (1888): 17ff. More popular in character was *"Indiens sagor på vandring genom världen", *Nordisk Tidskrift* 1884: 88–107.

[39] On *Edgren*, see Charpentier 1924: 66f.; SMK, II; B. Hildebrand in SBL, XII: 121–126.

After Edgren's departure, Sanskrit was again occasionally taught by Tegnér, but his work on the Swedish Bible committee took much of his time, and the chair of Oriental Languages was in the hands of changing deputies. In any case, the next name for Sanskrit at Lund is **Nils** Olof Mathias **Flensburg** (1855–1926). In 1888 he presented at Lund one of the first purely scholarly dissertations on Sanskrit in Sweden,[40] obtaining thus his Ph.D. and a docentship in Sanskrit. From 1887 he also worked as a schoolteacher at Lunds privata elementarskolan and continued there, even though he was made an extraordinary Professor of Sanskrit and Indo-European Linguistics in 1898 and an ordinary Professor with chair in 1909. His scholarly work belongs mainly to his early years.[41] As a professor he was more interested in Swedish culture and literature. He wrote poetry as well, but was never remarkable in this respect.[42]

Among Flensburg's students we must name **Ebbe** Oskar **Tuneld** (1877–1947), Sweden's first specialist of Pāli. He was a multifaceted linguist who had also studied at German universities (under Oldenberg *et al.*) and in Paris. After his doctoral dissertation on Buddhist philology had been accepted,[43] he was made a Docent of Indology at Lund in 1915. His main work, however, was the great Swedish dictionary of the Academy of Sweden, in which

---

[40] *Studier öfver den fornindiska tempusläran.* 178 p. Lund 1888. It deals with the use of imperfect and historical present in epic and classical Sanskrit, with examples from some episodes of the *Mahābhārata*, the *Pañcatantra* and the *Hitopadeśa.* To my regret he did not use the opportunity to thank his teachers in the preface, but probably he studied under Tegnér or Edgren (or both).

[41] **Studien auf dem Gebiete der idg. Wurzelbildung. Semasiologisch-etymologische Beiträge.* 1. *Die einfache Basis ter- im idg.* 11+115 p. Lund 1897; **Bidrag till Rigvedas mytologi. Om guden Pūṣan i Rigveda.* 20+49 p. (LUÅ, 5.4.) Lund 1909.

[42] On Flensburg, see Charpentier 1924: 68f.; B. Hildebrand in SBL, XVI (1966): 179f.; bibliography in LUM 1913 and 1924–25.

[43] *Recherches sur la valeur des traditions Bouddhiques palie et non-palie.* 11+239 p. Lund 1915.

he participated from 1905 until 1940, in 1920–40 as its editor-in-chief.[44]

Flensburg was succeeded in 1923 by his student John Kristian **Herbert Petersson** (1881–1927), docent since 1911. Petersson, however, was more an Indo-Europeanist than a Sanskrit scholar. His doctoral dissertation in 1911 dealt with Old Indo-Aryan,[45] but later on he mainly wrote on Indo-European, Balto-Slavic, Germanic and classical languages. In addition to Lund, he had studied at Rostock, Münster and Copenhagen.[46]

After Petersson's early death, the Lund chair was carried on for a long time through changing deputies (H. Smith, S. Wikander and G. Liebert). Then it became a chair of Comparative Linguistics, and was later completely abolished. In 1926–30 **Hannes** (Johannes Evelinus) **Sköld** (1886–1930), an Indo-Iranian scholar and linguist, taught as a docent at Lund. As a scholar he wholly deserved the chair, but his activity as a leftist politician made the authorities unwilling to accept him.[47]

More recently, a new interest in India at Lund University has developed around the chair of Comparative Religion represented

---

[44] On Tuneld, see Charpentier 1924: 70f.; A. Lindqvist in SMK, VIII (1955): 61f.; LUM 1924–25 & 1939 (with bibliography).

[45] *Studien zu Fortunatovs Regel. Beiträge zur altindischen Laut- und Sprachgeschichte.* 12+119 p. Lund 1911.

[46] On Petersson, see LUM 1924–25 and SMK.

[47] By Sköld: **Linguistic Gleanings.* 84 p. (LUÅ, 19.15.) Lund 1923; **Die ossetischen Lehnwörter im Hungarischen.* 114 p. (LUÅ, 20.4.) Lund 1925; **Nirukta. Its Place in Old Indian Literature, Its Etymologies.* 375 p. (Humanistiska Vetenskapssamfundet i Lund, Skrifter 8.) Lund 1926; **Papers on Pāṇini and Indian Grammar in General.* 50 p. (LUÅ, 21.8.) Lund 1926; **Untersuchungen zur Genesis der altindischen etymologischen Literatur, I–II.* 104+28 p. (LUÅ, 24.6 & 26.7.) Lund 1928–31; "Indo-Uralisch", *Finnisch-ugrische Forschungen* 18 (1927): 216–231; **Materialien zu den iranischen Pamirsprachen.* 319 p. (Humanistiska Vetenskapssamfundet i Lund, Skrifter, 21.) Lund 1936. Outside the field of Indo-Iranian studies he wrote his doctoral *dissertation on Serbo-Croatian dialects (1920) and published *two collections of poetry (1911) and *political works (1913, 1916, 1927). On Sköld, see LUM 1924–25 and Sven Swensson in SMK, VII (1954): 99f.

by Carl-Gustav Diehl (1906–1995; South Indian religion), Rune E. A. Johansson (1918–1981; Pāli), Jan Ergardt (1936–1992; Buddhism) and Olle Qvarnström (Jaina Studies).

5. GOTHENBURG

The Gothenburg University was founded as a private academic institute (högskola) in 1891 and became a state university in 1954. Sanskrit, which was then considered indispensable to linguistic studies, was taught from the very beginning. Part of the money for the institute came from the USA, and so came also its first Professor of Germanic Languages, our old acquaintance **Hjalmar Edgren**. His task was to establish the chair; in 1893 he was already back in Lincoln, but during this short period he also started the teaching of Sanskrit in Gothenburg. After retiring from Lincoln in 1901, he returned to Sweden and became a member of the Nobel committee until his death in December 1903.

It seems that after Edgren's departure there was a break of some years in the teaching of Sanskrit. It was permanently established as a part of the Gothenburg curriculum by Bror Per **Evald Lidén** (1862–1939). In contrast to the Indologist Edgren, Lidén was a comparativist, who methodically confined his studies to etymology[48] and never attempted popularizing his work. He obtained the chair of Sanskrit med jämförande indoeuropeisk språkforskning (the same title as at Uppsala and Lund) at Gothenburg in 1899, and in 1917 the chair was made ordinary.[49] Its history, however, belongs more to comparative linguistics than Indology, although Sanskrit was never wholly abandoned from its contents.

---

[48] The most important among his works were: **Studien zur altindischen und vergleichenden Sprachgeschichte*, 107 p. (Kungl. Humanistiska Vetenskapssamfundet, Skrifter, 6.1.) Uppsala 1897; **Ein baltisch-slavisches Auslautsgesetz*, 31 p. (GHÅ, 5.4.) Gothenburg 1899; **Armenische Studien*, 149 p. (GHÅ, 12.2.) Gothenburg 1906; **Studien zur tocharischen Sprachgeschichte*, 37 p. (GHÅ, 22.3.) Gothenburg 1916.

[49] On Lidén, see Frisk in SBL XXII (1979): 687–689; GHM 1916–41 (with bibliography).

After Lidén the chair was held in 1930–37 by **Georg Morgenstierne** (Georg Valentin Munthe af Morgenstierne; 1892–1978), the Norwegian linguist and specialist of Indo-Iranian border languages.[50] His extensive fieldwork and important publications are still well remembered and much used. After Morgenstierne had returned to Oslo to succeed Sten Konow there, the Gothenburg chair was held for a long time (1938–67) by Jöns Ivan **Hjalmar Frisk** (1900–1984), mainly known as a Greek linguist whose magnum opus was a Greek etymological dictionary (I–III, 1973–79). In Indology his name is mainly known for his excellent critical edition of the *Periplus maris Erythraei*, a Greek text about sailing to India in the first century AD.[51]

The next Indological chair in Sweden, at Stockholm University, was founded after the time span covered by this survey.[52]

6. RELIGIOUS STUDIES

The field of comparative religion has also shown some interest in ancient India. A pioneer of the field was Nathan Söderblom (1866–1931), scholar and archbishop, who in his studies also dealt with the Iranian religion. In 1907 he edited the massive anthology of translations called *Främmande religionsurkunder* (in 3 volumes), where India was mainly represented by Johansson. A colourful fig-

[50] On Morgenstierne, see GHM 1916–41; H. W. Bailey, JRAS 1979: 95f.; G. Buddruss, *Afghan Journal* 5(3) (1978): 109–111; *K. Kristiansen & I. Ross, bibliography, *Indo-Iranian Frontier Languages* 4 (1972); K. Kristiansen, *Lexicon grammaticorum*. Tübingen 1996, pp. 622f.; P. Skjærvø, ÅO 40 (1979); **Indo-Iranica. Mélanges présentés à Georg Morgenstierne*. Leiden 1962, with bibliography; *Bio-bibliographie de 134 savants*. (Acta Iranica, 20), 369ff. Leiden 1979.

[51] *Le Périple de la mer Érythrée, suivi d'une étude sur la tradition et la langue* (Göteborg Högskolas Årsskrift, 33.1 [1927]). On Frisk, see LUM 1939; GHM 1916–41 and 1942–54; *Vem är det?* 1983. After Frisk the Gothenburg chair was held in 1968–81 by Gösta Liebert (1916–1998), and in 1983–2000 by Folke Josephson. After him, the department was closed.

[52] The Stockholm chair was established in 1958 with Siegfrid Lienhard (1924–2011), first as lecturer and docent, professor in 1967–91, succeeded in 1993 by Claus Oetke.

ure was **Torgny Segerstedt** (1876–1945), a scholar and journalist in the centre of many controversies because of his unrelenting criticism of conservative theology and later of pro-Nazi politicians. His scholarly output mainly consists of comparative studies (a dissertation on the origin of polytheism), but also includes a study on the Vedic Asuras.[53]

An Indologist who became a scholar of religion was **Ernst Arbman** (1891–1959), on account of his Rudra book a Docent of Indian Philology and History of Religions at Uppsala from 1923, later Professor of History of Religions at Stockholm in 1937–58.[54] **Sigurd Lindquist** (1895–1943) is mainly remembered of his study of Yoga.[55] He was a minister and Docent (from 1934) of Psychology and History of Religions at Uppsala. **Sten Rodhe** (1915–2014) wrote his doctoral dissertation on the Vedic religion at Lund,[56] but then took a career as a schoolteacher.[57]

---

[53] "Les Asuras dans la religion védique", *Revue de l'Histoire des Religions* 57(2–3) (1908): 157–203; further: "Själavandringslärans ursprung", MO 4 (1910): 43–87 & 111–184. On Segerstedt, see J. Torbache's long article in SBL, XXXI (f. 155) (2002): 777–787, which, however, concentrates on the other sides of his career.

[54] Arbman's Indological work includes: diss. *Rudra. Untersuchungen zum altindischen Glauben und Kultus.* 313 p. Uppsala 1922; "Untersuchungen zur primitiven Seelenvorstellung mit bes. Rücksicht auf Indien", MO 1926: 85–226 & 1927: 1–185; "Tod und Unsterblichkeit im vedischen Glauben", *Archiv für Religionswissenschaft* 25 (1927): 339–387 & 26 (1928): 187–240. On Arbman, see UUM 1926 and 1936; E. B-n, SMK, I (1942): 120.

[55] Lindquist: "Zum Toxrïproblem", MO 18 (1918): 65–73; lic. diss. **Manikeismens religionshistoriska ställning*, I. 6+132 p. Uppsala 1921; diss. **Die Methoden der Yoga.* 233 p. Lund 1932; **Siddhi und Abhiññā. Eine Studie über die klassischen Wunder des Yoga.* 98 p. (UUÅ.) Uppsala 1935; "Till tolkningen av Bhagavadgītā", 19 p. (UUÅ 1941.7.); a few small articles. On Lindquist, see UUM 1936 and 1937–50.

[56] *Deliver us from Evil. Studies on the Vedic Ideas of Salvation.* 207 p. (Skrifter utgivna av Svenska sällskapet för missionsforskning, 2.) Lund 1946. Later he wrote some textbooks on religion and articles in Swedish, *inter alia* on meditation and Neo-Hindu movements in the West, and the book **Att komma till sig själv. Om olika former av meditation.* Stockholm 1978.

[57] The religious studies at Uppsala excelled more in Semitic and Iranian religions (H.-S. Nyberg, G. Widengren, H. Ringgren). Lund was mentioned above.

7. TRANSLATORS, SCHOOLMEN ETC.

Even when we can safely leave out of a survey of scholarly activities such people as theosophists, whose interest rarely attained any depth with respect to Sanskrit, a survey of Swedish Indology would be incomplete without a few names outside purely academic activities.

As in Germany, in Sweden, too, there were in the late 19th century schoolteachers interested in scholarly studies and in Sanskrit. Thus **August Zacharias Collin** (1833–1886) had originally been interested in modern languages, but after concluding his studies at Lund, he also became interested in Sanskrit. According to Charpentier, his early translation of the *Meghadūta*[58] was a poor accomplishment, but further studies under Roth at Tübingen in 1874–75 made him much better as a Sanskritist. Soon after his return he presented a selection from the *Ṛgveda* for the first time to the Swedish public, but this also seems to be the last contribution this teacher in Härnösand made to Indian studies.[59]

Collin's younger colleague at Härnösand school was **Carl Johan Blomberg** (1838–1890), a schoolman, journalist and politician and also much interested in Sanskrit and linguistics. During his study time at Uppsala University, there was, after the death of Tullberg, no teaching of Sanskrit at all, and he is said to have learnt the language from books. He never published anything about Sanskrit, although Charpentier deemed some of his posthumous papers well worth printing. In addition to Sanskrit, he also knew some Middle Indo-Aryan.[60]

---

[58] **Molnbudet.* 8+80 p. Helsingborg 1866.

[59] *"Om och ur Rigveda", *Ur vår tids forskning* 1877–78 (total 220 p.); further: *"Apahâravarmans äfventyr. Af Dandin", 33 p. (LUÅ 1867.) On Collin, see Charpentier 1924: 66; C. S. J. Collin in SBL, VIII (1929): 741–745.

[60] At least we can quote an article about comparative linguistics: *"Om qvantitet och accent i de indisk-europeiska språken", 68 p., in *Bilaga till Inbjudning till bivistande af årsexamen vid högre elementärlärovärk i Hernösand.* Hernösand 1877. On Blomberg, see Charpentier 1924: 65f.; H. Geijer in SBL, V (1925): 27–32 (with photo).

A productive translator of Sanskrit classics was Anders **Hilding Andersson** (1853–1918). He seems to have been a student of Tegnér, although the major part of his studies at Lund dealt with classical philology. This schoolman, who ended his career as school director in Lund, kept his interest in literature and translated many Latin classics into Swedish, but in addition to this, he was the most active and, according to Charpentier, the most distinguished translator of Sanskrit literature in Sweden. He introduced a number of Sanskrit classics to the Swedish public through his fluent, though occasionally rather free translations.[61]

While we are speaking of the history of Sanskrit studies in Sweden, it is perhaps not wholly out of place to mention briefly two Swedish translations published in Finland and done by Swedish-speaking Finns. Abraham **Herman Kellgren** (1822–56) was a student of Brockhaus and Burnouf and became the first Docent of Sanskrit at the University of Helsinki in 1849. Among his few Indological works there is a complete metrical Swedish translation of the Nala episode of the *Mahābhārata* published as a series of dissertations defended by his students.[62] Although mainly a scholar of Finno-Ugrian linguistics, **Otto Donner** (1835–1909) became in 1875 the first Professor of Sanskrit and Comparative Philology at Helsinki. His work, too, I have discussed elsewhere; here it is enough to mention a modest dissertation containing the lithographed Devanāgarī text and a free metrical Swedish translation of the Sītāharaṇa episode of the *Rāmāyaṇa*.[63]

---

[61] **Pärlbandet.* 76 p. Växjö 1892 (*Ratnāvalī*); *Den lilla lervagnen.* 133 p. Lund 1899 (*Mṛcchakaṭika*); **Likspökets tjugofem berättelser.* 244 p. Lund 1902 (*Vetālapañcaviṁśati*); **Urvaśī och hennes hjälte.* 60 p. Lund 1906 (*Vikramorvaśī*). On Andersson, see J. Mjöberg in SBL, I (1918): 760f. (with photo); Charpentier 1924: 67f.

[62] *Nala och Damayanti, en indisk dikt ur Mahâbhârata från originalet öfversatt och med förklarande noter försedd.* 30+8+200. Helsingfors 1852 (with a selection from *Amaruśataka* in an appendix). On Kellgren, see Aalto 1971: 42f. & 70–72; with more detail Karttunen 1991 & 1994, both with further references.

[63] *Sîtâharaṇam, episodium ur Râmâyaṇa.* Text, öfversättning och förklaringar. 40+71 p. Helsingfors 1865. On Donner, see Aalto 1971: 72–76 and Karttunen 1984.

APPENDIX 1:

Bibliography of Jarl Charpentier

- Etymologische Beiträge. *Beiträge zur Kunde der indogermanischen Sprachen ("Bezzenbergers Beiträge")* 30 (1906): 153–166.
- Zur indischen Wortforschung. Etymologische und exegetische Beiträge. *MO* 1 (1906): 17–42.
- [Trans. from Lithuanian] Hur de gamla litauerna levde. *MO* 1 (1906): 101–133. (from *Kaip senëji Lëtuvininkai gyvene.* Hrsg. von C. Cappeller. Heidelberg 1904).
- Slavische Etymologien. *MO* 1 (1906): 222–226.
- Kritische Bemerkungen zum urslavischen Entnasalierungsgesetz. *Archiv für slavische Philologie* 29 (1907): 1–10. (On N. Jokl, *ibid.* 28 [1906]: 1ff., with Jokl's "Antikritik", *ibid.* 29 [1907]: 11–49).
- Zur arischen Wortkunde. *Zeitschrift für vergleichende Sprachforschung* ("*Kuhns Zeitschrift*") 40 (1907): 425–477; 43 (1910): 161–168; 46 (1914): 25–46.
- Bemerkungen zu Rājaçekhara's Karpūramañjarī. *MO* 2 (1907–08): 226–230.
- Litauische Etymologien. *MO* 2 (1907–08): 23–35.
- *Studien zur indischen Erzählungsliteratur.* 1. *Paccekabuddhageschichten.* Dissertation, 9+174 p. (UUÅ, 4.) Uppsala 1908.
- Studien zur indischen Erzählungsliteratur. *ZDMG* 62 (1908): 725–747 (1. Das Hatthipālajātaka); *ZDMG* 63 (1909): 171–188 (2. Das Mātaṅgajātaka); *ZDMG* 64 (1910): 65–83 (3. Das Bhisajātaka); 397–429 (4. Devendra's ṭīkā zu Uttarajhayaṇa XXII. Ein jainistischer Beitrag zur Kṛṣṇa-Sage); *ZDMG* 66 (1912): 38–48 (5. Kleine Bemerkungen zur Jātakaliteratur).
- Kleine Beiträge zur armenischen Wortkunde. *Indogermanische Forschungen* 25 (1909): 241–256.
- Kleine Beiträge aus indischen Texten. *MO* 3 (1909): 72–75.
- Textstudien zu Mahāvastu. *MO* 3 (1909): 34–69.
- Ein Māgadhiwort im Mahāvastu. *MO* 3 (1909): 70–72 (vaseṭṭhā).
- Das Mārasaṁyutta im Mahāvastu. *WZKM* 23 (1909): 33–51.
- Über Rudra-Śiva. *WZKM* 23 (1909): 151–179.
- Bemerkungen über die vrātya's. *WZKM* 23 (1909): 355–388.
- *Buddha.* 96 p. (De största märkesmännen, 11.) Stockholm 1910.
- The leśyā-theory of the Jainas and Ājīvikas. In: *Festskrift tillegnad Karl Ferdinand Johansson*: 20–38. Gothenburg 1910.
- Zu Uttarajhayaṇa XXV. *WZKM* 24 (1910): 62–69.

- Zur Geschichte des Cariyāpiṭakā. *WZKM* 24 (1910): 351–415.
* *Kleine Beiträge zur indoiranischen Mythologie.* 87 p. (UUÅ 1911.2.) (1. Piśācas; 2. Verethragna).
- Avestische Etymologien. *Indogermanische Forschungen* 28 (1911): 153–157.
- Beiträge zur alt- und mittelindische Wortkunde. *Indogermanische Forschungen* 28 (1911): 157–188 & 29 (1911–12): 367–403.
- [Ed.] Le commentaire de Bhāvavijaya sur le neuvième chapitre de l'Uttarādhyāyanasūtra. *JA* 10(18) (1911): 201–255.
- Ṛgveda VIII, 100 (89). *WZKM* 25 (1911): 290–310.
- Bemerkungen über die vrātya's. *WZKM* 25 (1911): 355–388.
- *Die Desiderativbildungen der indoiranischen Sprachen.* 128 p. (Archives d'Études orientales, 6.) Uppsala 1912.
- Zur altindischen Etymologie. *MO* 6 (1912): 47–64, 118–160.
* Har Buddhalegenden öfvat inflytande på evangelieberättelserna? *Bibelforskaren* 29 (1912): 200–221?.
* Äṇkebränning i Indien. *Tidskrift för hemmet* 8 (1912): ???–???.
- Die altindischen Perfektformen vom Typus *dadāú*. *Indogermanische Forschungen* 32 (1913): 92–102.
- Ājīvika. *JRAS* 1913: 669–674.
- Zu den indischen Glossen bei Hesychius. *Zeitschrift für vergleichende Sprachforschung* 45 (1913): 90–94.
- Av. dūraoša-: ai. duróṣa-. *WZKM* 27 (1913): 235–244.
- Über eine alte Handschrift der Uttarādhyāyanaṭīkā des Devendragaṇi. *ZDMG* 67 (1913): 665–678.
- En indisk handbok i statslära from 300 f.Kr. *Nordisk Tidskrift* 1913: 353–369 (Arthaśāstra).
- Rabindranath Tagore. Några ord om hans religion, familj och diktning. *Nordisk Tidskrift* 1913: 541–552.
- A note on the Paḍariyā or Rummindei inscription. *Indian Antiquary* 43 (1914): 17–20.
- The date of Mahāvīra. *Indian Antiquary* 43 (1914): 118–123, 125–133, 167–178 (died 467 BC).
- Alt- und mittelindische Wortdeutungen. *MO* 8 (1914): 169–184.
- Sagengeschichtliches aus dem Arthaśāstra. *WZKM* 28 (1914): 211–240.
- Jainismen. *Nordisk Tidskrift* 1914: 485–509.
* Familjeförhållanden och familjeliv i samindoeuropeisk tid. *Tidskrift för hemmet* 10 (1914): ???–???.
- *De indoeuropeiska språken.* 4+253 p. (Aslerbergs populär-vetenskaplig bibliotek, 6–7.) Uppsala 1915.

– Lat. rāna Frosch. *Glotta* 6 (1915): 190–192.

– Zwei mittelindische Desiderativbildungen. *Indogermanische Forschungen* 35 (1915): 217–220.

– Indische Wörter mit den Endungen *-amba-*, *-imba-*, *-umba-*. *Indogermanische Forschungen* 35 (1915): 246–265.

– Die Hāṭhigumphā-Inschrift des Khāravela. *WZKM* 29 (1915): 208–230.

– [Ed. & trans.] Die Legende des heiligen Pārśva, des 23. tīrthaṅkara der Jainas aus Devendra's ṭīkā zu Uttarādhyāyana xxiii veröffentlicht und übersetzt. *ZDMG* 69 (1915): 321–359; 70 (1916): 271.

– Ashoka, det forntida Indiens berömdaste härskaren. *Nordisk Tidskrift* 1915: 119–138.

– De hinduistiska religionernas uppkomst. *Nordisk Tidskrift* 1915: 333–350.

– Kleine Bemerkungen zum Physiologus. In: *Aufsätze zur Kultur- und Sprachgeschichte vornehmlich des Orients Ernst Kuhn gewidmet*: 280–293. Breslau 1916.

– Beiträge zur alt- und mittelindische Wortkunde. *ZDMG* 70 (1916): 216–250.

* *Die verbalen* r-*Endungen der indogermanischen Sprachen.* 120 p. (Skrifter utgivna av Kungl. humanistiska vetenskapssamfundet i Uppsala, 18.4). Uppsala 1917.

– Griechische Etymologien. *Zeitschrift für vergleichende Sprachforschung* 47 (1916): 175–184.

– Die ethnographische Stellung der Tocharer. *ZDMG* 71 (1917): 347–388.

– Små bidrag till den grekiska etymologien. *Eranos* 17 (1917): 81–90.

– Marco Polo's närmaste föregångare och efterföljare. *Nordisk Tidskrift* 1917: 555–565.

– Zur altindischen Wortkunde. *WZKM* 30 (1917–18): 91–108.

– Zur italischen Wortkunde. *Glotta* 9 (1918): 33–69.

* Ein Beitrag zur Geschichte der Syphilis in Indien. *Nordiskt medicinskt arkiv* 2(51) (1918): ???–???.

– Heilige Fussabdrücke in Indien. *Ostasiatische Zeitschrift* 7 (1918–19): 1–30 & 179–200. (Of the Buddha and the Apostle Thomas).

– Slavische Etymologien. *Archiv für slavische Philologie* 37 (1918–20): 46–54.

– Altindisches Futurum II in imperfektischem Gebrauch. in: *Studier tillegnade Esaias Tegnér den 13 januari 1918*: 141–148. Lund 1918.

– Die Namen der Pāṇḍuiden am Hofe des Virāṭa. *ZDMG* 72 (1918): 224–226.

– Politiska och kulturella förbindelser mellan Grekland och Indien före Alexander den Store. *Nordisk Tidskrift* 1918: 466–493.

* Ett par äldre arbeten över hinduismen i ny bearbetning. *Svensk humanistisk tidskrift* 2 (1918): ???–???.

– [Trans.] *Franciskanermunken Vilhelms av Ruysbroeck resa genom Asien 1253–1255*, översatt och försedd med inledning och anmärkningar. 316 p. Stockholm 1919. (With long introduction, pp. 1–136).

– Some additional remarks on Vol I of Dr. Sven Hedin's "Southern Tibet". *Geografiska annaler* 1 (1919): 269–289. (With a rejoinder by Hedin: "Early European knowledge of Tibet", *ibid.* pp. 290–339).

– Zur alt- und mittelindische Wortkunde. *MO* 13 (1919): 1–54.

– Beiträge zur alt- und mittelindische Wortkunde. *ZDMG* 73 (1919): 129–158.

– Politiska och kulturella förbindelser mellan Grekland och Indien efter Alexander den Store. *Nordisk Tidskrift* 1919: 505–530.

* Ett par nyare engelska arbeten rörande indisk religion och kastväsen. *Svensk humanistisk tidskrift* 3 (1919): ???–???.

– [Ed.] *Uttarādhyāyanasūtra. Being the First Mūlasūtra of the Śvetāmbara Jains.* Edited with introduction, critical notes and a commentary. 409 p. (Archives d'études orientales, 18.) Uppsala 1920–22.

– [Trans.] *Ur Indiens klassiska litteratur.* Urval och översättning med inledning och anmärkningar. 3+239 p. Stockholm 1920. (Pp. 1–79 long introduction on literary history; pp. 81–107 selections from the *Buddhacarita*, pp. 109–127 selections from the *Kumārasambhava*, pp. 129–217 the *Mudrārākṣasa*, pp. 219–239 selections from the *Daśakumāracarita*).

– Cesare di Federici and Gasparo Balbi. *Geografiska annaler* 2 (1920): 146–161.

– Den vediska kulturens ålder. *Nordisk Tidskrift* 1920: 209–233.

– Indiska föreställningar om universum. *Nordisk Tidskrift* 1921: 129–145 & 209–224.

* *Die Suparṇasage. Untersuchungen zur altindischen Literatur- und Sagengeschichte.* 399 p. (Arbeten utg. af Vilhelm Ekmans Universitetsfond, 26.) Uppsala 1922.

– The history of the Jains. Chapter 6 in: E. J. Rapson (ed.), *The Cambridge History of India*, I: *Ancient India*: 150–170 Cambridge 1922.

– Quelques observations sur l'Ézour-Védam et son auteur. *JA* 11(20) (1922): 136–146.

– Upprorsrörelsen i Sydindien. *Nordisk Tidskrift* 1922: 194–216.

– Some remarks on the Hindu drama. *JRAS* 1923: 585–608. (Pp. 585–593 "The date of the Mudrā-Rākṣasa"; pp. 593–607 "The Author and Date of the Mṛc-chakaṭika.; pp. 607f. "A passage in the Dūta-vākya).

– Der Name Kambyses (Kaⁿbūjiya). *Zeitschrift für Indologie un Iranistik* 2 (1923): 140–152.

– Arbeten rörande Indiens religioner och språk under 1500- och 1600-talen. *Svenska Orientsällskapets Årsbok* 1 (1923): 12–26.

- *Stora Moguls dyñasti.* 225 p. Stockholm 1924.
- Preliminary Report on the "The Livro da Seita dos Indios Orientais" (The Brit. Mus. MS. Sloane, 1820). *BSOS* 2(4) (1924): 731–754. (On Father Fenicio).
- The Brit. Mus. MS. Sloane 2748A, a treatise on Hindu cosmology. *BSOS* 3(2) (1924): 317–342.
- The Brit. Mus. MS. Sloane 3290, the common source of Baldaeus and Papper. *BSOS* 3(3) (1924): 413–420.
- Cesare di Federici and Gasparo Balbi. *Indian Antiquary* 53 (1924): 49–61. (Revised from the 1920 article).
- A note on the Prathamasakha Brahmans. *Indian Antiquary* 53 (1924): 123–125.

* Supplementary notices on the discovery of the Vedas. *Journal of Indian History* 3 (1924): 161–187.

- A note from the Memoirs of Jahāngir. *JRAS* 1924: 440–442.
- Beiträge zur indoiranischen Wortkunde. *MO* 18 (1924): 1–45.

* Indiens självständighetssträvanden. *Ergo, Tidning för Uppsala studentkår* 1 (1924): ???–???.

- Något om den nyare Avestaforskningen. *Nordisk Tidskrift* 1924: 161–175.
- En helig man i det nutida Indien. *Nordisk Tidskrift* 1924: 409–416. (Vijaya Dharma Suri).
- Indologiska studier i Sverige. *Svenska Orientsällskapets Årsbok* 2 (1924): 55–72.
- Manikeiska miniatyrer från Centralasien. *Svenska Orientsällskapets Årsbok* 2 (1924): 73–100.

* *Zoroaster – life and times.* 36 p. Vizianagram 1927.

- *Indien: historia – religion – kastväsen.* 647 p. Stockholm 1925.
- [Trans.] *Indiska myter och sagor.* 260 p. (Myter och sagor.) Stockholm 1925. (Selected from the Veda, *Mahābhārata* and *Rāmāyaṇa*).
- The date of Zoroaster. *BSOS* 3(4) (1925): 747–755.
- Śakāra. *JRAS* 1925: 237–246.
- Thuggerna, en indisk kast av professionella mördare. *Svenska Orientsällskapets Årsbok* 3 (1925): 21–47.
- *Buddha, hans liv och lära.* 127 p. (Bonniers små handböcker i vetenskapliga ämnen, 12.) Stockholm 1926.
- *Jämförande indoeuropeisk språkvetenskap.* 205 p. (Bonniers små handböcker i vetenskapliga ämnen, 14.) Stockholm 1926.
- The original home of the Indo-Europeans. *BSOAS* 4(1) (1926): 147–170.

– Über den Begriff und die Etymologie von pūjā. In: *Beiträge zur Literaturwissenschaft und Geistesgeschichte Indiens. Festgabe H. Jacobi*: 276–297. Bonn 1926.

* Inledning + Det indoeuropeiska urhemmet + Iran och Indien till Alexander den Stores död. In: (Norstedts) *Världshistoria*, utg. av S. Tunberg och S. E. Bring. Del 1: De äldre orientaliska folken. Stockholm 1926.

– Remarks on the identification of some Jataka pictures. *BSOS* 4(3) (1927): 493–503. (In Chinese Central Asia).

– 1. Śūrpāraka; 2. Vitastā–Hydaspes. *JRAS* 1927: 111–120.

– St. Thomas the Apostle and India. *Kyrkohistorisk Årsskrift* 1927: 21–47.

– Amitraghāta. *JRAS* 1928: 132–135.

– A remark on two Indian names. *JRAS* 1928: 902–905. (1. Σισίκοττος, 2. Parṇadatta).

– Karl Ferdinand Johansson. *Indogermanisches Jahrbuch* 12 (1928): 324–329.

* (Norstedts) *Världshistoria*, utg. av S. Tunberg och S. E. Bring. Del 15. De asiatiska kulturerna. Av B. Karlgren och J. Charpentier. Stockholm 1926.

– Poison-detecting birds. *BSOS* 5(2) (1929): 233–242.

– Naicāśākha. *JRAS* 1930: 335–345. (RV 3.53).

– Antiochus, King of the Yavanas. *BSOS* 6(2) (Rapson Vol., 1931): 303–321.

– Indra. Ein Versuch der Aufklärung. *MO* 25 (1931): 1–28.

* Date of the Mudrārākṣasa. *Indian Historical Quarterly* 7 (1931): 629. (Short before the Hun invasion in the late 5th century).

* *Brahman, eine sprachwissenschaftlich-religionsgeschichtliche Untersuchung.* 4+138 p. (UUÅ 1932.8).

– Beiträge zur indischen Wortkunde. *MO* 26–27 (1932–33): 91–169.

– [Ed.] *The Livro da Seita dos Indios Orientais (Brit. Mus. Ms. Sloane 1820) of Father Jacobo Fenicio, S. J.*, Edited in Portuguese with an introduction and notes. 104+252 p. Paris 1933.

* Remarks on the fourth rock edict of Aśoka. *Indian Historical Quarterly* 9 (1933): 76–87.

The Indian Travels of Apollonius of Tyana. 66 p. (Skrifter utgivna av K. Humanistiska Vetenskaps-Samfundet i Uppsala, 29.3.) Uppsala 1934.

– Some notes on the Saundaranandakāvya. *JRAS* 1934: 113–119.

– "Irano-skythische" Eigennamen im Rigveda. *MO* 38 (1934): 59–71.

– Olof August Danielsson. *Indogermanisches Jahrbuch* 18 (1934): 327–332.

* William of Rubruck and Roger Bacon. *Geografiska annaler* 17 (1935): 255–267.

* Two short remarks on ancient Indian history. *Indian Historical Quarterly* 11 (1935): 529–536.

* *Catalogue of Manuscripts in European Languages Belonging to the Library of the India Office. Oriental and India Office Collections.* Vol. 1, Part 2: *The Mackenzie General and Miscellaneous Collections.* Compiled by J. S. Cotton, J. H. R. T. Charpentier & E. H. Johnston. With an introduction by David M. Blake. 78+713 p. London 1992. (Compiled 1911–35, printed in 1936, published only in 1992).

+ A great number of reviews in BSOS, GGA, JA, JRAS, MO, OLZ, WZKM, ZDMG etc.

APPENDIX II: Sanskrit and Comparative Linguistics in Swedish Universities 1838–1990

UPPSALA	LUND	GOTHENBURG
Professor i Sanskrit med jämförande indoeuropeisk språkforskning		
1838–53 Otto Fredrik Tullberg (Doc. ling. or., 1843 prof.)		
(1868? Lars Edman)	*(1862? Ernst Olbers)*	
1877/81–91 Axel Erdmann (1877–91 examinator i skr. & jämf. språkf, 1881–91 föreläsningar i sanskrit)	*1872–79 E. Tegnér (adjunkt i jämförande språkkunskap)*	
1880–92 Herman Napoleon Almkvist (eo. prof. i jämf. språkforskning)	*1884–89 E. Tegnér (professor linguarum orientalium)*	
1883–84 Olof August Danielsson (dep. eo. prof. i jämf. språkf.)	*1889–98 Nils Flensburg (doc.)*	
1886/93–1908 K. F. Johansson (doc., 1889–90 dep. eo. prof. i jämf. språkf. 1892–93 dep. eo. prof. i skr. & jämf. språkf., 1893–1908 eo. prof. i skr. & jämf. språkf.	*1898–1908 Nils Flensburg (eo.) of Germanic languages)*	*1890–93 Hj. Edgren (Prof.*
1908–26 Karl Ferdinand Johansson	1908–20 Nils Flensburg	*1899–1917 Evald Lidén (eo.)*
	1920–23 Herbert Petersson	1917–29 Evald Lidén
	1923–27 Herbert Petersson	
	1927–28 Helmer Smith	

1927–35 Jarl Charpentier	*1930–31 Helmer Smith*	1930–37 G. Morgenstierne
	1932–33 Kasten Rönnow	
1936–47 Helmer Smith	*1933–36 Helmer Smith*	*1937–38 Hjalmar Frisk*
1947–51 Hans Hendriksen	*1937–44 Hjalmar Frisk*	1938–67 Hjalmar Frisk
1951–53 Gösta Liebert (dep.)	*?1941?–49 Stig Wikander*	*1955–68 Gösta Liebert (eo.)*
1953–74 Stig Wikander	1949–69 Nils Holmer (jämf. språkf., särskilt indoeuropeisk)	1968–81 Gösta Liebert
1975–85 Nils Simonsson	–	1983–2000 Folke Josephson
1986–2003 Gunilla Gren-Eklund		
2004–09 William L. Smith		
Docentes:		
1886–93 Karl Ferdinand Johansson	1880–84 Hjalmar Edgren	
1873–91 Axel Erdmann	1888–98 Nils Flensburg (i sanskrit)	
1895–99 Evald Lidén	1915–40? Ebbe Tuneld (i indologi)	
1908–27 Jarl Charpentier	1911–23 Herbert Petersson (i jämf. ie. språkf.)	
1923–37 Ernst Arbman (indisk filologi & religionshistoria)	1921–36 Helmer Smith (i indologi)	
1928–43 Kasten Rönnow	1926–30 Hannes Sköld (1922–30 i slaviska språk)	1935–38 Hjalmar Frisk
1941–50 Nils Holmer (jämf. ie. språkf.)	1941–53 Stig Wikander	
1957–63 Nils Simonsson	1949–55 Gösta Liebert	
1972–81 Folke Josephson	–	
1980–86 Gunilla Gren-Eklund		198?–96 Claes Wennerberg

REFERENCES

AALTO, Pentti 1971. *Oriental Studies in Finland 1828–1918. The History of Learning and Science in Finland 1828–1918*. Helsinki: Societas Scientiarum Fennica.

—— 1991. Georg Carl von Döbeln's glossary of his Indian diary, *Studia Orientalia* 67: 127–145.

CARLQUIST, Gunnar (ed.) 1951. *Lunds stifts herdaminne. Från reformationen till nyaste tid.* (Serie II: Biografier, 3.) Lund: Gleerup.

CHARPENTIER, Jarl 1924. Indologiska studier i Sverige. *Svenska Orientsällskapets Årsbok* 2: 55–72.

DÖBELN, E. G. von & O. A. STRINDBERG 1856. *Några anteckningar om och af general von Döbeln*, I. Stockholm: Samson & Wallin.

DROIXHE, Daniel 1994. En attendant Bopp: une dissertation sur la convenance du Perse et du gothique de 1723. In: R. Sternemann (ed.), *Bopp-Symposium 1992 der Humboldt-Universität zu Berlin*: 53–71 (Indogermanische Bibliothek, dritte Reihe.) Heidelberg: Universitätsverlag C. Winter.

ELGENSTIERNA, G. M. 1926. *Den introducerade svenska adelns ättartavlor*, II. Stockholm.

FRÄNGSMYR, Tore 1976. *Ostindiska Kompaniet. Människorna, äventyret och den ekonomiska drömmen.* Höganäs: Wiken.

GHÅ = Göteborg Högskolans Årsskrift.

GHM = *Göteborg Högskolans Matrikel*:

– L. WÅHLIN & J. V. JOHANSSON: *GHM 1891–1916.* Gothenburg 1916.

– S. HALLBERG: *GHM 1916–1941.* (Göteborg Högskolas Årsskrift, 48.) Gothenburg 1942.

– N. SANDBERG: *GHM 1942–1954.* Gothenburg 1957.

KARTTUNEN, Klaus 1984. From the early days of Finnish Indology. Metrical translations from the Rigveda by Otto Donner. *Studia Orientalia* 55: 499–512.

—— 1991. Herman Kellgren – a bibliography. *Studia Orientalia* 67: 147–159.

—— 1994. From the early days of Finnish Indology II. Herman Kellgren. In: R. Sternemann (ed.), *Bopp-Symposium 1992 der Humboldt-Universität zu Berlin.* (Indogermanische Bibliothek, dritte Reihe): 105–132. Heidelberg: C. Winter.

—— 1997. From the early days of Finnish Indology III: Ivar Ulrik Wallenius. *Studia Orientalia* 82: 209–214.

—— 2003. South Asian Studies in Finland. *Newsletter of the IASS* 7: 17–25.

LJUNGBERG, P. A. 1880. *Västerås stifts herdaminne. Ny följd 1800–1880*, I: *Vestmanland*. Örebro: Allehandas förlag.

LUÅ = Lunds Universitets Årsskrift

LUM = *Lunds Universitets Matrikel*:

– Eva GERLE: *LUM, 1834–47*. Lund 1978.

– *LUM. Biografiska uppgifter öfver universitets styresmän, lärare och tjenstemän, 1879*. Lund 1879.

– C. af PETERSENS & A. MALM: *LUM*. Lund 1899.

– A. MALM & P. WILNER: *LUM, Läsåret 1924–1925*. Lund 1925.

– W. NORLIND & B. OLSSON: *LUM, 1939*. Lund 1939.

– W. NORLIND & M. PERSSON: *LUM, 1949–1950*. Lund 1951.

MO = *Le Monde Orientale*

OLÁN, Eskil 1923. *Ostindiska Compagniets Saga. Historien om Sveriges marknligaste handelsföretag*. 3rd edition. Gothenburg: Elanders Boktryckeri.

PAULY, E. 1992. Indisk filologi. In: *Københavns Universitet 1479–1979*, VIII: 511–566. Copenhagen: Sads Forlag.

SBL = *Svenskt biografiskt lexikon*, I–. Stockholm: Bonnier, 1918–.

SEGERSTEDT, Torgny T. 1976. Professuren i sanskrit med jämförande indoeuropeisk språkforskning. *Skrifter rörande Uppsala universitet*, B: *Inbjudningar*. (Acta Universitatis Upsaliensis): 12–19. Uppsala: Uppsala University.

SIMONSSON, Nils 1976. Sanskrit. In: Lennart Carlsson (ed.), *Faculty of Arts at Uppsala University. Linguistics and Philolophy*. (Uppsala University 500 Years, 6): 25–34. Uppsala: Uppsala University.

SMK = *Svenska män och kvinnor. Biografisk uppslagsbok*, I–VIII. Stockholm: Bonnier, 1942–55.

UAM = *Upsala Academies Matrikel*. (Predecessor of the UUM):

C. H. EKSTRAND, UAM 1832. Upsala 1832.

Aug. Th. LÅSTBOM, UAM 1841. Upsala 1841.

UUÅ = Upsala Universitets Årsskrift.

UUM = *Upsala Universitets Matrikel*:

– J. von BAHR & Th. BRANDBERG, *UUM*. Upsala 1896.

– Th. BRANDBERG & J. von BAHR, *UUM*. Uppsala 1906.

– Th. FRIES & E. von DÖBELN, *UUM, Höstterminen 1916*. Uppsala 1917.

– Th. FRIES & E. von DÖBELN, *UUM, Höstterminen 1926*. Uppsala 1927.

– Th. FRIES & E. von DÖBELN, *UUM, Höstterminen 1936*. Uppsala 1937.

– Å. DINTLER & Sune LINDQVIST, *UUM, 1937–1950*. Uppsala 1953.

ZETTERSTÉEN, Karl Wilhelm 1908. Report on the Manuscripts left by the late Professor O. F. Tullberg and now in the library of Uppsala University. *MO* 2 (1907–08): 66–83.

—— 1910. An old translation of the Ṛtusaṁhāra. *MO* 4: 1–23.

—— 1924. Semitiska studier i Sverige under de sista femtio åren, *Svenska Orientsällskapets Årsbok* 2: 5–54.

The Succession of Generations in Russian Sanskrit Studies (in the 19th–20th centuries)

SERGEI D. SEREBRIANY

This paper[1] is an attempt to present the history of Sanskrit studies in Russia in terms of personalities that made this history and the generations (or age groups) that can be discerned in its course.[2] Such an approach is justified, among other reasons, by the persistent "discontinuity" of the history of Indian studies in Russia. More than once, from generation to generation, there were gaps, or

[1] During the editorial work a number of additional references (mainly biographical sources) were suggested by the editor. In the footnotes such additions are marked accordingly. The English has been kindly checked by several colleagues, but the final responsibility for the style and grammar rests entirely with the author of the paper.

[2] In this paper, the concepts of "generation" or "age group" will not be defined rigorously in terms of time intervals. Differences between people of various ages have been determined (at least in Russia in the 19th and 20th centuries) not only and not so much by the sheer dates of their birth, as by patterns of historical (political, social) events variously spread through time. Meaningful time limits and intervals (i.e. boundaries between different age groups) should emerge as a result of the study, rather than be fixed at its beginning according to some general ideas about the succession of human generations.

It may be also noted that the paper is not going to present an exhaustive list of scholars involved in Sanskrit studies in Russia (nor exhaustive lists of achievements of the scholars who are mentioned). The task of the paper is just to outline a general pattern of "generational waves" within the overall framework of Russian history.

breaks of continuity. It is only in the second half of the 20th century that the tradition seems to have become truly cumulative.

Some years ago I was asked to write a short paper on the history of Sanskrit studies (more exactly, the studies of "ancient Indian literature") in 20th-century Russia (the USSR). In order to organize the data into a "narrative", I needed a "plot" or a pattern. I wish I could find (or "invent") one in terms of the history of ideas. But I failed to discern in the available data any pattern of this preferable kind (which does not exclude that it might be found later). Instead, I discerned a pattern of "generational waves" and described it in two papers in Russian (Serebriany 2002a; 2002b). This paper is an expanded version in English of those Russian papers.

The history of Sanskrit (Indian) studies in Russia during the last two centuries is part and parcel of the overall history of the country and may be best understood in the general context of this wider history[3]. In this paper, the succession of generations in Sanskrit studies in Russia will be compared, to an extent, with the succession of generations in other spheres of Russian culture, mostly in Russian literature (poetry), but also in music, painting and science. Sometimes references will be made to Western Indology, but not in a systematic way. In any case, my paper is but a tentative approach to a large theme.

---

[3] The history of Sanskrit studies in Russia and, for that matter, of Russian Indology in general is still to be written. In English one may refer to the article Roerich 1945, which is rather informative, but now dated and sometimes misleading (see a critique in Serebriany 2002a). Next, one should mention the book Bongard-Levin & Vigasin 1984. Unfortunately, this book mixes solid scholarship with propagandistic clichés (half-truths, half-lies and "figures of silence"). Both the paper and the book demonstrate to what extent the history of Indian (Sanskrit) studies was "ideologically dangerous" in the former USSR. Historical studies written by Aleksei Vigasin alone (or edited by him) in later years are more revealing and show the possibilities for future research (see e.g. Istoriya 1990: 318–349; Istoriya 1997: 392–433; Vigasin 1986; 2003; 2008). For older studies in Russian, see Bibliografiya Indii 1976: 32–58; 1982: 16–19.

THE ABORTIVE BEGINNING: GOTTLIEB SIEGFRIED BAYER

Oriental studies in general and Indian studies in particular were imported into Russia, along with other products of West European culture, during and following the reign of Peter I. Therefore the history of Sanskrit and Indian studies in Russia is, on the one hand, part of the *Rezeptionsgeschichte* of Indian (South Asian) culture and, on the other hand, part of the *Rezeptionsgeschichte* of Western scholarship and Western scholarly methods in the humanities. The foreignness of Indian studies in Russia is emphasized by the fact that through most of the 19th and even in the 20th century many Indologists in Russia were of German origin.

When, by a decree of Peter I, the Academy of Sciences was established in St. Petersburg in 1725, at first only foreigners (mostly Germans) were available for work at the new institution. As Sergej Ol'denburg bluntly put it in 1926 (the year is important, because both before 1917 and after about 1929 this kind of bluntness was hardly welcome):

> At the beginning of the 18th century there were no native scholars [*uchenykh/учёных* – which means, of course, both 'scholars' and 'scientists' – S.D.S.] in Russia, which is why they had to be invited from abroad; so for a long time foreigners, mainly Germans, outnumbered Russians [in the Academy]. Fortunately, the choice of foreigners was mostly lucky ... (Ol'denburg 1926: 784)

One of the first Germans to come (in 1726) was Theophilus (Gottlieb) Siegfried Bayer (1694–1738), a native of Königsberg (now Kaliningrad). An outstanding personality and a versatile scholar, he lived and worked in Russia during the last twelve years of his life (and died in St. Petersburg, at the age of 44, while preparing to go back to Germany). It was rather a critical period in the history of Russia: after the death of Peter I (in 1725) his "reforms" (in fact, revolutionary changes) were in many ways put to trial and, at least, had to be analysed and assessed anew. Officially, Bayer was invited to the Academy as a specialist in classical languages (i.e. Greek and Latin), but in St. Petersburg he, among other things, continued his research work on several Asian languages[4] and wrote important papers on the history of Russia, thus contributing to the formation of modern Russian consciousness.

In pre-Soviet Russian historiography Bayer, along with two other Germans, Gerhard Friedrich Müller (Miller in Russian, 1705–1783) and August Ludwig (von) Schlözer (1735–1809), was considered one of the founders of modern historical scholarship in Russia. As late as 1926 the Great Soviet Encyclopaedia called Bayer "one of the first serious researchers of ancient Russian history" (Anonyme 1926: 361). But in later Soviet books references to Bayer (and to the above-mentioned "*munitrayam*" in general) were mostly critical and even hostile (cf. e.g. Alpatov 1973; 1976; 1985, *passim*). Bayer was the first to identify the earliest rulers of Russia, the "Varangians" (in Russian *varyagi/варяги*) of old Russian annals (*letopisi/летописи*), as Scandinavians and thus started the long controversy known as the "Varangian problem". For some Russian contemporaries of Bayer (among them even for the great M. V. Lomonosov, 1711–1765), as well as for some Russian historians up to now, the fact (which seems to be indeed a fact) that the first rulers of Russia were foreigners would be a humiliation of national pride.[5] That is probably why no monograph on Bayer in Russia (and in Russian) has been published so far,[6] though there is

---

[4] Bayer was one of the first European Sinologists (cf. Lundbæk 1986). His major publication in St. Petersburg was *Museum Sinicum* (Bayer 1730), a compendium of information (as much as he managed to obtain) about the Chinese language. A long (even if probably not complete) list of Bayer's publications may be found in Pekarskij 1870: 194–196. Cf. also Babinger 1915. By the end of his life Bayer started working at an ambitious project, a huge Chinese–Latin dictionary, which remained uncompleted (cf. Lundbæk 1986: 188–203).

[5] On the state of the "Varangian problem(s)" in the 20th century, cf. e.g. Arne 1914; Stender-Petersen 1953; *Varangian Problems*; Lovmyan'skij 1985.

[6] In the 1930s the Russian Sinologist V. P. Taranovich did write a book about Bayer (Taranovich MS), but it was never published and is reported to be preserved in the archive of the Leningrad (now St. Petersburg) branch of the Institute of Oriental Studies (Bartol'd 1977: 32, 861; Aziatskij muzej 1972: 81; Istoriya 1990: 377, n. 60). It is remarkable that in the Russian histories of Orien-

a book in German (Babinger 1915) and a book in English by a Dane (Lundbæk 1986).

Bayer does deserve a special study, if only because he was not an insignificant figure in the Russian cultural landscape of the first post-Petrine decade. He was connected, one way or another, not only with some distinguished foreign members of the St. Petersburg Academy (e.g. with the famous French astronomer and geographer Joseph Nicolas Delisle [1688–1768; cf. Babinger 1915: 19–21] and with the great mathematician Leonhard Euler [1707–1783; cf. Bayer 1738]), but also with some key figures of Russian culture of that time: the historian (and statesman) Vasilij Tatishchev (1686–1750), the poet (and diplomat) Antiokh Kantemir (1708–1744)[7] and with Feofan Prokopovich (1681–1736), the theologian-cum-politician, one of the main ideologists of the reforms launched by Peter I (cf. Nichik 1977). Bayer's relations with Feofan seem to have been especially close: when a son of the Bayers died, Feofan wrote to his friend a consoling letter in Latin (Procopowicz MS); and after the death of Feofan Bayer wrote his biography (also in Latin: Bayer 1776). It was to Feofan Prokopovich that Bayer's magnum opus *Museum Sinicum* was dedicated.

---

tal studies in Russia the important contribution of Bayer to Russian historical scholarship is hardly ever mentioned (cf. Bartol'd 1977: 32; Aziatskij muzej 1972: 81, 235; Bongard-Levin & Vigasin 1984: 38; Istoriya 1990: 51–53; cf. also Livotova & Portugal 1966 and Vigasin 2008: 30–31).

Bayer is remembered in St. Petersburg by scholars of Greek and Roman antiquity. See e.g. a collection of papers: *Gotlib Zigfrid Bayer – akademik Peterburgskoj Akademii nauk. Sbornik statej* (St. Petersburg 1996) and a page about Bayer on the site "Sankt-Peterburgskie antikovedy" ["St. Petersburg scholars of classical antiquity"]: http://www.centant.pu.ru/spbant/db/bayer.html.

[7] Antiokh Kantemir, a son of the Moldavian prince (as well as a historian and a man of letters in his own right) Dmitrij Kantemir (1673–1723), is one of the earliest (if not *the* earliest) "modern" poet in the history of Russian literature. Cf. a letter (in Latin) from A. Kantemir to Bayer in Pekarskij 1870: 194. Here and further I do not give (as a rule) references to literature about Russian poets, composers, scientists etc., because I mention usually the most famous names, to be found in any general book on Russian literature, music, science etc.

Even before he came to Russia Bayer must have developed an interest in India. In St. Petersburg he managed to find two Indians to teach him an Indian language (not identifiable exactly).[8] There are at least three publications of Bayer related to Sanskrit and/or India (Bayer 1728; 1729; 1738). He is said to be the first in Russia to produce specimens of Devanagari in print. His study on the Greek kings in Bactria (Bayer 1738) was published together with a study on Indian ideas about time (*Doctrina temporum indica*) written by Christoph Theodosius Walther (1699–1741), a Danish missionary in Tranquebar. It shows that Bayer corresponded not only with Jesuits in China (cf. Lundbæk 1986, *passim*), but also with the Protestant mission in South India (at Tranquebar).[9]

In several respects, Bayer is a paradigmatic figure for the history of Indian studies (and probably the humanities in general) in Russia. The case of Bayer illustrates and emphasizes at least three important points:

1. The close connection of Indian studies in Russia with the world of European (Western) scholarship
2. The close connection between Indian studies and the general cultural (even political) situation in the country
3. The deplorable deficiency of our knowledge about the history of Indian studies in Russia, as well as the close connection between this history (and this knowledge) and "ideological" issues, some of them quite topical even now.

---

[8] P. P. Pekarskij gives the name of one of those Indians as "Sonhbara" (Pekarskij 1870: 189). His source is probably the unpublished autobiographical notes by Bayer himself, written in German (cf. Istoriya 1990: 377, n. 60). According to A. A. Vigasin, who could look into archives, the Indian in question transcribed his name (in signatures) as "Suhara" (Vigasin 2008: 66). In various scholarly publications it is stated that Bayer learned Sanskrit from his Indian informants. But most probably the Indians could teach him only one of North Indian dialects (cf. Vigasin 2008: 66–71).

[9] On the Lutheran mission at Tranquebar (Tarangambadi), in Tamilnadu, and its central figure, the German Bartholomäus Ziegenbalg (1682–1719), see Lehmann 1956.

One more point may be added: the persistent pattern of frustration that appears in the lives of many (though, fortunately, not all) Russian Indologists.

THE EARLY ENDEAVOURS: GERASIM LEBEDEV AND FRIEDRICH ADELUNG

In the 18th century, as far as we know, no other serious scholars of Sanskrit appeared in Russia.

Gerasim Stepanovich Lebedev (1749[10]–1817) is sometimes referred to as the first Russian scholar of Sanskrit or the first Russian Indologist (cf. Dasgupta 1957). Indeed, Lebedev was a contemporary of the first generation of British Indologists: W. Jones (1746–1794), Ch. Wilkins (1749–1836), H. Th. Colebrooke (1765–1837) and others. But, unlike these contemporaries of his, Lebedev, no doubt an outstanding personality in his own right, was not so much a scholar as a man of art[11] and a kind of adventurer,[12] in fact almost a misfit, a lonely figure without lasting consequences for Russian scholarship and Russian culture in general. He defected from a Russian diplomatic mission in Vienna (so in later Soviet terms he was a *nevozvrashchenets/невозвращенец*, 'one who has not returned [from abroad]') and for several years travelled through Europe on his own. In 1785 he went to India, first to Madras, then

[10] There seems to be some uncertainty about the exact year of Lebedev's birth, but according to M. I. Vorob'eva-Desyatovskaya "the majority of scholars agree that Lebedev was born in 1749" (Istoriya 1990: 319).

[11] Of a low origin (a son of a poor provincial priest) and ill-educated, he must have been a talented musician (playing cello): it was by musical performances that he earned his living in Europe and later in India.

[12] There is no full-fledged biography of Lebedev in Russian (nor in any other European language), but only a number of papers (cf. Bibliografiya Indii 1976: 49–50 [nos. 854–875]; cf. also Bongard-Levin & Vigasin 1984: 40–45; Istoriya 1990: 318–326; Vigasin 2008: 37–47). Lebedev's adventurous life has attracted writers. There is at least one novel in Russian about him, published in Moscow in 1959 (*Gerasim Lebedev* by V. Smirnova-Rakitina, cf. Bibliografiya Indii 1976: 50 [no. 871]). The modern Russian playwright Edvard Radzinskij (Эдвард [sic!] Радзинский) once wrote a play about the life of Gerasim Lebedev. The play was even staged, but without success.

to Calcutta. All in all Lebedev stayed in India for twelve years (1785–1797). In Calcutta he gave musical performances and learned Bengali, Hindustani as well as, to an extent, Sanskrit. But in today's Bengal Lebedev is remembered and revered as the founder of the first Bengali theatre (in Calcutta).[13]

By 1801 Lebedev returned to Russia (via South Africa and London). In London he got published (in English) his book on the spoken Calcutta Hindustani (Lebedev 1801; 1963), which seems to be his most lasting contribution to scholarship. In St. Petersburg, in 1805, he published (in Russian) a more ambitious book with a long (and rather clumsy) title, which may be rendered in English as 'An Impartial Review of the Systems of the Brahmans of East India, their Sacred Rites and Popular Customs' (Lebedev 1805). In modern terms, the book is a kind of cultural-anthropological study of Hinduism. Unfortunately, it is very naive, rather badly written and much below the level of sophistication achieved by that time in Western Indology.

But whatever expertise on Indian culture Lebedev could offer, there was hardly any demand for it in Russia of his time. Lebedev made an attempt to join the Academy of Sciences, but the Academy rejected him. Instead he made a more or less successful career at the "Asian Department" of the foreign ministry, working as a translator, mostly from English (Istoriya 1990: 323–324).

To place Lebedev in a broader cultural context, we may mention that he was a contemporary of Gavriil Derzhavin (1743–1816), the great Russian poet of the 18th century. There is a special study about their interaction at the beginning of the 19th century (Altshuler 1963).

Aleksandr Radishchev (1749–1802), the famous writer and poet and a kind of 18th-century counterpart of our 20th century "dissi-

[13] That is why the only scholarly book so far about Lebedev has been written in Bengali, by Hayat Mamud, a man of letters (and a poet) from Bangladesh who lived and worked in Moscow in the 1970s (Hayat Mamud 1985). This book is recently translated into Russian (Hayat Mamud 2012). See also Vasil'kov 2013.

dents", was Lebedev's coeval. But he did not live long enough to interact with Lebedev after the latter's return to Russia.[14]

To the same age group belonged Nikolaj Novikov (1744–1818), a great publisher and also a kind of "dissident". In 1788 he published in Moscow the *Bhagavadgītā*, translated into Russian from the English translation of Ch. Wilkins (Novikov 1788).[15] The translator was Aleksandr Petrov (c. 1760–1793),[16] a close friend of Nikolaj Karamzin (1766–1826), the (later) famous historian and man of letters. In 1792 Karamzin published parts of Kalidāsa's *Śakuntalā* in his own translation from G. Forster's German version (Karamzin 1792; cf. Grintser 1998).

Within the age group of A. Petrov and N. Karamzin we may also include the German scholar Friedrich Adelung (1768–1843), who in Russia was called Fedor Pavlovich Adelung.[17] A native of Stettin (and a nephew of the famous linguist Johann Christoph Adelung [1732–1806]), he moved to Russia in 1794. In the history of Russian scholarship F. Adelung is remembered as a distinguished historian[18] and bibliographer. But he took interest in San-

---

[14] Radishchev might have been i recentlyndeed interested in meeting Lebedev. In his famous book "A Journey from St. Petersburg to Moscow" (1790) Radishchev quoted G. T. F. Raynal's classical work *L'Histoire philosophique et politique des établissements et du commerce des Européens dans les deux Indes* (1770), comparing the Russian autocracy with the arbitrary rule of certain Indian potentates.

[15] For more details, cf. Serebriany 2002c.

[16] Very little is known about him. His short life deserves a special study.

[17] Germans domiciled in Russia usually got their first names russified (thus Friedrich might become Fiodor) and amplified with patronymics according to the Russian tradition: thus Adelung became Fiodor Pavlovich presumably because his father's name was (taken to have been) Paul (= Pavel in Russian).

[18] F. Adelung was one of those late 18th – early 19th century historians who started retrieving and reconstructing the history of Russia on the basis of rigorous documentary evidence (by way of thorough searches through archives, both in Russia and abroad). The master-mind and financial sponsor of this work was count Nikolaj Petrovich Rumyantsev (1754–1826), a son of the famous military commander Pyotr Rumyantsev-Zadunajskij (1725–1796), an illegitimate son of Peter I (cf. e.g. Kozlov 1981; Saraskina 2003). N. P. Rumyantsev's collections were the basis of what later became the State Lenin Library (now the Russian State Library) in Moscow, our counterpart of the Library of the Congress.

skrit too. As early as 1811 he wrote a short essay on the similarities between Sanskrit and Russian (Adelung 1811a; 1811b). Later he compiled a meticulous bibliography of Sanskrit texts published by the 1830s (Adelung 1830; 1837). Such works, certainly, get dated very soon, but, according to A. A. Vigasin, F. Adelung's bibliographical handbook was in use for several decades (Vigasin 1986: 271; Vigasin 2008: 74, 78–79; cf. also Windisch 1917: 96–97). N. Karamzin and F. Adelung belonged to the same generation (or age group) as the brothers Schlegel: August-Wilhelm (1767–1845) and Friedrich (1772–1829), the founders of Sanskrit (Indian) studies in Germany. But in Russia of that time (and for a long time to come) India did not evoke such an enthusiastic – and creative! – response as in Germany.

THE CONTROVERSIAL PATRON: COUNT SERGEJ UVAROV

With Count Sergej Semenovich Uvarov (1786–1855) we move a generation further.[19] Uvarov was a very controversial figure during his lifetime and remains so even today. He is probably most remembered as the author of the notorious formula "*pravoslavie – samoderzhavie – narodnost*'"[20], the ideological basis (motto) of the

---

It was mostly using the materials unearthed by count Nikolaj Rumiantsev and his collaborators that Nikolaj Karamzin wrote his famous "History of the Russian State" (*Istoriya gosudarstva rossijskogo*), a classic of Russian historical thought.

[19] It is probably worth mentioning here that in Russia the early scholars of things Tibetan, Mongolian and Buddhist belonged to the age group of Uvarov. I have in mind Isaac Jacob Schmidt (1779–1847) and P. L. Schilling von Canstadt (1786–1837).

[20] I.e. [Christian] orthodoxy – autocracy – but the last term is hardly translatable, as it was deliberately vague and polysemantic; *nārod* is of course "people" or, in German, "Volk", so the abstract noun *narodnost'* ("people-ness" or "Volkstum"?) may be understood as referring to any feelings, or ideas (ideals), or actions originating from and/or addressed to (and presumably aimed at the good of) the "people"; so we may render it as "being-with/feeling-with/thinking-with/acting-with-and-for-the-sake-of one's own people".

rule of Nicholas I (1825–1855). For Soviet historiography, he was an arch-reactionary, almost a non-person. No book about him has ever been written in Russia.[21] It is only now that we start to re-evaluate this figure and his place in our history (cf. Frolov 1999; see also Vigasin 1986: 268–269).

In any case, Uvarov was a remarkable personality. Brilliantly educated (among other places, at the University of Göttingen), he became president of the Academy of Sciences in 1818 (at the age of 32) and remained at this post till his death. In 1833–1849 he was also the minister of public education.

In 1810 (he was at that time the secretary of the Russian embassy in Paris) Uvarov submitted to the then minister of public education "A Project of an Asiatic Academy", written and published in French (Ouvaroff 1810; a Russian and a German translation appeared later: Uvarov 1811; Ouvaroff 1811). This was a very ambitious and, in fact, utopian project of establishing in Russia a great centre of Orientalist learning and research work. In this scholarly-cum-political utopia India occupied a prominent place.[22] The utopia, of course, never came true, but, as president of the Academy of Sciences in 1818–55, Uvarov did a lot for the development of Orientalist (including Indological) scholarship in Russia. It is at Uvarov's initiative that in 1818 the so-called "Asiatic Museum", a centre of Orientalist research, was founded (as part of the Academy). In the 20th century this "Museum" was renamed as "Institute of Oriental Studies" ("Institut vostokovedeniya"). Among other things, it is largely due to the support of Uvarov that the great project of the St. Petersburg Sanskrit dictionary (by O. Böhtlingk and R. Roth) was realized (cf. Vigasin 2003).

---

[21] The first full-fledged biography of Uvarov was written by an American scholar: Whittaker 1984 (a Russian translation of the book was published only in 1999).

[22] Cf. Vigasin 1986: 268–269; Vigasin 2008: 75–77; cf. also Aziatskij muzej 1972: 12. Uvarov was acquainted with and influenced by Friedrich Schlegel. Uvarov's "Projet" came out only two years later than F. Schlegel's famous book *Über die Sprache und Weisheit der Indier* (1808).

It was to Uvarov that 19th-century sanskritologists in Russia, R. Lenz, O. Böhtlingk and F. Bollensen, dedicated their works as to "the founder of Sanskrit studies in Russia" (cf. Vigasin 2003). Although Uvarov as the ideologist of the Russian Empire may be called a "state-nationalist" (or an "autocratic imperialist"), in his academic politics he was rather cosmopolitan and aware of the international nature of scholarship. It is against certain resistance within the Academy (as well as outside it) that he supported the publication of Böhtlingk's *Sanskrit–German* dictionary, a project which was not immediately related to Russia's "national interests" (cf. Vigasin 2003). Among Indological publications sponsored by the Academy we find books by foreign scholars as well (e.g. Bruce 1862).[23] A. A. Vigasin writes that Max Müller considered the possibility of publishing the *Ṛgveda* with the financial support of the St. Petersburg Academy, and only his strained relations with Böhtlingk made him change his plans (cf. Vigasin 2003).

Uvarov's *Projet d'une Académie Asiatique* was translated into Russian by the poet Vasilij Zhukovskij (1783–1852), one of the best Russian poets before Pushkin and one of Pushkin's teachers in poetry. V. Zhukovskij is a classic of poetic translations, mostly from German and English. Among other foreign poems he rendered into Russian (from the German translation by F. Rückert) the Nala-Damayantī story from the *Mahābhārata*.[24] This rendering was first published in 1844 and many times republished since then. It may not be widely read now, but an educated Russian is supposed to remember that the poetic piece is there.[25]

---

[23] Editor's note: Charles Bruce (1836–1920), a native of Scotland, was a student of R. Roth, but left Indology and in 1868 entered the ICS (Indian Civil Service), in which he made a very successful career (see *Who Was Who* 1916–1928).

[24] Zhukovskij's translation of Homer's *Odyssey* (first published in 1849) is a classic of Russian literature. But Zhukovskij did know Greek (as he did not know Sanskrit) and translated Homer's poem also with the help of a German translation.

[25] The history of translations from Sanskrit into Russian cannot be adequately treated in this paper and will only be touched from time to time. In fact, this his-

MORE GERMANS: J. A. B. DORN, ROBERT LENZ, FRIEDRICH BOLLENSEN

It is said that the first scholar to teach Sanskrit in Russia was a German, Johannes Albrecht Bernhard (in Russian Boris Andreevich) Dorn (1805–1881). He taught for some time (in 1829–1835) at the University of Kharkov (now Kharkiv in independent Ukraine). But this was only the beginning of his long and successful career in Russia.[26] Later he came to St. Petersburg, became a member of the Academy of Sciences and (the second) director of the Asiatic Museum (1842–1881).[27]

Sanskrit studies do not occupy a prominent place in the scholarly work of B. Dorn (as a scholar he seems to be remembered most for his historical and linguistic research work on Afghanistan and also as an Arabic scholar and numismatist). But as early as 1833 he published in Kharkov a remarkable book (in Latin!) titled "On the affinity of Slavic and Sanskrit languages" (Dorn 1833), quite a sophisticated study in the field of comparative linguistics, then only in *statu nascendi* (cf. Vigasin 1986: 271–272).

The first Sanskrit scholar born in the Russian Empire seems to have been a Baltic German named Robert Lenz (in Russian Robert Khristianovich Lents, 1808–1836)[28]. He was a student at the University of Dorpat/Derpt (now Tartu in Estonia) and then sent to

---

tory (as well as the overall *Rezeptionsgeschichte* of Indian letters in Russia) has not yet been studied properly. As the first general approach to the theme, a book by the American scholar Robert Stacy (1985) may be mentioned.

[26] On B. Dorn, see Bartol'd 1977, *passim*; Aziatskij muzej 1972, *passim*, Istoriya 1990: 254–258, 344–345; Vigasin 1986: 271–272; 2008: 79–82. See also Kulikova 1975.

[27] The first director of the Asiatic Museum was another German scholar, Christian Martin Fraehn (in Russian Khristian Danilovich Fren; 1782–1851). See Bartol'd 1977: 43–45 and *passim*; Aziatskij muzej 1972: 13–29 and *passim*; Istoriya 1990: 241–254.

[28] He was a younger brother of the famous physicist Emil Lenz (1804–1865) who also worked in Russia.

Berlin to study under F. Bopp. Lenz was a promising scholar,[29] but died much too early (at the age of 28).[30]

In this age group we should include one more German (from Germany), Friedrich (in Russian Fedor Fedorovich) Bollensen (1809–1896), who, like B. Dorn, taught Sanskrit in Russia (Kazan) and, like R. Lenz (and following his steps), brought out an edition-cum-translation (into German) of Kālidāsa's *Vikramorvaśīyam* (Bollensen 1846).[31]

R. Lenz, B. Dorn and F. Bollensen were contemporaries (and even coevals) of those age-groups in Russia which made "great leaps forward" in several spheres of culture. Aleksandr Pushkin (1799–1837) is the first figure in what we now call "classical Russian literature".[32] Next we may recall Nikolaj Gogol (1809–1852). In music, Mikhail Glinka (1804–1857) was probably the first to make Russian music a respected (and later admired) part of

---

[29] His most notable contribution to Sanskrit studies was an edition of Kālidāsa's *Vikramorvaśīyam* with notes and a translation into Latin (Lenz 1833a). This work (dedicated to S. Uvarov) was praised by F. Bopp (cf. Vigasin 1986: 272–273). R. Lenz was also the first to describe Sanskrit manuscripts preserved at the Asiatic Museum (Lenz 1833b).

[30] On Robert Lenz, see Bongard-Levin & Vigasin 1984: 65–68; Istoriya 1990: 326–329; Vigasin 1986: 272–274; Vigasin 2008: 83–87; Bibliografiya Indii 1976: 35, 50.

Editor's note: On Lenz, see also Klatt in *Allgemeine Deutsche Biographie* 18 (1883): 279; W. Lenz in *Deutschbaltisches biographisches Lexikon 1740–1960.* (Köln 1970): 447f.; L. Mseriants, K istorii sanskritologii v Rossii (Neizdannye materialy k biografii Roberta Lentsa i professora Pavla Yakovlevicha Petrova) *Novyi Vostok* 1922(1): 309–314; Windisch 1917: 144; G. A. Zograf, **Uchenye zapiski Leningradskogo gosudarstvennogo universiteta* 1960(2); **Recueil des actes de la séance publique de l'Académie impériale des sciences de Saint-Pétersbourg* 1836: 11–14.

[31] On Friedrich Bollensen, see Bibliografiya Indii 1976: 46; Vigasin 2008: 196.

Editor's note: On Bollensen, see also Windisch 1917: 375–379; *Biobibliograficheskij slovar' Kazan'* 1 (1904): 221–222 (defective); Neisser, *Allgemeine Deutsche Biographie* 47 (1903): 91–92; Neisser, *Bezzenberger's Beiträge* 24 (1899): 173–176 (with bibliography).]

[32] Apollon Grigor'ev (1822–1864) called Pushkin *nashe vse* (наше всё), which may be rendered in Sanskrit as *asmadīyam sarvasvam*.

European culture. In painting, the names of Karl Bryullov (1799–1852) and Aleksandr Ivanov (1806–1858) should be mentioned. In mathematics, a senior member of this age group was Nikolaj Ivanovich Lobachevskij (1793–1856), a lonely man of genius (ill-understood by his contemporary compatriots),[33] while Mikhail Vasil'evich Ostrogradskij (1801–1861/1862) is considered the founder of the continuous tradition of mathematics in Russia.

Had Robert Lenz lived longer and/or had Bernhard Dorn given more time to Sanskrit, a similar and simultaneous "great leap forward" might have taken place in Russian Indology as well. In the West, the senior coevals of Lenz and Dorn were, among others, Ch. Lassen (1800–1876) and Eugène Burnouf (1801–1852). But for Sanskrit studies in Russia it was still the time of humble beginnings. Most probably, there was not yet enough domestic demand for this kind of commodity.[34] After all, it was the age of the tsar Nicholas I (1796–1855, ruled since 1825), whose geopolitical interests (outside Europe) were directed not so much to India, as to the Caucasus and Constantinople.

OTTO BÖHTLINGK, PAVEL PETROV, KAETAN KOSSOVICH

Coming to the generation(s) born in the 1810s, we meet Mikhail Lermontov (1814–1841) and Aleksei K. Tolstoi (1817–1875), two of the greatest Russian poets; Vissarion Belinskij (1811–1848), Alexander Herzen (in Russian Aleksandr Gertsen, 1812–1870) and

[33] For about twenty years (1827–1846) Lobachevskij was the rector of Kazan University. It was under his rectorship that the chair of Sanskrit (the first in Russia) was opened there in 1842 (cf. Bongard-Levin & Vigasin 1984: 69; Istoriya 1990: 124, 338–339).

[34] At least in one other Orientalist discipline, Mongolian studies, something like a "great leap forward" was made in Russia by a scholar of this age group: Jósef Kowalewski (or, in Russian, Osip Kovalevskij, 1801–1878), a Pole, banished from Vilno (Vilnius) to Kazan in 1824. Kowalewski is considered one of the most important "Mongolists" of the 19th century (cf. Kotwicz 1948; Istoriya 1990: 278–281; Valeev 2004).

Mikhail Bakunin (1814–1876), the famous men of letters and "ideologists"; Ivan Goncharov (1812–1891) and Ivan Turgenev (1818–1883),[35] two of the greatest Russian prose writers. In the field of Oriental studies in Russia we may recall at least Anton Schiefner (in Russian Anton Antonovich Shifner 1817–1879), the Tibetologist,[36] and Vasilij Pavlovich Vasil'ev (1818–1900), the Sinologist (a pupil of Józef Kowalewski). Both have contributed significantly to Buddhist studies.[37]

In this age group, the towering figure in Sanskrit studies is of course Otto (in Russian: Otton Nikolaevich) Böhtlingk (1815–1904),[38] a German born in St. Petersburg (his ancestors had come to Russia during the reign of Peter I). O. Böhtlingk, probably more than anybody else, symbolizes the international nature of true scholarship in general and of the 19th-century Indology in particular. In 1833–35 he was a student at St. Petersburg University, but then moved to Germany where he studied under A. W. von Schlegel, Ch. Lassen and F. Bopp. For many years he lived and worked in Russia, associated with the Academy of Sciences, but in 1868 returned for good to his "historical homeland". In Germany

---

[35] Ivan Turgenev's years of life are exactly those of Karl Marx (1818–1883). Their coeval was the Russian tsar Alexander II "The Liberator" (1818–1881, ruled since 1855) who, unlike them, died a violent death (assassinated on the 1st of March [old style], 1881).

[36] Anton Schiefner was a linguist of many interests. He also contributed to the study of Sanskrit, of Caucasian languages and even of Finnish!

[37] On Schiefner, cf. e.g. Istoriya 1990: 288–289; Bibliografiya Indii 1976: 57. On Vasil'ev, cf. e.g. Istoriya 1990: 305–317; Istoriya 1997: 265–274; Bibliografiya Indii 1976: 46–47; Vasil'ev 1974.

Editor's note: On Schiefner also R. Rost, *Indian Antiquary* 9 (1880): 111–113; F. Wiedemann, *Bulletin de l'Académie impériale des sciences de St.-Pétersbourg* 26 (1880): 30–44 (with bibliography); JRAS 1880: Proceedings ix–xiii; bibliography in Livotova & Portugal' 1966; on Vasil'ev, V. V. Bartol'd, Istoricheskie i geograficheskie trudy V. P. Vasil'eva, *Aziatskij sbornik* 1918: Izv. 549–560; A. I. Ivanov, V. P. Vasil'ev kak sinolog, *Aziatskij sbornik* 1918: Izv. 561–566; A. Ivanovski (?), *Biograficheskij slovar' S.-Peterburgskogo universiteta* 1 (1896): 125–129; *Biobibliograficheskij slovar' Kazan'* 1 (1904): 222–225.

[38] According to E. Windisch, 19th-century Indology was dominated by three figures: O. Böhtlingk, R. Roth and A. Weber (Windisch 1917: 238).

he is considered a German scholar, but he also occupies a place of pride in the history of Russian Indology.[39]

Böhtlingk's coevals in Russia were Pavel Yakovlevich Petrov (1814–1874) and Kaetan Andreevich Kossovich (1814–1883).

P. Petrov seems to have been the first ethnic Russian to study and teach Sanskrit in Russia (first at the University of Kazan, then, from 1853, in Moscow). In 1828–32 he studied at Moscow University (together with the above-mentioned V. Belinskij who wrote admiringly about his brilliant friend), then at the University of St. Petersburg. As a promising scholar, he was sent to Germany, from where he visited France and Britain (1838–40). F. Bopp is reported to have been impressed by Petrov's personality (Istoriya 1990: 336). But after coming back to Russia (in 1840) Petrov was rather unsuccessful both in his formal career and in his scholarly achievements. He has left to posterity neither any major work, nor any *guruparamparā* in Sanskrit studies.

In 19th-century Russian literature the term "superfluous person (man)" (*lishnij chelovek* / лишний человек) was coined. This term

---

[39] Cf. e.g. Bongard-Levin & Vigasin 1984: 76–78; Istoriya 1990: 345–346; Vigasin 2003; 2008: 108–139; Bibliografiya Indii 1976: 45–46.

Editor's note: On Böhtlingk, see also Windisch 1917: 238–246; anonyme [according to *Bibliografiya Indii*, the author is Ol'denburg], *Materialy dlya biograficheskogo slovarya dejstvitel'nykh chlenov imperatorskoj Akademii Nauk* 1 (Petrograd 1915): 53–59 (with bibliography on pp. 54–59); Delbrück, *Berichte über die Verhandlungen der Königlich Sächsischen Gesellschaft der Wissenschaften, Philologisch-Historische Klasse* 56 (1904): 253–258; *Kern, *Museum* 1904: 322ff.; Kirfel, *Neue Deutsche Biographie* 2: 396–397; S. F. Ol'denburg in S. A. Vengerov (ed.), *Kritiko-biograficheskij slovar' russkikh pisatelej i uchionykh* 3 (St. Petersburg 1892): 216–220 & *Izvestiya Imperatorskoj Akademii Nayk* 5(20) (1904[5]): v–vi & *Zhurnal Ministerstva Narodnogo Prosveshcheniya* 353 (1904[5.4]): 41–47; R. Schmitt, *Lexicon Grammaticorum* (Tübingen 1996): 117–118; L. von Schroeder, *Reden und Aufsätze* 1913: 315ff.; Windisch, *Indogermanisches Jahrbuch* 3 (1915): 176–187; bibliography by S. F. Ol'denburg & K. G. Salemann, *Mélanges asiatiques* 10 (1892[2]): 247–256 & *Bulletin de l'Académie impériale des sciences de St.-Pétersbourg* (N.S. 3, 1894): 97–106; briefly in *Neue Deutsche Biographie* 1 (1995): 625; Otto Böhtlingk: *Briefe zum Petersburger Wörterbuch 1852–1885.* Hrsg. von Heidrun Brückner und Gabriele Zeller (Glasenapp-Stiftung, 45). Wiebaden: Harrassowitz, 2007.

denotes a certain social type (depicted in its many variants by Russian writers from Pushkin onwards) which, after and because of getting European education, cannot fit into Russian life. Petrov (as depicted by his contemporaries) looks very much like one more version of this very "superfluous person".[40] The life and character of Pavel Petrov deserves a special study.[41]

Kaetan Kossovich may be perceived as another version of "superfluous person". A son of a priest in Belorussia, he graduated from Moscow University where he studied classical Western languages, i.e. Greek and Latin, as well as some Oriental languages (Hebrew, Arabic, and Farsi). Later he studied Sanskrit, evidently without any teacher, from books. Kossovich was a protegé of Aleksej Khomyakov (1804–1860), a poet and one of the leading "Slavophiles". These "Slavophiles" (Khomyakov himself as well as others) took interest in Sanskrit as a "close relative" of Russian, but this interest remained amateurish and did not bring about any lasting scholarly achievements (cf. Vigasin 2003). Although Kossovich taught Sanskrit for many years at St. Petersburg University (since 1858), he too remained, as a matter of fact, an amateur

---

[40] On Petrov, cf. Roerich 1945: 73; Bongard-Levin & Vigasin 1984: 67–71; Vigasin 1986: 276–278; Istoriya 1990: 329–342; Bibliografiya Indii 1976: 55–56; Vigasin 2008: 89–103.

Editor's note: On Petrov, see also *Biograficheskij slovar' Moskovskogo universiteta* 2 (1855): 225–227; *Biobibliograficheskij slovar' Kazan'* 1 (1904): 236–237; G. F. Shamov, Sanskritologiya v Kazanskom universitete v pervoj polovine XIX v., *Problemy Vostokovedeniya* 1959(3): 117–122; A. S. Shofman, Russkij sanskritolog P. Ya. Petrov, *Ocherki po istorii Russkogo vostokovedeniya* 3 (1960): 126–146; A. S. Shofman, Sanskritolog P. Ya. Petrov v Kazanskom universitete, *Uchenye zapiski Kazanskogo gosudarsvennogo universiteta* 117(9) (1957): 53–58; a few notes by Mehlitz are given in his article on Trithen in *Zeitschrift für Indologie und Iranistik* 10 (1936): 277–287.

[41] One of the personal traits of P. Petrov (which seems to be rather common among Russians) was his inability to concentrate on any particular subject or field of study. Among other things, in his later years he turned to Arabic studies, but has not become an outstanding Arabist either.

Sanskritologist.[42] His life, like the life of Pavel Petrov, also deserves a special study.[43]

The failure of Petrov and Kossovich as scholars is sometimes explained by the general "backwardness" of Russia of that time, more exactly, by the lack of interest in Russian society for Sanskrit and Indian culture. Be as it may, it was only in later generations that really creative Sanskrit scholars did appear among Russians.

IVAN MINAEV AND HIS AGE-GROUP

Some of the greatest figures of Russian culture were born in the 1820s. Here we need only mention Fedor Dostoevskij (1821–1881) and Lev Tolstoi (1828–1910). But Russian Indology had to wait till the 1840s.

Ivan Pavlovich Minaev (1840–1890), a pupil of K. Kossovich (as well as of V. Vasil'ev), is sometimes called the founder of Russian Indology.[44] In any case he seems to have been the first (ethnic)

[42] On Kossovich, cf. Bongard-Levin & Vigasin 1984: 71–73; Vigasin 1986: 278–280; Istoriya 1990: 347–349; Bibliografiya Indii 1976: 48–49; Vigasin 2008: 94–97, 116–122, 135–139.

Editor's note: On Kossovich, see also JRAS 15 (1883), Proceedings: xxiii–xiv; I. B.; *Zhurnal Ministerstva Narodnogo Prosveshcheniya* 1883 March 226: 35–42; A. Ya. Garkavi, *Izvestiya Imperatorskogo Arkheologicheskogo Obshchestva* 10: 433–487; M. O. Marks, *Russkaya Starina* 52 (1886): 605–620; S. F. Ol'denburg, *Biograficheskij slovar' S.-Peterburgskogo universiteta* 1 (1896): 346–354; S. Ol'denburg, *Russkij biograficheskij slovar'*, IX (Knappe–Kyuhel'beker, 1903): 301–303.

[43] Like P. Petrov, K. Kossovich could not limit his interests to Sanskrit and Indian studies. Among his publications there are studies on the Avesta and ancient Persian inscriptions (cf. e.g. Istoriya 1990: 348). He was also a scholar of Hebrew. It may be worth mentioning that Kaetan's brother, Ignatij Kossovich (1808–1879), a scholar of Greek and Latin, an alumnus of Vilnius University and a professor at Warsaw University, at least once tried his hand in translating from Sanskrit: in 1851–52 he got published his Russian translation of the Nala-Damayantī episode from the *Mahābhārata* (see Bibliografiya Indii 1976: 369 [no. 7507]).

[44] On Minaev, cf. Kotovskij 1967; Aziatskij muzej 1972: 238–239; Bongard-Levin & Vigasin 1984: 82–97; Istoriya 1997: 392–406; Bibliografiya Indii 1976: 52–53; Vigasin 2008: 140–191; Ajrapetov *et al.* 2010 (especially the contributions of Ya. V. Vasil'kov, A. A. Vigasin and T. N. Zagorodnikova).

Russian Indologist to gain recognition among Western colleagues.[45] He was also the first Russian professional Indologist to travel in India.[46] His interests were many, but the main one was in Buddhism, which may be explained by the tradition of Buddhist studies in Russia and by the fact that the Russian Empire had some Buddhist populations.

It is usually (and justly) said that I. Minaev lived too short a life (only fifty years). But it may be noted that his coeval, the great composer Pyotr Chaikovskij (1840–1893) lived not much longer. Roughly to the same age group belonged the great composers A. Borodin (1834–1887), M. Musorgskij (1839–1881) and N. Rimskij-Korsakov (1837–1910), as well as M. Balakirev (1837–1910) and Ts. Kyui (Цезарь Антонович Кюи; 1835–1918). They are collectively known as "the mighty five" (in Russian "*moguchaya kuchka*"/могучая кучка, 'the mighty handful'). At that time there was no "mighty group" yet in Russian Indology, but only rather lonely scholars at various universities. Three more names may be recalled: Vincenz (in Russia: Vikentij Ivanovich) Scherzl (1843–1906) taught Sanskrit in Kharkov and Odessa,[47] Friedrich (Fedor Ivanovich) Knauer (1849–1917 or, according to other

---

[45] After graduating from St. Petersburg University Minaev studied in Europe for five years (1863–68).

[46] On Minaev's travels, cf. Istoriya 1997: 397–403; Minaev 1960. It is worth noting that Minaev's first trip to India (in 1874–75) was financed by St. Petersburg University, but the other two trips (in 1880 and 1885) were sponsored by the Military ministry (cf. Istoriya 1997: 401). This shows that by Minaev's time Indian studies in Russia became strategically topical (or at least perceived as such by military authorities).

[47] V. Scherzl was born in Bohemia, then the Austro-Hungarian Empire, now the Czech Republic. On him, cf. Istoriya 1997: 78; Bibliografiya Indii 1976: 57.

Editor's note: On Scherzl, see also *Dvadtsatipyatiletie Imperatorskago Novorossijskago universiteta* (Odessa 1890): 279–280; *Ènciklopedichnyj slovar'* 38 (1908): 529.

sources, 1918) in Kiev,[48] and Leopold von Schröder (1851–1920) in Dorpat (Tartu) (he moved to Vienna in 1894).[49]

Probably the time was not yet ripe for Sanskrit studies to thrive as a specific branch of the humanities in Russia. Thus, at least three among I. Minaev's contemporaries who, as students, studied Sanskrit with P. Petrov at Moscow University, later became eminent scholars in other fields. Fedor Evgen'evich Korsh (1843–1915) is said to have composed poems in Sanskrit, but he is remembered now more as a specialist in classical (i.e. Greek and Latin) as well as Slavic languages.[50] Filipp Fedorovich Fortunatov (1848–1914) published his thesis on *Sāmaveda-Āraṇyaka* in 1875, but later became a great authority on comparative Indo-European linguistics.[51] Vsevolod Fedorovich Miller (1848–1913) studied the

---

[48] Friedrich Knauer was a native of Bessarabia (now independent Moldova). On him, cf. Bongard-Levin & Vigasin 1984: 100–101; Bibliografiya Indii 1976: 48; Vigasin 2008: 194–195; Cherkaz'yanova 2008.

Editor's note: On Knauer, see also *Album Academicum Dorpatense 1801–1889*, no. 9096; *Ukrains'ka radians'ka enciklopediya* 6 (1961), s.v.; scattered information in L. von Schröder, *Lebenserinnerungen* (Vienna 1921).

[49] Leopold von Schröder, a nephew of Otto Böhtlingk, was a Baltic German, born in the Russian Empire. Later he became Professor in Vienna and a very famous (some would say notorious) Indologist in the German speaking world. On him, cf. Vigasin 2008: 192–194.

Editor's note: On von Schröder, see also his own *Lebenserinnerungen* (Vienna 1921, with bibliography on pp. 276–287); Frauwallner, *Anzeiger der Österreichischen Akademie der Wissenschaften* 98 (1961): 84–89; *Deutsch baltisches biographisches Lexikon 1710–1960* (Vienna 1970); briefly *Deutsche Biographische Enzyklopädie* 9 (1998): 149.

[50] On F. Korsh as an Indologist, cf. e.g. Bongard-Levin & Vigasin 1984: 99; Istoriya 1997: 27; Bibliografiya Indii 1976: 48; Vigasin 2008: 200.

Editor's note: On Korsh, see also *Xaristeria, sbornik statej v cest' F. E. Korsha* (1896); A. N. Kononov, *Biobibliograficheskij slovar' otechestvennykh tyurkologov. Dooktiabr'skij period* (Moscow 1974): 194–195 with further references; N. K. Dmitriev, *Fedor Evgen'evich Korsh* (Moscow 1962, with bibliography); R. Lewicki, *Lexicon grammaticorum* (1996): 526.

[51] On F. Fortunatov as an Indologist, cf. e.g. Bongard-Levin & Vigasin 1984: 97–98; Istoriya 1997: 24–25; Bibliografiya Indii 1976: 56; Vigasin 2008: 197–198.

Veda(s) (and the Avesta too) in Germany, but later his most important work was in the field of Slavic (and Iranian) languages.[52] So, this age group was not at all poor in great names in the humanities (as well as in science). We may also recall, among others, Aleksandr Veselovskij (1838–1906), the famous literary historian, and Vasilij Kluchevskij (1841–1911), the equally famous historian of Russia. The famous Ukrainian linguist Afanasij Potebnia (1835–1891) may also be included in this age group.[53] As for science, suffice it to recall the name of the great chemist Dmitrij Mendeleev (1834–1907).

SERGEJ OL'DENBURG, FEDOR STCHERBATSKY AND OTHERS

It was only the generation of I. Minaev's pupils that yielded names of a similar stature in the field of Sanskrit and Indian (Indological) studies. I mean of course, in the first place, Sergej Fedorovich

---

Editor's note: On Fortunatov, see also R. Lewicki, *Lexicon Grammaticorum* (1996): 303–304; M. Vasmer, *Indogermanische Jahrbuch* 8 (1920/21): 266–269 (with bibliography on pp. 270–271).

[52] On V. Miller as an Indologist, cf. e.g. Bongard-Levin & Vigasin 1984: 98–99; Istoriya 1997: 25–26; Bibliografiya Indii 1976: 51–52; Vigasin 2008: 198–200.

Editor's note: On Miller, see also B. A. Kaloev, *V. F. Miller – Kavkazoved (Issledovanie i materialy)* (Ordzhonikidze 1963, life, photo, letters); S. F. Ol'denburg, *Russkaya mysl'* 1913(12): 39–41 (an obituary).

[53] A figure apart is Dmitrij Nikolaevich Ovsyaniko-Kulikovskij (1853–1920) who followed Potebnia in the field of linguistics and literary studies. He started his scholarly career as a student of Sanskrit (and Vedic mythology), but later switched over to the history of Russian literature and culture, as well as to general linguistics and what now would be called "literary theory". On Ovsyaniko-Kulikovskij as an Indologist, cf. e.g. Bongard-Levin & Vigasin 1984: 101–102; Istoriya 1997: 79–80; Bibliografiya Indii 1976: 53–54; Vigasin 2008: 201–203.

Editor's note: On Ovsyaniko-Kulikovskij, see also R. Lewicki, *Lexicon Grammaticorum* .(1996): 684–685; Pamyati D. N. Ovsyaniko-Kulikovskogo, *Nachala* 1922(2): 5–42; see also *Biobibliograficheskij slovar' Kazan'* 1 (1904): 142–143.

Ol'denburg (1863–1934) and Fedor Ippolitovich Shcherbatskoj[54] (often Shcherbatsky, Stcherbatsky or Shcherbatskoy; 1866–1942). Among other things, it is worth noting that both belonged to the elite of the Empire. (all earlier Russian Indologists had been of modest origins). It seems that by the end of the 19th century Indology in Russia acquired a higher prestige.

S. Ol'denburg was an outstanding (and in a way paradigmatic) figure in Russian culture and public life of the first third of the 20th century. One of the leaders of the constitutional-democratic party, in the fateful summer of 1917 he was for some time the minister of education in the Provisional government of A. Kerenskij. From 1904 up to 1929 he was the "permanent secretary" of the Academy of Sciences.[55] Both Ol'denburg and Shcherbatsky, like many other representatives of the pre-revolutionary Russian intelligentsia, after 1917 came to collaborate with the new "powers that

---

[54] In Russian this aristocratic family name sounds actually "Shcherbatskój" (with the stress on the last syllable). In Lev Tolstoi's "Anna Karenina" we meet prince Shcherbatskoj and his family.

[55] There are two books (collections of jubilee speeches and papers) devoted to Ol'denburg: one published in 1934, to celebrate "the 50th anniversary of his scholarly and public activity: 1882–1932" (*Ol'denburg Festschrift* 1934); another one in 1986, which included the speeches pronounced in 1984, on the occasion of the 50th anniversary of his death (*Ol'denburg Gedenkschrift* 1986). Neither in 1932/34 nor in 1984/86 anything like the whole truth could be possibly told. Nevertheless, the former book is more informative, the latter one more rhetorical. Both include bibliographies of Ol'denburg's publications. Cf. also Istoriya 1997: 406–415; Bibliografiya Indii 1976: 54–55; Vigasin 2008: 205–236. It was only at the beginning of the 21st century that an attempt to write a biography of Ol'denburg was undertaken by the historian Boris Kaganovich; see Kaganovich 2006. This excellent and revealing book has a significant and honest subtitle: "An attempt at a biography". See also the review of this book by the author of the present article: Serebriany 2007.

With Ol'denburg and Shcherbatsky we cross the fatal time limit of 1917. On the scholars active in the field (and in the country) after that year one may consult the "Dictionary of our country's orientalists" by S. D. Miliband (1995; 2008). This "Dictionary" may be complemented with the martyrologue compiled by Ya. Vasil'kov and M. Sorokina (2003).

be" in the hope to "civilize" them, but were eventually crushed in the process.[56]

S. Ol'denburg is remembered first of all as an efficient organizer of research. Probably his most lasting achievement has been the well known Bibliotheca Buddhica: thirty volumes in forty years (1897–1937).

F. Shcherbatsky hardly needs a detailed introduction in this paper. He seems to be the Russian Indologist who is best known outside Russia, probably because he wrote and got published his "*granthatrayam*" in English (Stcherbatsky 1923; 1927; 1930–32). A biographical study of Shcherbatsky, the man and the scholar, is still a desideratum.[57]

To the same age group there belonged Dmitrij Nikolaevich Kudryavskij (1867–1920). He studied comparative linguistics and Sanskrit at St. Petersburg and Jena (under B. Delbrück); since 1898 he was a professor of German and comparative linguistics at the University of Yur'ev (Dorpat/Derpt, now Tartu in Estonia). Among D. N. Kudryavskij's contributions to Sanskrit studies is a fine translation of the *Hitopadeśa* into Russian published in Yur'ev in 1908–1909 (see Istoriya 1997: 46–47; Vigasin 2008: 195–196).

In the West, the age group of Ol'denburg and Shcherbatsky is represented, among others, by Sylvain Lévi (1863–1935), a friend

---

[56] The whole story (of Ol'denburg's case) remains to be told. For the first approaches to the theme, cf. Kaganovich 1994; Alpatov & Sidorov 1997; Kaganovich 2006: 151ff.

[57] On Shcherbatsky, cf. *Shcherbatsky Gedenkschrift* 1972; Bongard-Levin & Vigasin 1984: 126–143; Istoriya 1997: 416–424; Vasil'kov 1989; Bibliografiya Indii 1976: 57–58; Vigasin 2008: 237–443.

Editor's note: On Shcherbatsky, see also *Indian Historical Quarterly* 20 (1944): 102–103; JRAS 1943: 118–109; N. P. Anikeev, *Vestnik istorii mirovoj kul'tury* 1957(2): 241–245; P. V. Bapat, ABORI 24 (1943): 284–285; V. I. Kal'yanov, *Izvestiya AN SSSR* 5 (1946[3]): 245–252; I. M. Kutasova, *Sovetskoe vostokovedenie* 1958(3): 136–143; N. Yu. Lubotskaya, *Narody Azii i Afriki* 1967(3): 195–196; D. S. Ruegg, *Journal of Indian Philosophy* 1 (1971): 213–216; *A. N. Zelinskij, *Strany i narody Vostoka* 5 (1967): 236–257. Further, *Papers of Th. Stcherbatsky*. Translated for the first time into English by Harish C. Gupta, edited with an introduction by Debiprasad Chattopadhyaya. (Soviet Indology Series, 2.) Calcutta 1969.

of Ol'denburg,[58] and Moritz Winternitz (1863–1937). In Russia, this age group yielded a number of eminent Orientalists: P. Kokovtsov (1861–1942), N. Marr (1865–1934), A. Snesarev (1865–1937), B. Turaev (1868–1934), V. Bartol'd (1868–1930), A. Krymskij (1871–1942). In Russian poetry, it was the generation of "elder symbolists": Fedor Sologub (1863–1927), Vyacheslav Ivanov (1866–1949), Konstantin Bal'mont (1867–1942). Bal'mont, at the beginning of the 20th century, rendered into Russian (from West European translations) the three plays of Kālidāsa and the *Buddhacarita* of Aśvaghoṣa. In Russian prose literature, it was the age group of Anton Chekhov (1860–1904), Maksim Gorkij (1868–1936) and Ivan Bunin (1870–1952), the first Russian Nobel prize winner in literature (1933). In Russian politics, alas, it was the age of the last tsar Nicholas II (1868–1918) and of Vladimir Ulyanov-Lenin (1870–1924).

Many Russians of these generations left the country with the "first wave" of the post-revolutionary emigration. The junior colleague of Ol'denburg and Shcherbatsky, Alexander Wilhelm (Baron) von Staël-Holstein (1871–1937),[59] a Baltic German, after 1917 remained and died in China.[60] He studied Mahāyāna texts, comparing Sanskrit, Chinese and Tibetan versions.[61]

---

[58] The correspondence between S. Lévi and Ol'denburg, as well as between S. Lévi and Shcherbatsky was recently published in France (Bongard-Levin *et al.* 2002)

[59] In Russia(n) he was called Aleksandr Avgustovich, and his surname re-transliterated from Russian may look as Stal'-Gol'shtein.

[60] He was a professor of Sanskrit in Peking. A. von Staël-Holstein's mother-land was actually Estonia. In the 1920s and 1930s he often visited independent Estonia, but must have never reappeared in Soviet Russia.

[61] A. von Staël-Holstein was almost coeval with the great composer Sergej Rakhmaninov (1873–1943) who also emigrated after 1917. On A. von Staël-Holstein, cf. Bongard-Levin & Vigasin 1984: 103, 105; Istoriya 1997: 426–428; Bibliografiya Indii 1976: 131, 139; Vigasin 2008: 503–506.

Editor's note: On Staël-Holstein, see also *Deutsch-Baltisches Biographisches Lexicon 1710–1960* (Vienna 1970); S. Elisséeff, *Harvard Journal of Asiatic Studies* 3 (1938): 1–8; *E. Schierlitz, *Monumenta Serica* 3(1) (1938): 286–291: *J. Schubert, *Artibus Asiae* 7 (1937): 227–230; Märt Läänemets, *Homeland (Kodumaa)*, April 8, 1987.

A special case is that of Pavlo Ritter (In Russian Pavel Ritter, 1872–1939), a German from Ukraine, who studied and later taught Sanskrit at Kharkov University.[62] Before 1917 he translated from Sanskrit into Russian, among other works, Kālidāsa's *Meghadūta* (the translation unsurpassed till now). But after 1917 he seems to have switched over to translating into Ukrainian.[63]

S. Ol'denburg and F. Shcherbatsky nearly succeeded in establishing a tradition of Sanskrit (predominantly Buddhist) studies in Russia. But their success was rather short-lived.

THE GENERATION THAT SQUANDERED ITS INDOLOGISTS[64]

The next age group in Russia are those who were born from the late 1870s to early 1880s and up to the mid-1890s. These people were lucky enough to mature and got educated before 1917 (or even 1914). Those of them who did not perish or emigrated proved to have enough guts to survive during the "Soviet" years and even brilliantly realize themselves one way or another. It is this age group that yielded the greatest names in 20th century Russian poetry: Aleksandr Blok (1880–1921), Andrej Belyj (1880–1934), Velimir Khlebnikov (1885–1922), Nikolaj Gumilev (1886–1921),

---

[62] P. Ritter was a student of D. Ovsyaniko-Kulikovskij.

[63] In the 1920s Bolshevik authorities encouraged the development of Ukrainian language and culture (later they had second thoughts and started persecuting "Ukrainian nationalists"). The life and work of P. Ritter (like those of A. Potebnia and D. Ovsyaniko-Kulikovskij) must be studied in the context of Russian-Ukrainian cultural relations and, probably, as examples of Russian-Ukrainian biculturalism (in Ritter's case it might have been even Russian-Ukrainian-German triculturalism). Kharkov, where Ritter (like A. Potebnia and D. Ovsyaniko-Kulikovskij) lived and worked, was a predominantly Russian city with the Ukrainian "hinterland". On P. Ritter, cf. Bongard-Levin & Vigasin 1984: 102; Istoriya 1997: 80–81; Bibliografiya Indii 1976: 56; Vigasin 2008: 203.

Editor's note: On Ritter, see also **Professor P. G. Ritter (1872–1939). Zbirnik biografichnikh ta bibliografichnikh materialiv*. Harkiv 1966 (in Ukrainian) and Y. Zavhorodniy in the present volume.

[64] An allusion to the famous paper by Roman Jakobson "On a Generation that Squandered its Poets" ("О поколении, растратившем своих поэтов", 1931).

Anna Akhmatova (1889–1966), Boris Pasternak (1890–1960), Osip Mandelshtam (1891–1938), Marina Tsvetaeva (1892–1941), Vladimir Mayakovskij (1893–1930) as well as some others. In Russian prose literature, we may recall Mikhail Bulgakov (1891–1940) and Isaak Babel (1894–1940).[65]

It is this age group that has given us the "stalwarts of Soviet Orientalist studies": the turkologists V. Gordlevskij (1876–1956), S. Malov (1880–1936) and A. Samojlovich (1880–1938), the Sinologist V. Alekseev (1881–1951), the Arabist I. Krachkovskij (1883–1951), the Mongolist B. Vladimirtsov (1884–1931), the historian of the "Ancient East" V. Struve (1889–1965), the Iranist E. Bertels (1890–1957) and the Japanologist N. Konrad (1891–1970).[66]

For Indology it was one of the difficult periods. One more junior colleague of Ol'denburg and Shcherbatsky, Nikolaj Dmitrievich Mironov (1880–1936), who studied in Strassburg under E. Leumann, emigrated after 1917 and died in emigration, evidently not having realized his full potential.[67] Otto (alias Otton Ottonovich) Rosenberg (1888–1919), one more Baltic German and a very promising scholar of Buddhism,[68] died while trying to escape Russia plagued with the civil war.[69] Another pupil of the

---

[65] Here we may also recall two great composers: Igor Stravinskij (1882–1971) and Sergej Prokof'ev (1891–1953).

[66] It is also the age group that gave Russia some of the most well known political figures of the 20th century: Iosif Dzhugashvili-Stalin (1879–1953) and Lev (Leib) Bronshtein-Trotskij (1879–1940), on the one hand, and Nikita Khrushchov (1894–1971), on the other.

[67] On Mironov, cf. Bongard-Levin & Vigasin 1984: 237–239; Istoriya 1997: 425; Bibliografiya Indii 1976, index; Vigasin 2008: 499–503.

[68] Shcherbatsky called him "the most gifted pupil of mine" (cf. Istoriya 1997: 428).

[69] Otto Rosenberg was (or at least was believed by many in Russia to have been) a relative (a brother or a cousin?) of Alfred Rosenberg (1893–1946), one of the leading ideologists of German national-socialism, the author of the notorious book "The Myth of the 20th century". On Otto Rosenberg, cf. Istoriya 1997: 428–430; Vigasin 2008: 444–498. Some of his works were republished in 1991 (Rosenberg1991).

same masters, Mikhail Izrailevich Tubyanskij (1893–1937) (one of the first of many Jews in 20th-century Russian Indology) was executed during the "Great Terror".[70]

Yet another pupil of Ol'denburg and Shcherbatsky (and yet another Russian Jew) was a bit more lucky: Nadine Stchoupak, née Nadezhda Steinberg, (1886–1941) emigrated to France as early as 1908 and studied in Paris under Antoine Meillet and Sylvain Lévi. Later she worked with Louis Renou and died in Paris.[71]

For Rozalia Iosifovna (alias Osipovna) Shor (1894–1939) and Boris Aleksandrovich Larin (1893–1964), Sanskrit was just one of their manifold interests. Their contributions to Sanskrit studies are masterly, but very limited in scope.[72]

Editor's note: On Rosenberg, see also K. Kollmar-Paulenz & J. S. Barlow, *Otto Ottonovich Rosenberg and his Contribution to Buddhology in Russia*. (Wiener Studien zur Tibetologie und Buddhismuskunde, 41.) Vienna 1998.

[70] Tubyanskij's contributions to Sanskrit studies proper were not numerous. But he was probably the first in Russia to study Bengali and definitely the first to translate Rabīndranāth Tagore's writings (mostly prose) into Russian straight from the original. In the late 1920s he went to Mongolia and switched over to the study of Buddhism after Mongolian and Tibetan sources. (Cf. Aziatskij muzej 1972: 162–165; Bibliografiya Indii 1976, index). The date of his death is sometimes given as 1943 (so says the official document graciously presented to his relatives in the 1950s, during the Khrushchovian "rehabilitance"). But most probably he was shot soon after his arrest in 1937 (so in Vasil'kov & Sorokina 2003: 378–379).

[71] See Bongard-Levin *et al.* 2002: 164, n. 321. See also Mazon 1945; Kaganovich 2005.

[72] Both Shor and Larin probably deserve special studies as two paradigmatic (though in different ways) figures of the humanities during the Soviet period.

Rozalia Shor was a Jewess born in Lithuania (in the city of Kaunas). Before 1917 a Jewish woman in Russia could not possibly make a career which Rozalia Shor managed to make under the "Soviet" regime. She must have combined the advantages of her pre-revolutionary secondary education (probably at a gymnasium) with the social advantages available to her after the revolution. After the disaster of 1917 the class of educated Russians was heavily decimated. In the vacuum thus created there were drawn a lot of Jews who were educated enough and quite willing to work under the new regime (which welcomed them because they mostly had not been connected with the *ancien régime*). Rozalia Shor was evidently one of such Jews. In 1921 she graduated from the historico-philological faculty of Moscow University where she studied European literature and general linguistics, which included Sanskrit. In the 1920–30s she was one of the leading

Boris Leonidovich Smirnov (1891–1967) was a medical doctor, exiled to Ashkhabad (Turkmenistan). A self-taught Sanskrit scholar, he started publishing his translations from the *Mahābhārata* only in the late 1950s. This was a work of love and devotion, very important for its time, but rather dated now.[73]

It so happened that the leading "Soviet" Indologist in this age group was Aleksej Petrovich Barannikov (1890–1952). In his earlier years he studied Sanskrit, but in the 1930s made his career by criticizing Ol'denburg and Shcherbatsky as "reactionaries" who preferred the "dead" Sanskrit to the living "languages of the people". He established Hindi studies at Leningrad University and, among other things, translated Tulasīdāsa's *Rāmacaritamānasa*

Soviet scholars in the humanities. The long list of her publications includes mostly works on European literature and general linguistics. But there are also some papers on the Vedic language and Sanskrit narrative literature. R. Shor translated from Sanskrit into Russian "Selected stories from the *Pañcatantra*" (Moscow, 1930) and the "Twenty-five stories of Vetāla" (Leningrad, 1939). Cf. Serebryakov 1962: 342–344; Bibliografiya Indii 1976, index.

Boris Larin was born in Poltava, in the very heart of Ukraine. His father was a teacher, who later became a priest (cf. Larin's short autobiography in Larin 1977: 214–215). In 1910–1914 Larin studied at Kiev University: old Russian literature with V. Perets, comparative linguistics and Sanskrit with F. Knauer. In 1916 he came to St. Petersburg (then Petrograd) and, among other things, studied Sanskrit with Shcherbatsky. His list of publications (Larin 1977: 215–222) includes works on Russian, Ukrainian and Lithuanian languages (especially on lexicography and dialectology). A number of his publications is connected, one way or another, with Sanskrit (or Vedic). His translation of a portion from Vāmana's *Kāvyālaṁkāra* (published in 1957, but probably done earlier) is a masterpiece of philological work. It is indeed a pity that Larin has not done more in the field of Sanskrit. Larin's biography leaves an impression that he was a scholar of a great potential, but deliberately kept a low profile in order to be on the safe side. In the "Soviet" time to be a son of a priest was almost a crime in itself.

Editor's note: On Larin, see also V. I. Kal'yanov, *Narody Azii i Afriki* 1964(4): 276–277; R. Lewicki, *Lexicon grammaticorum* 1996: 549–550.

[73] On B. Smirnov, cf. Bibliografiya Indii 1976: 56 & index. His biography is also a desideratum.

Editor's note: On Smirnov, see also P. A. Grintser, *Sovetskoe vostokovedenie* 1958(6): 151–152.

into Russian doggerel (published in 1948).[74] His preface to the translation, though, was for many years and for many people an important source of information about Indian cultural heritage.

It would not be out of place here to tell briefly the sad story about two other Indologists of this age group, the Mervarts, husband and wife.[75] He was German, born in Mannheim, in 1884, as Gustav Hermann Christian Meerwarth. But in 1911 we find him in Russia, in St. Petersburg, teaching German at a gymnasium. In 1912 he became a citizen of Russia and converted to Orthodox Christianity. In Russia he was called German Khristianovich or Aleksandr Mikhajlovich Mervart. She was born in St. Petersburg, in 1888, as Ludmila Aleksandrovna Levina. Her father, a military doctor, was sent to India in 1897 to fight the plague together with the famous doctor Vladimir Khavkin (alias Waldemar Mordecai Wolff Haffkine, 1860–1930). Under the influence of her father she got interested in India and later "infected" her husband with this interest. In the spring of 1914 the Mervarts were sent to South Asia by the Academy of Sciences to collect materials for the Museum of Ethnography. They stayed in Ceylon (now Sri Lanka) and India till 1918 and came back home to a different country. After many troubles and hardships they returned in 1924 to St. Petersburg (in that very year renamed Leningrad) and worked there several years, describing what they had managed to bring from South Asia, doing other research work as well as teaching. But by the late 1920s the Bolshevik government decided to tame the Academy of Sciences, and Aleksandr Mervart fell victim to the ensuing witch-hunt. He was arrested as a German spy and a member of a counter-revolutionary organisation, sentenced to five years of imprisonment and in 1932 died in a prison camp. Ludmila Mervart, also arrested

---

[74] Here and further for the detailed bibliographical information I may refer the reader to the two books of "Bibliography of India" (Bibliografiya Indii 1976 & 1982), to the "Dictionary" of S. D. Miliband (Miliband 1995) and to the martyrologue compiled by Ya. Vasil'kov and M. Sorokina (2003).

[75] On the Mervarts, see Vigasin 2008: 507–537; Vasil'kov & Sorokina 2003: 265ff.

in 1930 and also sentenced to five years of imprisonment, fortunately survived and from 1944 till her death in 1965 lived in Moscow. She is remembered as the founder of Indonesian studies in Russia.

Aleksandr Mervart, among other things, may be called the founder of Tamil studies in Russia. But he also has to his credit some publications related to Sanskrit studies.

THE LOST GENERATION: THE KILLED OR EXILED

Next we come to those who were born by the very end of the 19th century and in the 1900s. The critical year, the borderline between different age groups, seems to be 1895. Those born from this year onwards had to mature during the troubled time of World War I, the Civil War and the early 1920s; if they managed to survive through this ordeal (and remained in the country), they might have faced the state terror of the late 1920s and the 1930s. Here are some paradigmatic figures of this age group.

The poet Sergej Esenin (1895–1925) sided, though half-heartedly, with the Bolsheviks, but committed suicide in 1925.

The philosopher Mikhail Bakhtin (1895–1975) was arrested in 1928 and banished (for five years) to Kazakhstan in 1929 for "private lecturing on idealist philosophy". After the banishment he did his best to keep quiet and far enough from the capitals, playing the role of a "Literaturwissenschaftler" (a role more acceptable to the Soviet establishment). It is only by the end of his life, that he was discovered by younger people and hailed almost as a prophet (rather to his own surprise).

Vladimir Nabokov (1899–1977) emigrated with his parents after 1917 and became a famous American writer.

Nikolaj Zabolotskij (1903–1958), one of the best 20th-century Russian poets, was arrested in 1938 and almost driven to insanity by tortures; fortunately, he survived and was sentenced only to banishment (released in 1946).

Dmitrij Likhachov (1906–1999) graduated from Leningrad University in 1928 and soon was arrested as a member of a religious group; spent several years in a prison camp on the "Solovki"; from the 1940s to 1950s he became a leading authority on Old Russian literature (playing up the official "russophile" ideology); by the end of his life Likhachov turned almost into a symbol of Russian intelligentsia; under and after Gorbachev he was one of the most often heard critics of the "Soviet" regime in terms of "culture".

Dmitrij Shostakovich (1906–1975) is one of the greatest 20th-century composers. His relations with the "Soviet" regime were uneven and ambiguous, but at least he was never persecuted. His posthumous memoirs revealed his long-standing aversion against the regime.

To the same age group there belonged many outstanding cultural figures whose relations with the "Soviet" establishment might have been as complex and ambiguous as in the case of D. Likhachov and D. Shostakovich. Aleksandr Kolmogorov (1903–1987) is considered one of the greatest mathematicians of the 20th century. Yulij Khariton (1904–1996), the physicist, was the main architect ("the father") of the Soviet A-bomb.[76]

It is also this age group that provided Russia with the leading politicians of post-Stalin and post-Khrushchev era. To name only the three: Mikhail Suslov (1902–1982), Aleksej Kosygin (1904–1980) and Leonid Brezhnev (1906–1982).

For Sanskrit scholars, the pupils of Ol'denburg and Shcherbatsky, born in the 1900s, life was harsh. Evgenij Evgen'evich Obermiller (1901–1935) was the luckiest: he died a natural death in his early thirties. Andrej Ivanovich Vostrikov (1902–1937) fell victim of the "Great Terror". Boris Vladimirovich Semichov (1900–1981) spent many years in camps and banishment and could not realize himself fully. Of this age group, it was only Vladimir Ivanovich Kal'yanov (1908–2001) who, surviving in Russia, es-

---

[76] It may be noted that the father of American A-bomb, J. Robert Oppenheimer (1904–1967), was exactly Khariton's coeval.

caped imprisonment and premature death. He translated several books of the *Mahābhārata* (but the quality of his translations is vehemently questioned by younger scholars).[77]

George Roerich (1902–1960, in Russian Yurij Nikolaevich Rerikh), one of the sons of the painter Nicholas (Nikolaj Konstantinovich) Roerich (1874–1947), also belonged to this generation. Like Vladimir Nabokov, he survived in emigration, in Western Europe, India and the U.S.A., but, unlike Nabokov, came back to Russia in 1957 and died in Moscow, having considerably stimulated the development of Indology in his motherland.[78]

THE AGE-GROUPS DECIMATED BY WORLD WAR II

In the second half of the 20th century several generations of Indologists in general and Sanskrit scholars in particular appeared in Russia.

In the fateful 1917 there was born Igor Dmitrievich Serebryakov (1917–1998), a peculiar and rather lonely figure in our Indology. He translated a lot from Sanskrit, but has not proved to be an artful translator.[79] I should also mention Grigorij Fedorovich Il'in

[77] When Kal'yanov died in January 2001, no fellow Indologist attended the funeral. Kal'yanov is held responsible for the dire fate of his colleagues. He is also reported to have been an instrument of harassing Shcherbatsky in the late 1930s. It is up to St. Petersburg Indologists to tell the sad story in full.

[78] The Roerichs were (and continue to be) a very controversial family whose true story only begins to be told. The father, Nikolaj Roerich, appears to have been rather a sinister personality. He entertained an utopian idea of establishing a "Buddhist state" in Central Asia. In this connection he evidently came in touch with Soviet secret services, intending to "use" them, but most probably was instead "used" himself. The son, Yurij Roerich, was an earnest scholar, but his life must have been doomed by the macabre follies of his parents. The circumstances of his returning to Russia are rather unclear (he might have been forced to return). The circumstances of his death are surrounded with suspicions and legends. Some people believe that he was actually killed (poisoned?), either because he proved to be "ideologically alien", or for some other reason.

[79] I. D. Serebryakov had the advantage of personal experience of India. From the late 1950s he lived and worked in India for years in various official capacities (in 1964–69, as a correspondent of the newspaper *Pravda*). Other Russian

(1914–1985), a historian of ancient India who worked with Vedic and classical Sanskrit sources.

These two scholars belonged to the generations which were decimated by World War II. In Russian poetry this age group is represented by Aleksandr Tvardovskij (1910–1971), Semen Lipkin (1911–2003),[80] Vadim Shefner (1915–2002)[81] as well as several well known poets of the so-called "war generation", born in the early 1920s.[82] Among prose writers suffice it to name Aleksandr Solzhenitsyn (1918–2008). In the humanities at large the most famous name is perhaps Yurij Mikhajlovich Lotman (1922–1994). In this age group, there are also some scholars of modern Indian languages, e.g. Evgenij Petrovich Chelyshev (b. 1921), who for many years was the Soviet "Indologist-in-chief".

Many of those born in the early 1920s (in fact, up to 1927) perished young at the fronts of the war. It is not by chance that in this particular age group, that is among those who were born before 1927, we have only women scholars of Sanskrit.

Vera Aleksandrovna Kochergina (b. 1924) studied Sanskrit at Moscow University with Mikhail Nikolaevich Peterson (1885–1962), a distinguished linguist, and has taught Sanskrit for many years at her alma mater.[83] Professor Kochergina wrote a Sanskrit

---

Indologists, after 1917 and till the 1960s, or even till later, could not, as a rule, go to India (nor, for that matter, to any other foreign country).

[80] S. Lipkin earned his living by translations. Among other things, he rendered parts of the *Mahābhārata* into rhymed Russian verses and ventured to translate anew Kālidāsa's *Śakuntalā* and *Meghadūta* (using word-by-word translations from Sanskrit that had been prepared for him by an Indologist).

[81] He translated into Russian the poetic parts of Śūdraka's *Mṛcchakaṭika* (see further, note 84).

[82] One of these poets, David Samojlov (1920–1990), wrote:

«Мне выпало горе родиться в двадцатом,
В проклятом году и в столетье проклятом ...»
"Mne vypalo gore rodit'sya v dvadtsatom,
V proklyatom godu i v stolet'e proklyatom ..."
['I have had the ill luck to be born in the twentieth,
In the damned year and in the damned century ...']

[83] V. Kochergina wrote an interesting book about her teacher (Kochergina 1996).

text-book for students and compiled a Sanskrit-Russian dictionary (the only *complete* Sanskrit-Russian dictionary available so far).

Tat'yana Evgen'evna Katenina (1926–1987) for many years taught Sanskrit, as well as Hindi and Marathi, at Leningrad University. Most of her published works have been about Hindi and Marathi, but at least one very remarkable paper was devoted to linguistic theories in ancient India.

Oktyabrina Fedorovna Volkova (1926–1988) was an alumna of Leningrad University, but later lived in Moscow and taught Sanskrit to many people (including the author of this essay) in the kitchen of her flat.[84] From the St. Petersburg / Leningrad tradition she inherited a deep interest in Buddhism. She did not publish much, but her very important contribution was the Russian translation of Āryaśūra's *Jātakamālā*, the translation which had been started long ago by A. P. Barannikov, but finalized and edited by O. F. Volkova in 1962. She is also reported to have translated the *Laṅkāvatārasūtra*, but the translation remains unpublished. In the 1970s and early 1980s Buddhism was frowned upon by Soviet authorities, and there was little hope to get published a translation of a Buddhist *sūtra*.

BLESSED BY THE THAW

The next age group was doubly lucky: they were born too late to be enlisted in the army during the war, and their formative years coincided with the "thaw" after Stalin's death, when Khrushchev

---

[84] Cf. the obituary written by T. Elizarenkova (1989) and Lysenko 2006. O. Volkova's father was a Soviet general and, according to the family tradition, belonged to one of the small Finno-Ugric ethnic groups which lived on the territory where St. Petersburg was founded. Oktyabrina herself, referring to her father, called this people "chukhontsy" (чухонцы); her younger sister Inna preferred the ethnonym "izhortsy" (ижорцы), while a brother of them insisted on the ethnonym "ингерманландцы" (in English: Ingrian Finns). According, again, to the family tradition, the surname "Volkov(a)" (which in Russian is connected with the word "volk" [волк] / 'wolf') was a translation from the original Finnish "Susi" ('Wolf'). See Lysenko 2006: 7.

made friends with India. As if all of a sudden we have got indeed a "mighty group" of Sanskrit scholars in both capitals. In Leningrad there were educated Vladimir Svyatoslavovich Vorob'ev-Desyatovskij (1927–1956),[85] Èduard Naumovich Tyomkin (b. 1928) and Vladimir Gansovich Èrman (b. 1928).[86] In Moscow we have Pavel Aleksandrovich Grintser (1928–2009),[87] Vladimir Nikolaevich Toporov (1928–2005),[88] Tat'yana Yakovlevna Elizarenkova

---

[85] In 1944–45 he served in the army and participated in military actions in Romania, Hungary and Czechoslovakia. His early death might have been caused by the hardships during the war. V. Vorob'ev-Desyatovskij was a thorough scholar of Sanskrit and Tibetan. But he also had a fine literary taste. Among other things, he masterly translated into Russian the *Mṛcchakaṭika* of Śūdraka (the poetic parts were translated by the poet V. Shefner).

[86] Vladimir Èrman has been teaching Sanskrit at St. Petersburg (Leningrad) University for many years. He also has to his credit a number of translations from Sanskrit. Recently he has translated the sixth book of the *Mahābhārata* (including the *Bhagavadgītā*). This translation was published in 2009 (Èrman 2009). It is for the first time that Russian readers got a scholarly and commented translation of the *Bhagavadgītā* (into lucid Russian prose) done by an expert in Sanskrit. Professor Èrmán's father was Estonian, hence the unusual patronymic.

[87] To present adequately the work of Pavel Grintser, one would have to write a special paper. For many years he studied the *Mahābhārata*, the *Rāmāyaṇa*, narrative literature in Sanskrit, the Sanskrit drama, the *alaṁkāraśāstra*, and also wrote on the subject of comparative literature. By the end of his life (unfortunately, too late in his life) he started translating Valmiki's *Rāmāyaṇa* into Russian. In 2006 the translation of the first two books (the Bālakāṇḍa and the Ayodhyākāṇḍa) was published (Grintser 2006). Before his death (in 2009) Pavel Grintser completed the translation of the third book and of most of the fourth one. This is the first scholarly translation of the poem into Russian. But the translation is not only scholarly; it is also highly artistic and may be considered, in my opinion, a valuable contribution to Russian literature. On P. Grintser, see now Kudelin & Lidova 2008.

[88] Vladimir Toporov was indeed a polymath, a specialist in many languages and many subjects. The list of his publications is a thick book in itself. One of his first Indological works was a translation from Pali into Russian (with an introduction and commentaries) of the *Dhammapada* (first published in 1960). It is, in my opinion, one of the best translations of any Indian text into Russian. In 1960, the book was published in the resurrected series "Bibliotheca Buddhica", with Yurij Roerich as the "beantwortlicher Redacteur". As the oral tradition relates, the bosses of that time got infuriated. They took the publication of the *Dhammapada* (a "religious text"!) as an "ideological diversion". One of the bosses summoned Yurij Roerich and scolded him. The scholar died soon after that meeting. And V. N. Toporov gave up Buddhist studies for many years. On

(1929–2007),[89] Vyacheslav Vsevolodovich Ivanov[90] (b. 1929), and Aleksandr Yakovlevich Syrkin (b. 1930),[91] all of them the students of Professor Mikhail Peterson at Moscow University.[92]

It is worth noting that this particular age group (those born in the late 1920s and up to the early 1930s) is not rich in poets (in any case, in famous poets).[93]

Toporov, besides the "Bibliographies of India" and the "Dictionary" of S. D. Miliband, cf. also *Polytropon* (1998).

[89] Tat'yana Elizarenkova's special field was the Vedic language and the *Ṛgveda* in particular. By the beginning of the 2000s she completed her full translation of the *Ṛgvedasaṁhitā* (the first ever done into Russian). For this work she was awarded, in January 2004, the order of Padma Shri by the government of the Republic of India. T. Elizarenkova was also a scholar of Pali. Together with V. N. Toporov (her husband) she wrote a book on the Pali language (Elizarenkova & Toporov 1965; 2003). In 1976 also an English translation of the book was published in Moscow. On Elizarenkova, see now the obituary by Ya. V. Vasil'kov (2009). See also Kulikov & Rusanov 2008.

[90] Vyacheslav Ivanov (a son of the eminent Soviet writer Vsevolod Ivanov [1895–1963]) is also a polymath. From the early 1960s he and V. N. Toporov were among the leaders of our "structuralist" (alias "semiotical") movement, a kind of non-political scholarly opposition to the Soviet establishment. It is in this "structuralist-semiotical" vein that the two scholars wrote a book on Sanskrit (Ivanov & Toporov 1960), in 1968 published in an English translation as well. Since the 1990s V. Ivanov lives both in the USA and in Russia.

[91] Aleksandr Syrkin is a master of translations. He translated into Russian the *Pañcatantra* in Pūrnabhadra's version (the translation first published in 1958), several most important Upaniṣads (in the 1960s), the *Kāmasūtra* (first published in 1993), Jayadeva's *Gītagovinda* (published in 1995), the whole of the *Dīghanikāya* (not yet published) and other texts. In 1977 A. Syrkin emigrated to Israel, but in the 1990s used to visit his native Moscow and to get his books (re)published here.

In this context one more scholar, one more emigré, of this age group must be mentioned: Aleksandr Moiseevich Pyatigorskij (1929–2009), a philosopher and a scholar of Tamil and Buddhism. In the 1960s and early 1970s he was a very conspicuous figure in Moscow intellectual life. In 1974 he left for London (and for many years taught at the SOAS), but since the 1990s reappeared in Russia from time to time and got his books published here.

[92] To the same generation there belonged Georgij Aleksandrovich Zograf (1928–1993), our leading specialist in the languages of South Asia (cf. Vasil'kov & Gurov 1995).

[93] Nevertheless, some names may be mentioned: Valentin Berestov (1928–1998), Vladimir Kornilov (1928–2002), Inna Lisnyanskaya (b. 1928) ... We may surmise that the circumstances of life favorable for the formation of scholars

The next decade, on the contrary, produced both not a few poets and quite a number of Sanskrit scholars. Here we may differentiate between two age groups. The first, those born in the early 1930s: Evgenij Mikhajlovich Medvedev (1932–1985), a historian of ancient India, Grigorij Maksimovich Bongard-Levin (1933–2008), Viktoriya Viktorovna Vertogradova (b. 1933), Margarita Iosifovna Vorob'eva-Desyatovskaya (b. 1933).[94] Their famous counterparts in poetry are Evgenij Evtushenko (b. 1933) and Andrej Voznesenskij (1933–2010).[95] The other age group are those born in the second half of the 1930s.[96] Here suffice it to name Yuliya Markovna Alikhanova (b. 1936) and Svetlana Leonidovna Neveleva (b. 1937).[97]

BORN IN THE 1940s

Between generations (as well as between countries) there stands Boris Leonidovich Ogibenin (b. 1940), who emigrated to France in the early 1970s.[98] In this respect he is somewhat similar to the Iosif

---

might have been not as favorable for the formation of poets. Here we may also recall Èdison Denisov (1929–1996) who is now considered one of the most important composers of the 20th century.

Two famous politicians, Mikhail Gorbachev (b. 1931) and Boris Yeltsin (El'tsyn, 1931–2007), may be considered either belonging to this age group or falling between this and the next one.

[94] Two more names should be mentioned here. Mikhail Sergeevich Andronov (1931–2008) was our major specialist in the Tamil language and Dravidian linguistics. Leonid Borisovich Alaev (b. 1932), though not strictly speaking a Sanskrit scholar, is a distinguished historian of India and Indian culture, an important figure in our Indology.

[95] Here we may also mention the great composer Alfred Schnitke (1934–1998). Another famous composer, Sofiya Gubaidulina (b. 1931), is just a bit older.

[96] In between the two groups we may place Nikita Vladimirovich Gurov (1935–2009), one of the leading St. Petersburg Indologists. His interests extended from the Proto-Indic culture to the Vedas, Sanskrit and Dravidian languages.

[97] David Ben'yaminovich Zil'berman (Silberman, 1938–1977), a pupil of O. Volkova and A. Pyatigorskij, was a promising scholar of Indian philosophy. He was forced to emigrate to the USA in 1974 and perished there in a road accident.

[98] Now in French his surname is written as Oguibenine.

Brodskij (1940–1996), who also occupies a peculiar place in the history of our poetry and also emigrated in the early 1970s.[99]

During (and immediately after) World War II comparatively few babies were born (and in the 1970s–80s many of that generation went away with the so-called "third wave" of emigration), but among the "children of the war" there are also some Sanskrit scholars. After 1917 this age group was the first who could go to India during their university years.

Vsevolod Sergeevich Sementsov (1941–1986) was the first professional Sanskrit scholar in Russia who translated the whole of the *Bhagavadgītā*. One of his translations, in verses, was first published in 1985 and republished in 1999.[100] Another translation, in prose, together with his translation of Rāmānuja's commentary on the *Gītā*, has remained in a manuscript.[101]

Boris Alekseevich Zakhar'in (b. 1942) is a linguist *par excellence*, a scholar of Sanskrit, Pāli, Hindi, Kashmiri and other South Asian languages. He translated a lot from Sanskrit and Pāli and takes a particular interest in Sanskrit grammatical tradition. Recently he translated into Russian the first *āhnika* of Patāñjali's *Mahābhāshya* and the Sanskrit grammar of Varadarāja. Both translations are accompanied with very detailed commentaries. B. A. Zakhar'in is head of the department of South Asian languages at the Institute of Asian and African Studies, Moscow State University. He has regularly attended the World Sanskrit Conferences, each time contributing papers on the vyākaraṇa tradition.

Yaroslav Vladimirovich Vasil'kov (b. 1943) is a specialist in the *Mahābhārata* and related subjects. As mentioned above, he,

---

[99] The late Valerij Isaevich Rudoj (1940–2009), his colleague Elena Petrovna Ostrovskaya (b. 1954) and their group of "buddhological" scholars, though residents of St. Petersburg, also occupy a very special "territory" in our Indology. This group studied and studies Buddhism and "Indian philosophy" in a rather esoteric way, almost without any contacts with other Indologists.

[100] Cf. http://omnamahshivaya.narod.ru/libr/bhgitasem/index.htm.

[101] Aleksandr Mikhajlovich Dubyanskij (b. 1941), our leading specialist in the Tamil language and culture, also belongs to this age group.

together with S. L. Neveleva, has translated into Russian several books of the *Mahābhārata*. Since 2003 Ya. V. Vasil'kov has been a vice-president of the IASS. In 2010 he got published a big book in Russian titled "Myth, Ritual and History in the Mahābhārata", a fruit of many years of devoted and painstaking research work.

Aleksei Alekseevich Vigasin (b. 1946) is an outstanding historian of ancient India. His studies in (and translations from) the *Arthaśāstra* and various Dharmaśāstras are remarkable contributions to Sanskrit scholarship. He was the first to prepare a complete Russian translation of Aśoka's inscriptions. At present Vigasin is head of the department of South Asian history at the Institute of Asian and African Studies, Moscow State University.

Andrej Mikhajlovich Samozvantsev (1949–2009) was also a historian who studied the *Arthaśāstra* and Dharmaśāstras. He took particular interest in the ancient Indian law and the theories of property.

The author of this paper (b. 1946) is a philologist, a student of South Asian languages, literature(s) and culture(s) in general. As for Sanskrit studies, my most notable achievements have been a translation into Russian of Vidyāpati's *Puruṣaparīkṣā* and of several chapters from Rājaśekhara's *Kāvyamīmāṃsā*.

Aleksandr Aleksandrovich Stolyarov (b. 1946) is a student of Indian epigraphy (mostly in Sanskrit). Now he has become the director of the recently established Centre for South Asian Studies at the Russian State University for the Humanities (Moscow).[102]

---

[102] In 1946 at least two well known politicians were born: Boris Berezovskij, the "king-maker" of the late 1990s, and Vladimir Zhirinovskij, one of the symbols of the absurdity of our post-Soviet politics. Zhirinovskij, incidentally, graduated from the Institute of Oriental Languages (Moscow State University), where he studied the Turkish language. Patriarch Kirill (Cyril), the present (since 2009) Primate of the Russian Orthodox Church, was also born in 1946.

As to poetry, an exemplary (paradigmatic) figure for this generation is probably Igor' Irten'ev (b. 1947), a "postmodernist" poet who writes only in an ironic vein.

Vladimir Nikolaevich Romanov (1947–2013) was a historian of Indian culture. His latest work was a translation (with a study) of parts of the *Śatapathabrāhmaṇa* (published in 2009).

Andrej Anatol'evich Terent'ev (b. 1948) is a student of Jainism and Buddhism, especially of Buddhist art. He translated into Russian a number of Jaina philosophical texts, but now concentrates on Buddhist philosophy.

BORN IN THE SECOND HALF OF THE 20th CENTURY

But it was only among those who were born in the 1950 and later that a whole group of scholars appeared who came to study Indian philosophy in a systematic way.[103] Several of them have been PhD students of the late G. M. Bongard-Levin.

In Moscow there works Valerij Pavlovich Androsov (b. 1950), a historian of Buddhist philosophy. He has translated into Russian several major works of those ascribed to Nāgārjuna and has written several monographs on Buddhist thought.

---

[103] We may say, it is the generation of Vladimir Putin, (the former and present) president of Russia, born in 1952. There are already a number of quite well known poets in this generation. One of them, Nina Iskrenko (1951–1995) wrote: «Мы дети скучных лет России» / "My deti skuchnykh let Rossii" ('We are the children of Russia's boring years'), echoing the line of Aleksandr Blok: «Мы дети страшных лет России» / "My deti strashnykh let Rossii" ('We are the children of Russia's terrible years'). Another poet of the same generation, Evgenij Bunimovich (b. 1954), wrote:

«В пятидесятых – рождены,
в шестидесятых – влюблены,
в семидесятых – болтуны,
в восьмидесятых – не нужны ...»
"V pyatidesyatykh – rozhdeny,
v shestidesyatykh – vlyubleny,
v semidesyatykh – boltuny,
v vos'midesyatykh – ne nuzhny ..."
('In the fifties [we were] born,
in the sixties [we] fell in love,
in the seventies [we were] chatterboxes,
in the eighties [we became] superfluous').

Another Muscovite, Vladimir Kirillovich Shokhin (b. 1951), by now has become our major authority on Indian philosophy as well as on comparative philosophy. He has translated into Russian the basic texts of Sāṃkhya and Nyāya and has written a number of fundamental works on the history of Indian (Hindu and Buddhist) philosophy.

Andrej Vsevolodovich Paribok (b. 1952), now teaching at St. Petersburg University, is also a student of Buddhism and a philosopher in his own right. He translated from Pāli into Russian the *Milindapañha* and a number of texts from the Pāli canon.

Viktoriya Georgievna Lysenko, who works at the Institute of Philosophy[104] in Moscow, is a scholar of many interests. She used to devote most of her time to early Buddhist thought and to the Vaiśeṣika system. She has translated into Russian the *Padārtha-dharmasaṃgraha* of Praśastapāda with the commentary *Nyāya-kandalī* by Śrīdhara and has written a number of monographs. Now V. G. Lysenko takes special interest in Indian epistemology and translates from Sanskrit works on this subject.

Her fellow student at the Moscow State University was Natal'ya Vasil'evna Isaeva, a great admirer of Śaṅkara. For many years N. V. Isaeva was working at a translation of Śaṅkara's *Brahma-sūtrabhāṣya*, but now she lives mostly in France and seems to have given up that ambitious project. Natal'ya Alekseevna Kanaeva teaches Indian philosophy at various places in Moscow and has written a very interesting text-book on the subject, as well as a monograph on Buddhist logic. Their younger colleague Aleksej Vladimirovich Pimenov studied Mimāṃsā. But now he lives somewhere in America, and we have not heard from him for quite some time.

At the Institute of Philosophy in Moscow there is the M. K. Gandhi Chair of Indian Philosophy, where students are taught Sanskrit so that they could read Indian philosophical texts in the original. In 2009 scholars working at the Institute of Philosophy

[104] Part of the Russian Academy of Sciences.

published a huge (950 pages!) volume in Russian under the title "Indian Philosophy. An Encyclopedia. Edited by M. T. Stepaniants". The volume is a fruit of collective endeavours of scholars from Moscow and St. Petersburg. It is devoted predominantly to pre-modern Hindu, Buddhist and Jaina thought.

But among those who were born in the 1950s and later studied Sanskrit, not everybody has been taken by Indian philosophy. Thus, Sergej Vsevolodovich Kullanda (b. 1954) studies, among other things, Sanskrit inscriptions in Java. Dmitrij Nikolaevich Lelyukhin (b. 1956) studies ancient Indian inscriptions and is an enthusiast of digitizing his sources. Natal'ya Vladimirovna Aleksandrova uses her knowledge of Sanskrit to study the works of Chinese Buddhist pilgrims (Faxian and Xuanzang) in India. Elena Valer'evna Tyulina is a scholar of puranas. She has translated into Russian the *Garuḍa-purāṇa*. Yuliya Georgievna Kokova teaches Sanskrit and Hindi at St. Petersburg University; the sphere of her research interests is Indian mythology as reflected in puranic literature.

Among people born still later, in the 1960s and 1970s, there are also Sanskrit scholars of various interests.[105] Natal'ya Rostislavovna Lidova[106] concentrates, in Moscow, on the study of the *Naṭyaśāstra*. Leonid Igorevich Kulikov (b. 1964), a student of T. Y. Elizarenkova, has been taken by Vedic studies and pursues them mostly in Leiden. Sergej Sergeevich Tavastsherna (b. 1965)[107] teaches Sanskrit and Pāli at St. Petersburg University and investigates the intricacies of Sanskrit grammar.

Maksim Albertovich Rusanov (b. 1966) is a connoisseur of poetry in Sanskrit, Prakrits, Farsi and Urdu. He has written a monograph on the Sanskrit kāvya and translated into Russian the *Sattasaī* of Hāla. Now he is head of the department of the philology

---

[105] For this age group I do not dare suggest counterparts from other spheres of Russian culture.

[106] She was a PhD student of P. A. Grintser.

[107] He is a scion of a Swedish-Finnish family; the original spelling of the name was Tawaststjerna.

of Southern and Central Asia at the Russian State University for the Humanities in Moscow.

Sergej Vladimirovich Pakhomov (b. 1968) teaches non-Western and comparative philosophy at the philosophical faculty of St. Petersburg University. His favorite subject is Tantric philosophy.

Natal'ya Anatol'evna Zheleznova (Moscow) has become our major specialist in Jaina thought. She has written a brilliant monograph on the teaching of Kundakunda and has got a special award from Indian Jainas. Kseniya Dmitrievna Nikol'skaya (Moscow), a student of A. A. Vigasin, continues her teachers's research on the *Arthaśāstra*. Vladimir Pavlovich Ivanov (b. 1973) studies, in St. Petersburg, the philosophy of Sanskrit grammar. Ruzana Vladimirovna Pskhu (Moscow) has published a study of Rāmānuja's *Vedārthasaṃgraha*.

A case apart is Andrej A. Ignat'ev (b. 1977) who lives in the city of Kaliningrad[108]. He studied Sanskrit at the University there, in the late 1990s, under Professor A. N. Khovanskij, who was actually a professor of mathematics and an amateur Sanskritist. Since the early 2000s A. A. Ignat'ev regularly publishes in Kaliningrad translations of various puranic texts and sends them to fellow Indologists to Moscow, St. Petersburg, and probably elsewhere.

Both in Moscow and St. Petersburg, the two traditional centres of Sanskrit studies in Russia, there are already still younger scholars active in the field. But theirs must be quite a new chapter in the history of Russian scholarship. So I would stop my review here.

REFERENCES

ADELUNG, F. von 1811a. *Rapports entre la langue sanscrite et la langue russe. Présentés à l'Académie impériale russe*. St. Petersburg: Drechsler.

—— 1811b. *O skhodstve sanskritskogo yazyka s russkim* [On the similarities between Sanskrit and Russian]. St. Petersburg.

[108] The former Königsberg in the former Eastern Prussia, the city of Immanuel Kant.

—— 1830. *Versùch einer Literatur der Sanskrit-Sprache*. St. Petersburg: Kray.

—— 1837. *Literatur der Sanskrit-Sprache*. Zweite durchaus verbesserte und vermehrte Ausgabe. St. Petersburg: Kray.

AJRAPETOV, A. G., A. A. VIGASIN & T. YU. MACHULOVSKAYA (eds.) 2010, *Minaevskie chteniya. Materialy nauchnoj konferentsii (Tambov, 25 noyabrya 2009 g.)* [Readings on Minaev. Materials from à conference held in Tambov, Nov. 2009]. Tambov: Tambovskij gosudarstvennyi universitet.

ALPATOV, M. A. 1973: *Rùsskaya istoricheskaya mysl' i Zapadnaya Evropa. XII–XVII vv.* [Russian historical thought and Western Europe. The 12th–17th c.]. Moscow: Nauka.

—— 1976. *Russkaya istoricheskaya mysl' i Zapadnaya Evropa. XVII – pervaya chetvert' XVIII v.* [Russian historical thought and Western Europe. The 17th – the first quarter of the 18th c.]. Moscow: Nauka.

—— 1985. *Russkaya istoricheskaya mysl' i Zapadnaya Evropa. XVIII – pervaya polovina XIX v.* [Russian historical thought and Western Europe. The 18th – the first half of the 19th c.]. Moscow: Nauka.

ALPATOV, V. M. & M. A. SIDOROV 1997. Dirizher akademicheskogo orkestra [The conductor of the academic orchestra]. *Vestnik rossijskoj akademii nauk* 67(2).

AL'TSHULER, M. G. 1963. Lebedev i Derzhavin [Lebedev and Derzhavin]. *Narody Azii i Afriki* (Moscow) 1963(4): 126–129.

Anonyme 1926 = Bajer, Gotlib-Zigfrid (1694–1738). In: *Bol'shaya sovetskaya èntsiklopediya* [Big Soviet Encyclopaedia], IV: 361–362. Moscow: Sovetskaya èntsiklopediya.

ARNE, T. 1914. *La Suède et l'Orient. Études archéologiques sur les relations de la Suède et de l'Orient pendant l'âge des Vikings*. (Archives d'études orientales, 8.) Uppsala: Appelbergs.

Aziatskij muzej – Leningradskoe otdelenie Instituta vostokovedeniya AN SSSR. Moscow: Nauka, 1972.

BABINGER, F. 1915. *Gottlieb Siegfried Bayer (1694–1738). Ein Beitrag zur Geschichte der morgenländischen Studien im 18. Jahrhundert*. München: J. Schön.

BARTOL'D, V. V. 1977. *Raboty po istorii vostokovedeniya*. (Sochineniya, 9) [Works on the history of Oriental studies (Works, 9)]. Moscow: Nauka.

BAYER, T. S. 1728. Elementa litteraturae brahmanicae, tangutanae, mungalicae. Cum 10 tabulis aeri incisis. *Commentarii Academiae scientiarum imperialis petropolitanae* 3: 389–422. St. Petersburg.

—— 1729. Elementa litteraturae brahmanicae, tangutanae, mungalicae. Cum 9 tabulis aeri incisis. *Commentarii Academiae scientiarum imperialis petropolitanae* 4: 289–301. St. Petersburg.

—— 1730. *Museum Sinicum, in quo Sinicae Linguae et Litteraturae ratio explicatur.* St. Petersburg: Typographia Academiae Imperatoriae.

—— 1738. *Historia regni graecorum Bactriani, in qua simul Graecorum in India coloniarum vetus memoria explicatur. Accedit Christophori Theodosii Waltheri, Missionarii regii Danici, Doctrina temporum indica cum paralipomenis (et Leonardi Euleri, De Indorum anno solari astronomico).* St. Petersburg: Academia scientiarum imperialis petropolitanae.

—— 1776. *Vita Theophanis Procopowitsch.* Nordische Nebenstunden, hrsgn von J. B. Scherer, Th. I. Frankfurt: Bey J. G. Fleischer (cf. Nichik 1977: 185).

Bibliografiya Indii. Dorevolutsionnaya i sovetskaya literatura na russkom yazyke i yazykakh narodov SSSR, original'naya i perevodnaya [The bibliography of India. Prerevolutionary and Soviet literature in the Russian language and the languages of the people of the USSR, both original and translated (up to 1967)]. Moscow: Nauka, 1976.

Bibliografiya Indii, 1968–1975. Sovetskaya i perevodnaya literatura [The bibliography of India, 1968–1985. Soviet and translated literature]. Moscow: Nauka, 1982.

BOLLENSEN, F. (trans.) 1846. *Vikramorvaśī, das ist Urwasi, der Preis der Tapferkeit, ein Drama Kalidasa's in fünf Akten ... Herausgegeben, übersetzt und erläutert von F. Bollensen.* St. Petersburg: Gräff.

BONGARD-LEVIN, G. M. & A. A. VIGASIN 1984. *The Image of India. The Study of Ancient Indian Civilisation in the USSR.* Moscow: Progress.

BONGARD-LEVIN, G. M. & R. LARDINOIS & A. A. VIGASIN (eds.) 2002. *Correspondances orientalistes entre Paris et Saint-Pétersbourg (1887–1935).* (Mémoires de l'Académie des Inscriptions et Belles-Lettres; 26.) Paris: Boccard. [Letters written by S. Lévi and other French scholars to S. Oldenburg and F. Shcherbatsky.]

BRUCE, C. 1862. *Die Geschichte von Nala. Versuch einer Herstellung des Textes.* St. Petersburg: Kaiserliche Akademie der Wissenschaften.

CHERKAZ'YANOVA, I. V. 2008. *Nemtsy – rossiiskie uchenye v gody pervoi mirovoi voiny: epizody iz istorii Akademii Nauk.* http://www.nbuv.gov.ua/portal/Soc_Gum/Pni/2008/08ivcozu.pdf.

DASGUPTA, R. K. 1957. G. S. Lebedev (1749–1817): The first Russian Indologist. *Russian Slavonic Papers* (Oxford) 7: 1–16.

DORN, B. 1833. *De affinitate linguae slavicae et sanskritae.* Khar'kov [the name of the city on the title page is printed in Russian].

ELIZARENKOVA, T. Ya. 1989. Pamyati Oktyabriny Fedorovny Volkovoj [In memoriam of Oktiabrina Fiodorovna Volkova]. *Narody Azii i Afriki* 1989(2): 209–210.

ELIZARENKOVA, T. Ya. & V. N. TOPOROV 1965. *Yazyk pali* [The Pali language]. Moscow: Nauka.

ELIZARENKOVA, T. Ya. & V. N. TOPOROV 2003. *Yazyk pali*. 2nd ed. Moscow: Vostochnaya literatura.

ÈRMAN, V. G. (trans.) 2009. *Makhabkharata. Bkhishmaparva*. Moscow: Ladomir, Nauka. (An electronic version is available at: http://www.bolesmir.ru/index.php?content=text&name=o377.)

FROLOV, È. D. 1999. Graf Sergej Semenovich Uvarov i akademicheskij klassitsizm [Count S. S. Uvarov and academic classicism]. In: *Peterburgskaya Akademiya nauk v istorii akademij mira. K 275-letiyu Akademii nauk. Materialy mezhdunarodnoj konferentsii* [The St. Petersburg Academy of Sciences in the context of the history of other academies in the world. On the 275th anniversary of the Academy of Sciences. Materials of an international conference], II: 275–285. St. Petersburg: Sankt-Peterburgskij nauchnyj tsentr Rossijskoj Akademii Nauk.

GRINTSER, P. A. 1998. "Sakontala" Karamzina [The "Sakontala" by Karamzin]. In: *Polytropon. K 70-letiyu Vladimira Nikolaevicha Toporova* [For the 70th birthday of V. N. Toporov]: 537–566. Moscow: Indrik.

—— (trans.) 2006. *Ramayana, I–II. Kn. I – Balakanda (Kniga o detstve); kn. Ajodh'yakanda (Kniga ob Ajodh'e).* (Seriya "Literaturnye pamyatniki"). Moscow: Ladomir, Nauka (An electronic version is available at: http://www.bolesmir.ru/index.php?content=text&name=o540.)

HAYAT MAMUD 1985. *Gerasim Stepanovich Lebedef* (in Bengali). Dhaka: Bangla Academy.

—— 2012. *Gerasim Stepanovich Lebedev. Perevod s bengal'skogo* [Gerasim Stepanovich Lebedev. A translation from Bengali]. Translated by E. K. Brosalina, E. A. Kostina & A. L. Sladkov. Ed. by E. K. Brosalina & Ya. V. Vasil'kov. Yaroslavl': Akademiya 76.

Istoriya 1990 = *Istoriya otechestvennogo vostokovedeniya do serediny XIX veka* [History of Oriental studies in our country up to the middle of the 19th century]. Moscow: Vostochnaya literatura RAN, 1990.

Istoriya 1997 = *Istoriya otechestvennogo vostokovedeniya s serediny XIX veka do 1917 goda* [History of oriental studies in our country from the middle of the 19th century up to 1917]. Moscow: Vostochnaya literatura RAN, 1997.

IVANOV, V. V. & V. N. TOPOROV 1960. *Sanskrit*. Moscow: Izdatel'stvo vostochnoj literatury.

KAGANOVICH, B. S. 1994. Nachalo tragedii. Akademiya nauk v 1920-e gody po materialam arkhiva S. F. Ol'denburga [The beginning of the tragedy. The Academy of sciences in the 1920s after the materials of S. F. Oldenburg's archive]. *Zvezda* (St. Petersburg) 1994, no. 12.

—— 2005. Nadezhda Oseevna Shchupak. Zhizn i Sud'ba. *Odissei. Chelovek v istorii – 2005*: 241–261. Moscow: Nauka. (An electronic version is available at: http://www.odysseus.msk.ru/numbers/?year=2005&id=83.)

—— 2006. *Sergej Fedorovich Ol'denburg. Opyt biografii*. St. Petersburg: Feniks.

KARAMZIN, N. (trans.) 1792. Stseny iz Cakontaly, indijskoj dramy [Scenes from Śakutalā, an Indian drama]. *Moskovskij zhurnal* [Moscow journal] 6(2): 125–156 & 6(3): 294–323.

KOCHERGINA, V. A. 1996. *Professor M. N. Peterson*. Moscow: Filologiya.

KOTOVSKIJ, G. G. (ed.) 1967. *Ivan Pavlovich Minaev. Sbornik statej* [A collection of articles]. Moscow: Nauka.

KOTWICZ, W. 1948. *Józef Kowalewski, orientalista (1801–1878)*. Wrocław: Wrocławskie Towarzystwo naukowe.

KOZLOV, V. P. 1981. *Kolumby rossijskikh drevnostej* [The Columbuses of Russian antiquities]. Moscow: Nauka.

KUDELIN, A. P. & N. R. LIDOVA (eds.) 2008. *Donum Paulum. Studia Poetica et Orientalia k 80-letiyu P. A. Grintsera*. Moscow: Nauka.

KULIKOV, L. & M. RUSANOV (eds.) 2008. *Indologica. T. Ya. Elizarenkova Memorial Volume*, I. (Orientalia et Classica. Papers of the Institute of Oriental and Classical Studies, 20.) Moscow: Russian State University for the Humanities.

KULIKOVA, A. M. 1975. B. A. Dorn i universitetskoe vostokovedenie v Rossii [B. A. Dorn and the oriental studies in Russian universities]. *Narody Azii i Afriki* 1975(2): 220–228.

LARIN, B. A. 1977. *Istoriya russkogo yazyka i obshchee yazykoznanie. Izbrannye raboty* [History of the Russian language and general linguistics. Selected works]. Moscow: Prosveshchenie.

LEBEDEV, G. S. 1801. *A Grammar of the Pure and Mixed East Indian Dialects, with Dialogues Affixed, Spoken in All the Eastern Countries, Methodically Arranged at Calcutta, According to the Brahmenian System, of the Shamscrit Language. Comprehending literal explanations of the compound words, and circumlocutory phrases, necessary for the attainment of the idiom of that language, etc. Calculated for the use of Europeans. With remarks on the errors in former grammars and dialogues of the mixed dialects called Moorish or Moors, written by different Europeans; together with a refutation of the assertions of Sir William Jones, respecting the Shamscrit alphabet; and several specimens of Oriental poetry, published in the Asiatic Researches*. London: J. Skirven.

—— 1805. *Bespristrastnoe sozertsanie sistem Vostochnoi Indii bramgenov, svyashchennykh obryadov ikh i narodnykh obychaev*. St. Petersburg.

—— 1963. *Grammar of the Pure and Mixed East Indian Dialects*. Ed. by Mahadev Prasad Saha. Calcutta: K. L. Mukhopadhyay.

LEHMANN, A. 1956. *Es begann in Tranquebar. Die Geschichte der ersten evangelischen Kirche in Indien*. 2nd ed. Berlin: Evangelische Verlagsanstalt.

LENZ, R. (trans.) 1833a. *Urvasia, fabula Calidasi. Textum sanscritum edidit, interpretationem latinam et notas illustrantes adiecit Robertus Lenz*. Berolini: F. Dümmler.

LENZ, R. 1833b. *Bericht über eine im Asiatischen Museum der Kaiserlichen Akademie der Wissenschaften zu St.-Petersburg deponierte Sammlung Sanskrit-Manuscripte*. St. Petersburg: Buchdrückerei der kaiserlichen Akademie der Wissenschaften.

LIVOTOVA, O. E. & V. B. PORTUGAL' 1966. *Vostokovedenie v izdaniyakh Akademii nauk 1726–1917* [Oriental studies in the publications of the Academy of Sciences]. Moscow: Nauka.

LOVMYAN'SKIJ, Kh. 1985. *Rus' i normanny* [Russia and Normans]. Moscow: Progress. [A Russian translation, with commentaries, of the Polish book: Henryk Łowmiański. *Zagadnienie roli normanów w genezie państw slowiańskich*. Warszawa 1957.]

LUNDBÆK, K. 1986. *T. S. Bayer (1694–1738). Pioneer Sinologist*. (Scandinavian Institute of Asian Studies Monograph Series, 54.) London: Curzon Press.

LYSENKO, V. G. (ed.) 2006. *Smaranam. Pamyati Oktyabriny Fedorovny Volkovoj. Sbornik statej*. [Smaranam. On the memory of O. F: Volkova: Collection of articles]. Moscow: Vostochnaya literatura RAN.

MAZON, A. (ed.) 1945. *Nadine Stchoupak, 1886 – 1941. In memoriam*. Paris: Imprimerie Union.

MILIBAND, S. D. 1995. *Biobibliograficheskii slovar' otechestvennykh vostokovedov s 1917 g*. [Biobibliographical dictionary of our country's orientalists since 1917], I–II. 2nd ed. Moscow: Nauka.

—— 2008. *Vostokovedy Rossii, XX – nachalo XXI: Biobibliograficheskij slovar'* [Russian Orientalists from the 20th to the early 21th c.: Biobibliograhical dictionary], II. Moscow: Vostochnaya literatura RAN.

MINAEV, I. P. 1960. *Travels in and Diaries of India and Burma*. Tr. by H. Sanyal. Calcutta.

NICHIK, V. M. 1977. *Feofan Prokopovich*. (Seriya "Mysliteli proshlogo") Moscow: Mysl'.

NOVIKOV, N. (trans.) 1788. *Baguat-Geta, ili besedy Krishny s Arzhunom …* 1788. Moscow.

OL'DENBURG, S. 1926. Akademiya Nauk SSSR [The Academy of Sciences of the USSR]. In: *Bol'shaya sovetskaya èntsiklopediya* [Big Soviet Encyclopaedia], I: 783–790. Moscow: Sovetskaya èntsiklopediya.

Ol'denburg-Festschrift 1934 = *Sergeyu Fedorovichu Ol'denburgu. K pyatidesyatiletiyu nauchno-obshchestvennoj deyatel'nosti 1882–1932. Sbornik statej*. Leningrad: Izdatel'stvo Akademii Nauk SSSR.

Ol'denburg-Gedenkschrift 1986 = *Sergej Fedorovich Ol'denburg. Uchenyj-vostokoved*. Moscow: Nauka.

OUVAROFF, S. 1810. *Projet d'une Académie asiatique*. St. Petersburg: Pluchart.

—— 1811. *Ideen zu einer asiatischen Akademie*. Traduit du français par Hauenschild. St. Petersburg: Pluchart.

PEKARSKIJ, P. P. 1870. *Istoriya imperatorskoj Akademii Nauk v Peterburge* [History of imperial Academy of Sciences in Petersburg], I. St. Petersburg: Tipografiya imperatorskoj Akademii Nauk.

Polytropon. K 70-letiyu Vladimira Nikolaevicha Toporova [For the 70th birthday of V. N. Toporov]. Moscow: Indrik, 1998.

Procopowicz MS = Theophanes Procopowicz, *Ad Theophilum Sigefridum Baijerum pro exstincto filio dolentem*. Manuscript: Central Scientific Library of the Academy of Sciences of Ukraine. (Cf. Nichik 1977: 180.)

ROERICH, G. N. 1945. Indology in Russia. *Journal of the Greater India Society* 12(2): 69–98.

ROSENBERG, O. O. 1991. *Trudy po buddizmu* [Works on Buddhism]. Ed. by A. N. Ignativich. Moscow: Nauka.

SARASKINA, L. I. 2003. *Graf N. P. Rumiantsev i ego vremya / Count Nikolai Rumyantsev and His Time*. Moscow: Nash dom. [Bilingual edition.]

SEREBRIANY, S. D. 2002a. Yu. N. Rerikh i istoriya otechestvennoj indologii [Yu. N. Roerich and the history of Indology in our country]. In: *Peterburgskij rerikhovskij sbornik* [St.-Petersburg Roerich Collection], V: 20–77. St. Petersburg: Izdatel'stvo Sankt-Petersburgskogo universiteta.

—— 2002b. Drevneindijskaja literatura [Old Indian literature]. In: *Izuchenie literatur Vostoka. Rossiya, XX vek* [Studying the literatures of the Orient. Russia, the 20th century]. Moscow: Vostochnaya literatura RAN.

—— 2002c. The Bhagavadgita in ussia: Notes towards the Rezeptionsgeschichte. *EVAM. Forum on Indian Representations* (New Delhi) 1(1&2): 234–247.

—— 2007. Nauka i vlast' v Rossii. Aktual'nye razmyshleniya nad sovremennoj knigoj: Kaganovich B. S., Sergej Fedorovich Ol'denburg. Opyt biografii, SPb., 2006. In: *Odissej. Chelovek v istorii – 2007*: 356–375 Moscow: Nauka. (An electronic version is available at: http://www.odysseus.msk.ru/numbers/?year=2007& id=16.)

SEREBRYAKOV, I. D. (ed.) 1962. Izbrannye trudy russkikh indologov-filologov [Selected works of Russian Indologists-philologists]. Moscow: Izdatel'stvo vostochnoj literatury.

SHCHERBATSKY, Th. 1923. *The Central Conception of Buddhism and the Meaning of the Word "Dharma"*. London: The Royal Asiatic Society.

—— 1927. *The Conception of Buddhist Nirvāna*. Leningrad.

—— 1930–32. *Buddhist Logic*, I–II (Bibliotheca Buddhica, 26.) Leningrad: Izdatel'stvo Akademii Nauk SSSR.

Shcherbatsky-Gedenkschrift 1972 = *Indijskaya kul'tura i buddizm – Indian Culture and Buddhism. Sbornik statej pamyati akademika F. I. Shcherbatskogo*. Moscow: Nauka.

STACY, R. H. 1985. *India in Russian Literature*. Delhi: Motilal Banarsidass.

STENDER-PETERSEN, A. 1953. *Varangica*. Aarhus: Bianco Lunos bogtrykkeri.

Taranovich MS = V. P. Taranovich, *Akademik T. Z. Bajer i ego trudy po vostokovedeniyu. K 200-letiyu so dnya smerti Bajera* [Academician T. Z. Bayer and his works on Oriental studies. On the bicentenary of his death] Manuscript: Arkhiv vostokovedov, SPb-oe otdelenie Instituta vostokovedeniya, fond 102, opis' 1, no. 2.

UVAROV, S. S. 1811. Mysli o zavedenii v Rossii Akademii aziatskoj [Thoughts about establishing in Russia an Asiatic Academy]. *Vestnik Evropy* [Messenger of Europe] (Moscow) 55(1–2).

VALEEV, R. M. (ed.) 2004. *Mongoloved O. M. Kovalevskij. Biografiya i nasledie (1801–1878)*. Kazan': Alma-Lit.

Varangian Problems. Report on the First International Symposium on the Theme The Eastern Connections of the Nordic Peoples in the Viking Period and Early Middle Ages, Moesgaard, University of Aarhus, 7th-11th October 1968. (Scando-Slavica, Supplementum 1.) Kopenhagen: Munksgaard, 1970.

VASIL'EV, L. S. (ed.) 1974. *Istoriya i kul'tura Kitaya. Sbornik pamyati akademika V. P. Vasil'eva*. Moscow: Nauka.

VASIL'KOV, Ya. V. 1989. Vstrecha Vostoka i Zapada v nauchnoj deyatel'nosti F. I. Shcherbatskogo [The meeting of East and West in the scholarly work of F. I. Shcherbatsky]. *Vostok – Zapad. Issledovaniya, perevody, publikatsii*, IV: 178–265. Moscow: Nauka.

—— 2009. T. Ya. Elizarenkova (1929–2007). *Newsletter of the International Association of Sanskrit Studies* 2009: 32–34.

—— 2013. Chto novogo my uznali o zhizni Gerasima Lebedeva v Indii: predvaritel'nye itogi (New data on Gerasim Lebedev's life in India:

Preliminary results]. *Zografskij sbornik* 3: 260–286. St. Petersburg: Kunstkamera.

VASIL'KOV, YA. V. & N. V. GUROV (eds.) 1995. *Sthapakashraddha. Sbornik statej pamiati G. A. Zografa* [Sthāpakaśraddhā. A collection of papers in memoriam of G. A. Zograf]. St. Petersburg: Tsentr Peterburgskoe Vostokovedenie.

VASIL'KOV, YA. V. & M. SOROKINA 2003. *Lyudi i sud'by. Biobibliograficheskij slovar' vostokovedov – zhertv politicheskogo terrora v sovetskij period* [People and fates. Biobibliographical dictionary of orientalists – victims of political terror during the Soviet period]. St. Petersburg: Peterburgskoe vostokovedenie.

VIGASIN, A. A. 1986. Izuchenie Indijskoj kul'tury v Rossii v pervoj treti XIX v[eka] [The study of Indian culture in Russia during the first third of the 19th century]. In: P. V. Kutsobin (ed.), *Indiya 1984. Ezhegodnik* [India – 1984. The Yearbook]. Moscow: Nauka.

—— 2003. Delo o sanskritskom slovare [The case of the Sanskrit dictionary]. *Vestnik drevnei istorii* [Herald of ancient history] 2: 194–210.

—— 2008. *Izuchenie Indii v Rossii (ocherki i materialy).* [Indian studies in Russia (essays and materials)]. Moscow: Izdatel'stvo Stepanenko.

WHITTAKER, C. 1984. *The Origins of Modern Russian Education. An Intellectual Biography of Count Sergei Uvarov, 1796–1855.* DeKalb: Northern Illinois University Press.

WINDISCH, E. 1917. *Geschichte der Sanskrit-Philologie und indischer Altertumskunde*, I (Grundriss der indo-arischen Philologie und Altertumskunde, I.1.) Strassburg: Trübner.

Corpus of Ukrainian Translations of Sanskrit Texts

YURIY ZAVHORODNIY

India's cultural, religious and philosophical tradition is one of the richest and oldest in the world.[1] It is widely accepted that language is the essence of culture, and a common language – Sanskrit – unites many Indian texts dating from the Vedic period to the Epic and Classic periods. Before studying original Sanskrit texts or their translations into other languages, it will be useful for any student of ancient Indian culture to find out if there are translations available in his or her own language.

Unfortunately, Indian studies in contemporary Ukraine do not exist as a full-fledged discipline, because the tradition was destroyed in the 1930s under the Stalin regime. The world community of scholars appears to think that Sanskrit texts have not been studied in Ukraine and that no Sanskrit texts have been translated into Ukrainian.[2] But is that really the case?

The following table summarizes my research on the existing Ukrainian translations of Sanskrit texts. It contains the name of the translator, the title of the translated Sanskrit text and the date of its first publication with notes on whether the translation was done directly from Sanskrit and, if not, on the source from which the text was translated into Ukrainian.

---

[1] See Potter 1995, section 1.2. In this fundamental research Potter points out the books dealing with the issue. The book contains more than 10.000 titles that were published in various European languages about Indian philosophy (both critical research and publications of Sanskrit texts).

[2] See Banerji 1989: 602.

Author	Text	Date of the First Publication and Notes
Ivan Franko (1856–1916), an eminent Ukrainian poet, writer, translator, thinker and benefactor	<u>From</u>: *Mahābhārata* translation of four fragments without source identification (this has been supplied by me).	
	1. Manu and the Flood. Āraṇyakaparvan, chapter 185, ślokas 2–52.	1. *Zhytie i slovo* 4 (1896): 295–298 (L'viv). <u>Source</u>: A. Hoefer, *Indische Gedichte in deutschen Nachbildungen*, I, pp. 31–42. Leipzig 1844.
	2. Sunda and Upasunda. Ādiparvan, chapters 201–203 (partially).	2. *Zhytie i slovo* 5 (1896): 362–367 (L'viv). <u>Source</u>: F. Bopp, *Ardschuna's Reise zu Indra's Himmel nebst anderen Episoden des Maha-Bharata*. Aus dem Sanskrit im Urversmasse übersetzt. Zweite durchgesehene Ausgabe, pp. 36–45. Berlin 1868.
	3. Śakuntalā. Ādiparvan, chapter 65 (partially).	3. *Zhytie i slovo* 6 (1897): 22–32 (L'viv). <u>Sources</u>: P. E. Foucaux, *Sakountala, traduction libre*. Paris 1894; the translation of M. N. Dutt.
	4. Death of Hiḍimba. Ādiparvan, chapters 139–142 (partially).	4. *Literaturna spadschina*, I: 215–222. Kyiv: AN URSR, 1956. <u>Source</u>: F. Bopp, *Ardschuna's Reise zu Indra's Himmel nebst anderen Episoden des Maha-Bharata*, pp. 14–27. Berlin 1868. ("Death of Gidimba" was translated by I. Franko in 1875.)

	<u>From</u>: *Mārkaṇḍeyapurāṇa*, translation of two fragments without source identification (this has been supplied by me).	
	1. The Tsar Vipaścit in Hell. Chapters 13–15 (partially).	1. *Zhytie i slovo* 6 (1896): 15–21 (L'viv). <u>Sources</u>: *The Markandeya Purana*, translated by F. E. Pargiter, I (Bibliotheca Indica, New Series, 700): 72–76, 88–91. Calçutta: The Asiatic Society of Bengal, 1878. (References in the version of I. Franko); F. Rückert, "Der gute König in der Hölle", *ZDMG* 12 (1858): 336–340.
	2. Tsar and Ascetic. Chapters 7–8 (free translation).	2. I. Franko, *Z vershyn i nizyn*. L'viv 1893, pp. 429–468. <u>Source</u>: F. Rückert "Die Sage von König Hariscandra", *ZDMG* 13 (1859): 103.
	<u>From:</u> *Pañcatantra*, translation of four tales and one book without source identification (this has been supplied by me).	
	Hare and Bear – 1.8. Crow and Adder – 1.6. Painted Fox – 1.10. Crows and Owls – 3. Fable about Fable – 1.12.	*Dzvinok* 9 (1897): 141–144 (Hare and Bear); 10 (1897): 145–147 (Crow and Adder); 19 (1898): 281–287 (Painted Fox); 20 (1898): 297–312; 21 (1898): 321–329; 22 (1898): 338–341; 23 (1898): 353–358; 24(1898): 376–378 (Crows and Owls); 24 (1898): 378–383. (L'viv).

		Sources: Th. Benfey, *Pantschatantra, fünf Bücher indischer Fabeln, Märchen und Erzählungen*. Leipzig, 1859; L. Fritze, *Pantschatantra, ein altes indisches Lehrbuch der Lebensklugheit in Erzählungen und Sprüchen*. Leipzig 1884.
Lesya Ukrainka (Larysa Petrivna Kosach-Kvitka) (1871–1913), an eminent Ukrainian poet, writer, translator and benefactor	From: *Ṛgveda*, translation of twelve hymns without source identification. Eleven hymns were identified by professor M. Ya. Kalinovich in 1927. RV 1.32, 50, 113, 123; 2.4; 10.14, 16, 17, 18, 129, 154. One hymn to Agni without source identification. (Free translation)	L. Ukrainka, *Starodavnia istoria skhidnykh narodiv*. Katerynoslav 1918, pp. 17–24. Source: L. Menard, *L'historie des anciens peuples de L'Orient*. Paris 1883; probably German and French translations by A. Ludwig and S. A. Langlois (according to the correspondence of L. Ukrainka with her uncle M. Drahomanov [1841–1895, an eminent Ukrainian philosopher, historian, public figure, publicist]).
Pavlo Ritter (1872–1939), an eminent Ukrainian specialist in Indian culture, linguist and translator	From: *Ṛgveda*, translation of twenty hymns. The hymns were identified by A. Kovalivs'ky in 1966 and more precisely by me. RV 1.1, 154; 2.38; 3.33; 4.42, 51; 5.83; 6.27, 54; 7.89, 103; 8.29; 9.112; 10.34, 95, 119, 127, 129, 146, 186.	All translations by P. Ritter are from Sanskrit. The hymns RV 1.1, 154; 2.38; 4.42, 51; 5.83; 6.27, 54; 7.103; 8.29; 9.112; 10.34, 95, 119 were published in: "Rigveda.

		Vybrani gimny (Pereklad z vediis'kogo sanskrytu ta prymitky Pavla Rittera)". *Vsesvit* 11 (1976): 128–150. The hymns RV 10.127, 129, 146, 186 were published in: P. Ritter, "Chotyry gimny z Rig-vedy". *Skhidnyi svit* 1 (1927): 186–188. The hymns RV 3.33 and 7.89 were published in: *Golosy Starodavn'oi Indii. Antologiia davn'oindiis'koi literatury. Pereklad iz sanskrytu, uporiadkuvannia Pavla Rittera.* Peredmova I. Serebriakova. Kyiv: Dnipro, 1982, pp. 94–96, 102. Sources: Unknown.
	From: *Atharvaveda*, translation of three hymns. The hymns were identified by A. Kovalivs'ky in 1966. AV 4.16; 6.105; 12.1.	In: *Golosy Starodavn'oi Indii*, pp. 115–123. Source: Unknown.
	From: *Śatapathabrāhmaṇa*, translation of two fragments. One was identified by me: 1.1.	In: *Golosy Starodavn'oi Indii*, pp. 124–128. Source: Unknown.
	From: *Maitrāyaṇīsaṃhitā*, translation of two fragments. Unidentified.	In: *Golosy Starodavn'oi Indii*, p. 129. Source: Unknown.

	Kaṭha-Upaniṣad, complete translation.	In: *Golosy Starodavn'oi Indii*, pp. 133–147. <u>Source:</u> Unknown.
	<u>From</u>: *Mahābhārata*, translation of thirteen fragments without source identification (which has supplied by me).	<u>Source:</u> The Calcutta edition.
	Ādiparvan, chapters 65–69 (in chapter 69 the ślokas 45–51 were not translated).	In: *Golosy Starodavn'oi Indii*, pp. 151–163.
	Vanaparvan, chapter 50, ślokas 1–31,	ibid., pp. 163–167.
	chapter 57, ślokas 1–23,	ibid., pp. 167–170.
	chapter 58, ślokas 1–34,	ibid., pp. 170–174.
	chapter 59, ślokas 1–25,	ibid., pp. 174–177.
	chapter 60, ślokas 1–38,	ibid., pp. 178–182.
	chapter 61, ślokas 1–125,	ibid., pp. 182–187.
	chapter 62, ślokas 1–43,	ibid., pp. 187–194.
	chapter 74, ślokas 1–24, chapter 75, ślokas 1–27,	ibid., pp. 194–199.
	chapter 110, ślokas 1–36, chapter 111, ślokas 1–22, chapter 112, ślokas 1–19, chapter 113, ślokas 1–25 (correspondence incomplete).	ibid., pp. 199–208.

	Udyogaparvan, from chapter 131; śloka 6 to chapter 134, śloka 36.	ibid., pp. 208–213.
	Dronaparvan, chapter 159, ślokas 8–50, chapter 161, ślokas 1–14, chapter 163, ślokas 21–49 (correspondence incomplete).	ibid., pp. 213–218.
	<u>From</u>: *Rāmāyaṇa*, translation of ten fragments from different books, without source identification.	ibid., pp. 219–247. <u>Source</u>: The Bengal recension of Paris edition.
	Translation of Kālidāsa's lyric poem *Meghadūta*.	P. Ritter, *Khmara-vistun (Megha-dūta). Staroindiis'ka elegiia Kalidasy*. Pereklad z sanskryts'koi movy z vstupnoiu statteiu i prymitkamy, Kharkiv: Vseukrains'ka naukova asotsiatsiia skhodoznavstva, vydavnytstvo Proletariy, 1928. <u>Source</u>: Unknown

	Translation of fifteen verses of Bhartṛhari: *Nītiśataka* 15, 16, 64. *Vairāgyaśataka* 18, 43, 48, 49, 50, 62. *Śringāraśataka* 40, 42, 75. (The verses, except for three, were identified by me.) Translation of Kālidāsa's epic poem *Kumārasambhava*.	P. Z. Ritter, "Bkhartrhari". *Skhidnyi svit* 3–4 (1928): 260–263. <u>Source</u>: A. Thumb, *Handbuch des Sanskrit*, II, pp. 51–57, ū 1, 2, 6, 10–13, 15–17, 19–22, 26. Heidelberg 1905. Archival materials (Kyiv).
Gnat Khotkevich (Gnat Galaida) (1877–1938), a well-known Ukrainian writer, actor, art critic and translator	*Śakuntalā* by Kālidāsa, complete translation.	*Kalidasa. Shiakuntalia.* Translation with preface and notes of G. Khotkevich. Kharkiv 1929. 200 p. <u>Sources:</u> *Calidasa Sacuntala, drame en sept actes, mele de prose et de vers.* Traduit par Abel Bergaigne et Paul Lehugeur. Paris 1884; *Kalidasa's Sakuntala. Ein indisches Schauspiel.* Aus dem Sanskrit und Prakrit metrisch übersetzt von Ernst Meier. Hildeburghausen 1867; *Sakuntala. Indijskaya drama Kalidasu.* Perevod s sanskritskogo A. Putyaty. Moscow 1879; *Kalidasa. Dramy. Perevod K. Bal'monta so vstupitel'nym ocherkom S. Ol'denburga.* Moscow 1916. Gnat Khotkevich is reported to have studied Sanskrit and may have used original Sanskrit texts.

Let us analyse the data contained in the table. It can be seen that the first translation from Sanskrit into Ukrainian was done in 1875. This translation was not from the original text, but from a German translation. The first piece of Indian literature that attracted the attention of Ukrainian translators was the Ādiparvan, the first book of the *Mahābhārata*. Ivan Franko, an eminent Ukrainian writer, was the first translator, thus initiating the incorporation of Indian literary heritage into the Ukrainian culture. Although he produced the first translation in 1875, it was published only in 1956. The first publication of one of his translations was accomplished in 1893; it was a free translation of a fragment from the *Mārkaṇḍeyapurāṇa* titled "Tsar and Ascetic". In addition to the *Mahābhārata* and Purāṇic literature, Franko paid attention to the famous framed fables of the *Pañcatantra*. Not knowing Sanskrit, he resorted to existing European translations of Sanskrit texts, primarily those by the prominent scholar Franz Bopp.

The first twelve hymns of the *Ṛgveda*, the most ancient piece of Indian literature, were exposed in Ukrainian by Lesya Ukrainka and published in 1918 after her death. Like I. Franko, she used existing European translations of Sanskrit texts.

Gnat Khotkevich produced the first complete Ukrainian translation of the *Śakuntalā*, probably the best piece of the eminent Indian poet and dramatist Kālidāsa. This translation was published in 1929. While translating this piece Khotkevich made use of the existing German, French and Russian translations. He is also reported to have been acquainted with Sanskrit.

Pavlo Ritter was the first person to translate into Ukrainian from Sanskrit originals. Due to his professional and translation skills, masterpieces of Vedic, Epic and Classic Sanskrit were finally rendered into Ukrainian. He worked with ten out of the thirteen pieces that were translated into Ukrainian between 1870 and 1920. Unfortunately, most of his translations were published long after his death.

Thus, interest of Ukrainians in ancient Indian culture was first evinced by I. Franko and culminated in the activities of P. Ritter. Individuals who took a deep interest in ancient India were concentrated mostly in two Ukrainian cities, Lviv and Kharkiv. Altogether thirteen Indian texts were introduced to Ukrainian culture. Most popular of them were the *Ṛgveda* (L. Ukrainka and P. Ritter), the *Mahābhārata* (I. Franko and P. Ritter) and works by Kālidāsa (P. Ritter and G. Khotkevich). The most popular parts within these texts were the famous cosmogonic hymn of the *Ṛgveda* (10.129) (L. Ukrainka and P. Ritter) and the *Śakuntalā* episode of the Ādiparvan, the first book of the *Mahābhārata* (I. Franko and P. Ritter).

The Ukrainian translators took no notice of Sanskrit texts belonging to religious and philosophic schools of ancient India nor of such texts as the *Arthaśāstra*, *Hitopadeśa*, *Śukasaptati*, *Kathāsaritsāgara*, the works of Bāṇa, etc.

Ukrainian scholars were about to engage in scholarly research of Sanskrit texts, but this development was aborted with Stalin's repressions in the 1930s. Today, interest in Sanskrit texts is being revived in Ukraine. I hope that this collection of data on Ukrainian translations of ancient Indian texts from 1870 to 1920 may help in this and can be included into the world heritage of Sanskrit studies. A recent archival hint to P. Ritter's translation of Kālidāsa's "Birth of the War-God" (*Kumārasambhava*) suggests that the scope of existing Ukrainian translations of ancient Indian texts may be even wider than presently known.

REFERENCES

BANERJI, S. C. 1989. *A Companion to Sanskrit Literature*. Delhi: Motilal Banarsidass.

FRANKO, Ivan 1977. *Zibrannya tvoriv u pyatydesyaty tomakh*. Kyiv: Naukova Dumka.

KHOTKEVICH, Gnat 1929. *Kalidasa. Shakuntala*. Kharkiv.

POTTER, Karl H. (ed.) 1995. *Encyclopedia of Indian Philosophies*, I. Delhi: Motilal Banarsidass.

RITTER, Pavlo 1961. Translations and comments. In: *Antolohiya Literature Shkodu*. Kharkiv: Kkarkivs'kyi Derzhavnyi Universytet.

UKRAINKA, Lesya 1975. *Zibrannya tvoriv u tvanadtsyaty tomakh*, II. Kyiv: Naukova Dumka.

The History of Indology in Denmark

KENNETH G. ZYSK

The term "Indology" is a made-up word, which means the study of India. It first appeared in English in October 1888,[1] about the same time that Danish "Indologi" and German "Indologie" were in fashion. In most of Europe, including Denmark, Indology is understood to be the study of the history, the literature, and the culture of the people of India, with a special reference to the ancient period, and its languages.[2] Today, Indology is often replaced by "Indian Studies", which is much broader in scope, including also social and anthropological studies of Indian cultures. Denmark in general and the University of Copenhagen in particular have a long and distinguished history of Indology.

The story begins as an oft-overlooked chapter in the history of Denmark's colonial period in the 17th century. In 1620, the explorer **Ove Giedde** (1594–1660) reached the east coast of India and established a colony at a place known as Trankebar (now called Tharangambadi), located in the modern Indian state of Tamilnadu, about 150 km south of Chennai. From 1620 to 1845, when it was turned over to the British, Trankebar served as a centre of Danish

---

[1] Simpson & Weiner 1989: 885.

[2] Else Pauly (1992: 511) provides the following definition in Danish: "'Indologien' er en videnskab uden naturlige grænser; som universitetsfag har studiet forskellige områder (med tilsvarende benævnelser) rundt i verden, de fleste steder som i Danmark med vægt på det på kendskab til sanskrit og andre ældre sprogtrin baserede filologiske arbejde."

activity in India. In 1755, I. C. Soetmann established a satellite colony, called Serampore or Frederiksnagore, near Calcutta in Bengal, which also was eventually transferred to the British in 1845. A third and rather insignificant colony was established on the Nicobar Islands, just south of the Andamans in the Indian Ocean, after Denmark ousted the Austrians in 1784. It too was transferred to the British in the middle of the 19th century. Since the Danish interest was primarily trade, the Danes on the Nicobars did not contribute to the history of Danish Indology.[3]

Like those of the other colonial powers – England, France, and Portugal – Denmark's chief efforts were centred in trade and missionary work. In order to convert the indigenous Indians to Christianity, missionaries devoted a good deal of their time to learning regional languages and to translating the Bible's New Testament and part of the Old Testament into those languages. This, of course, opened up an entirely new world to those educated, European priests who were sent abroad. They began to describe the different languages and develop pedagogic tools in the form of grammars and dictionaries. One such priest was **Jacob Worm** (1642–1692/93), who, instead of being executed for insulting the king, was deported to Trankebar, where he engaged himself in translating the Bible into Tamil.

The "Danske evangelisk-lutherske mission blandt hinduerne"[4] was created in 1706. Although Danish in name, Germans actually manned the early missions in India. Priests were trained at the "Franckesche Stiftungen" in Halle and ordained in Copenhagen before being sent to Trankebar.

One of the first to be dispatched was **Bartholomæus Ziegenbalg** (1683–1719) from Pulnitz, who learned Portuguese and Tamil and published a Tamil grammar in Latin in 1716, which was one of the first western-language grammars of an Indian Dravidian language. Based on only the 119 Tamil texts in his possession,

---

[3] See *Vore Gamle Tropekolonier*, VI: 227–244; VII: 183–196, 247–259.

[4] "Danish Evangelical-Luthern Mission Among the Hindus".

Ziegenbalg wrote the *Bibliotheca Malabarica*, which, when published in 1708, became the first European contribution to the history of Tamil literature (Zvelebil 1974: 2). A few further contributions to South Indian languages and cultures followed from later missionaries, but it was not until **Carsten Niebuhr** (1733–1815) visited India on his return from Yemen that Danish contributions to the study of India came into the mainstream of continental Indology.

Beginning in September 1763, Carsten Niebuhr spent fourteen months on the West Coast of India, recovering from a case of fever he developed on the way from the Middle East. He stayed with the British in Bombay, but, as he regained his strength, he ventured out along the coast reaching as far as Surat on the river Tapti near the opening to the Bay of Cambay in the modern state of Gujarat. The first 80 pages of the second part of the first volume of his *Reisebeschreibung nach Arabien und andren umliegenden Ländern*[5] (1778) are devoted to describing the Indian people, their customs, and their important religious places, such as the famous cave temples of Elephanta located in the Bay of Bombay. Unlike the South Indian Dravidian culture and language around Trankebar, Bombay in the modern state of Mahara**ṣ**ṭra and Surat in Gujarat are dominated by speakers of North Indian languages, of which Sanskrit is the oldest known example.

In the 18th century, the discipline of Oriental Studies was established in Europe. Beginning with Sir William Jones' widely received description of the similarities between Sanskrit, Persian and Greek, the interest in Sanskrit began to grow, with German comparative philology leading the way. A Danish student of this school of thought was **Rasmus Rask** (1787–1832), who distinguished himself as one of the leading scholars in the current linguistic field with his studies of Nordic and Icelandic languages and mythologies.

[5] "Travels through Arabia and Other Neighbouring Lands".

Rask immediately understood the importance of Sanskrit after hearing the words of Rasmus Nyerup, who, as professor of the history of literature, gave lectures on Indian literature and mythology at the University of Copenhagen. It is said that he inspired Rask to study and master Sanskrit with the words

> det var ikke nok at vide, hvad der stod i Edda; man måtte spørge, hvordan det kom til at stå der, og for at få svar måtte man kunne sanskrit[6] (Pauly 1992: 521).

Born in the little town of Brændekilde, southwest of Odense on the island of Fyn, Rask distinguished himself as a gifted linguist and received a royal scholarship to travel to Finland, Russia, the Middle East, and India to collect data in support of his theory about the language families. In this connection, he travelled to India and Ceylon from 1820 to 1823. After a tortuous visit to India, he returned to Denmark with notebooks and a good collection of handwritten original works that would become crucial for the development of Indian and Iranian philology in Denmark.[7] He began his linguistic explorations in Bombay on 29 September 1820, and following in the footsteps of Niebuhr sailed up to Surat. From there, he travelled by boat on the rivers and by foot overland to Serampore before sailing south to Trankebar. Like Niebuhr before him, Rash took copious notes on aspects of the people's languages and customs. He spent time in Madras, recuperating from illness, before reaching the Danish colony in South India. In October 1821, he sailed on to Ceylon (modern Śrī Laṅkā). He lived nine months on the island, where the oldest school of Buddhism, Theravāda, is still practised. He lived most of the time in the capital city, Colombo, where he devoted his time to learning Pali and Singhalese. The first is the language of the Theravāda scriptures, known as the Pali Canon, and the second is the indigenous language of the island kingdom. Both find their roots in Sanskrit. He acquired

[6] "It was not enough to know what is in the Edda, one must ask how it came to be there, and to answer that, one should learn Sanskrit."

[7] See Zysk 2010.

many palm-leaf manuscripts written in the Pali language, and these would eventually be used for the editions of several books of the Pali Canon, published by the Pali Text Society in London. These publications opened up an entirely new field of Indology that focused on Middle Indian languages, with a special emphasis on Pali, and paved the way for the more recent discipline of Buddhist Studies. Rask departed Colombo on 19 August 1822, and arrived home in Denmark on 5 May 1823; five months later, he died. Because of Rasmus Rask, the University of Copenhagen became committed to Indology, and thus another chapter of its history began. Indology under different names has been a research and degree-granting discipline at the University of Copenhagen for over 160 years; and many distinguished scholars and educators have been associated with the subject.

Carl Theodor Johannsen (1804–1840) was the first person to teach Sanskrit at the University of Copenhagen. Originally trained in Arabic, he received the royal appointment as professor of Oriental Languages in Copenhagen on 23 February 1833. He taught Hebrew, Arabic, and Sanskrit.

About the same time, **Lars Nannestad Boisen** (1803–1875), a theologian and orientalist trained in Bonn and in Paris, published the first Danish translations of extracts from the Sanskrit epics, *Rāmāyaṇa* and *Mahābhārata*, and from the didactic stories of the *Hitopadeśa*, in his "Flowers of the Orient" (*Østerlandske Blomster*) in 1834.

In 1841, **Martin Johannes Hammerich** (1811–1881) was appointed to the University of Copenhagen's newly established position of docent in "Indian and Oriental Languages and Literature" (Indisk-orientalske sprog og litteratur); and in 1845, he made the first Danish translation directly from Sanskrit of the famous play *Abhijñānaśākuntala* by the celebrated Indian poet Kālidāsa. More than fifty years earlier, the play's first appearance in German translation inspired the poet Goethe to borrow a device of Indian dramaturgy for the prologue to his *Faust*. The English translation by Sir William Jones, which appeared in 1789–90, served as the basis for both the German translation and Hans West's Danish translation, which, under the title *Cálidás Sacontalá eller Den uheldige Ring*,[8] was published in 1793, two years after the German rendering.

The first professorship of Indian and Oriental Philology (Indisk-østerlandsk filologi) at the University of Copenhagen was given to **Niels Ludvig Westergaard** (1815–1878) on 29 September 1845. He distinguished himself in Sanskrit lexicography and in the deciphering of ancient Indian inscriptions, which he collected during a three-year expedition to India from 1841–44. He also prepared a Sanskrit reader and grammar in Danish and compiled a catalogue of Indian manuscripts held in the Royal and University Libraries. Westergaard produced several students whose contributions provided different shades to the picture of Danish Indology. The most well-known among them was **Søren Sørensen** (1848–1902). He is recognised for his pioneering studies of the Indian epic, *Mahābhārata*, and for his still useful *Index to the Names in the Mahābhārata*.

The shift from Sanskrit to Middle Indic and Pali Studies began with the appointment of **Michæl Viggo Fausbøll** (1821–1908) to succeed Westergaard in 1878. A priest's son, born into a Sønderjysk farming family, Fausbøll initially had difficulty at the University of Copenhagen, but eventually found his home in the study of languages, and received the gold medal for a defence of one of Martin Hammerich's theories about Sanskrit syntax. His study of Sanskrit prepared him to take on Rask's Pali manuscripts, which lay in the University's library. He studied these handwritten documents with extreme skill and diligence and developed a system for transcribing into Roman letters the Sinhala script in which the Pali scriptures were written. This system, for the most part, is still used for the publication of Pali-texts and for the use of Pali words in scholarly articles and papers.

---

[8] "Kālidāsa's Śākuntala or The Unlucky Ring".

His *opus magnum* was the six-volume edition of the *Jātaka* with its commentary, which was begun in 1873 and completed with an index volume prepared essentially by Dines Andersen in 1897. It was published by the Pali Text Society, as part of its complete edition of the Buddhist Pali Canon. Fausbøll's edition of the *Jātaka* served as the basis for the numerous translations of the stories of the Buddha in a former life and was the reference text for establishing the connections between these stories and the *Fables of Aesop*, *The Stories of the 1001 Arabian Nights*, and the later Sanskrit children's literature of the *Pañcatantra* and *Hitopadeśa*. It was probably his recollection of stories from this Indian didactic literature that prompted Christian H. Kalkar, a respectable theologian, to report to H. C. Andersen that he will soon receive a copy of his *Eventyr*, translated into Sanskrit! It is said that upon receiving this information, Andersen became thoroughly delighted. Although his *Eventyr* have appeared in many different languages, Sanskrit, to my knowledge, is, unfortunately, not one of them.

In addition to his studies and teaching of Sanskrit and Pali, Fausbøll had an avid interest in folklore and contributed regularly to the *Journal of the Mahabodhi Society* in Calcutta.

Towards the end of his academic career, Fausbøll produced a bright scholar and eventual co-worker named **Dines Andersen** (1861–1940), who was instrumental in making Pali part of the curricula of most Indology programmes in Europe and abroad by publishing a reader and glossary of Pali in 1907. It is still used as a principal tool for teaching Pali.

Like Rasmus Rask, Andersen came from a small country town on the island of Fyn, where his father was a millwright and his foster father a blacksmith. A priest who was a friend of his family helped him to study at the Odense Latinskole, which helped to prepare him for entrance into the University of Copenhagen, where he studied Latin, Greek and Danish. He eventually became interested in Indic languages and received his doktorgrad in 1892 with a thesis on the use of verbs in the *Chāndogya-Upaniṣad*.

He was employed at the University Library, and eventually was put in charge of the Pali manuscripts, to which he devoted most of his scholarly efforts. He was appointed professor of Indology in 1903, and served as the principal authority for numerous projects that dealt with India and Buddhism, until his retirement in 1928. His pedagogical material and critical essays on Pali language and literature paved the way for the *Critical Pali Dictionary*, which some consider to be the most significant Danish contribution to Indological scholarship.

The *Critical Pali Dictionary* owes its origins to the work of **Vilhelm Trenckner** (1824–1891), a fairly well-off teacher of orphans at a school in Copenhagen, who, after learning Persian and Arabic, undertook the study of the Pali manuscripts from the Rask collection. Through the Pali Text Society, he published an edition of the post-canonical *Milindapañha*, or the Questions of King Menander, an account of the discussions between the Greco-Bactrican king and the Buddhist monk Nāgasena, and the first volume of the canonical text, *Majjhimaṇikāya*, or the Buddha's Middle-Length Sayings. His greatest contribution to Pali studies, however, is his unpublished glossary of words in the Pali Canon, written on slips of thin paper used to separate the cigars he loved to smoke, and his transcriptions of several books from the Pali Canon, using his own system of transliteration. He was not only a careful scholar, but also a man with sharp and piercing wit. While returning from a two-year visit to England, he wrote the following to Fausbøll, who was on his way to England:

> At den engelske Politik er i en forbavsende Grad egoistisk og kræmmeragtig, vil De snart opdage, så snart den engelske tåge rigtig er forsvunden fra Deres Øine[9] (Pauly 1992: 549).

---

[9] "You will soon discover that the English politics is to an astonishing degree egotistical and mercenary, when the English fog is really removed from your eyes."

Thanks to these pioneering efforts of Trenckner and the surprisingly poor quality of the Pali Text Society's *Pali-English Dictionary* (1921–25), Dines Andersen with the help of Helmer Smith, professor of Sanskrit and Comparative Linguistics at the University of Uppsala, began the *Critical Pali Dictionary* under the sponsorship of Danish Royal Academy of Sciences (Det Kongelige Danske Videnskabernes Selskab) in 1924. Although this project has gone through many ups and downs since its inception, it has finally come to an end with the publication of vol. 3.8, under the editorship of Oskar von Hinüber in 2011. After eighty years, a total of 36 fasciculi in three volumes has been published, covering the latters *a* through *ka*, or about one-fourth of the Pali alphabet. The volumes are now distributed by the Pali Text Society. Even though incomplete, the great value of this dictionary is the breadth of semantic meanings available from the examination of words in all their various contexts.

A new phase of Indology in Denmark began with one of the most versatile Danish scholars of India, **Poul Tuxen** (1880–1955), the son of the Classicist, Søren Ludvig Tuxen. Poul was an accomplished violinist, who studied with Dines Andersen and the German Indologist Ernst Windisch in Leipzig. He received the gold medal in 1905 (published in 1944) for his work *Kvinden i det gamle Indien*[10], in which he used a variety of Sanskrit sources; and in 1911, he defended his doktordisputats, entitled *Yoga: En Oversigt over den systematiske Yogafilosofi på grundlag af Kilderne*[11]. Moving easily in many genres of Sanskrit literature and through several of the ancient Indian languages, he prepared many translations into Danish and wrote extensively on Sanskrit and Indian culture for both the scholar and the general reader. More than any Indologist before or after him, Tuxen made Indian literature, culture and thought accessible to Danish people. He spent the winter of 1921–

[10] "The Woman in Ancient India".

[11] "An Overview of Systematic Yogic Philosophy on the Basis of Original Sources".

22 in the Southeast Asian Buddhist countries of Śrī Laṅkā and Thailand. This sojourn gave him a deeper and richer understanding of the living tradition of Theravāda Buddhism, which became reflected in his writings on Buddhism. He was named to the professorship of Indology (Indisk filologi) in 1928 to succeed Dines Andersen and, like nearly every professor since, worked in some capacity for the *Critical Pali Dictionary*. A persistent eye-disease caused him to withdraw from his teaching duties in his last years as a professor, but he has left a rich Danish legacy of writing on India.

Hans Hendriksen (1913–1989) succeeded Tuxen as the professor of Indology and shifted the emphasis from philology to linguistics. Originally interested in the old Indo-European language of Hittite, Hendriksen managed to find work as contributor to the *Critical Pali Dictionary*, and in 1944 defended his doktordisputats, entitled "Syntax of the Infinite Verb-forms of Pali". In 1947, he succeeded Helmer Smith as professor of Sanskrit at the University of Uppsala, but in 1951, was called back to the University of Copenhagen to succeed Poul Tuxen as professor of Indology. His interest in linguistics resulted in the three volume *Himachali Studies* (1976–86), which included the grammar, texts, and vocabulary of the modern Indian dialects of the Himachal regions of India, which lie in the mountain valleys along the border of Tibet and Kashmir.

In 1960, Hendriksen was given a small sum of 1000 kr. per year to buy books and to start a library for the newly created Institute of Indic Philology. By 1979, when the contribution had increased to 49.000 kr., per annum, the library had nearly 4000 books and journals, and was considered to be one of the better collections of Indic materials in Northern Europe.

In 1971, Dr **Ivo Fišer** (1929–2004), a doktorant from the University of Prague, was appointed as the first non-Scandinavian lektor at the Institute of Indic Philology. He taught Sanskrit, Pali, and a variety of courses on Indian history and culture. Before his death, he published works on various aspects of the social life in ancient India, with a focus on the literary tradition of Indian Erotics (Kāmaśāstra). Since this subject has been considered "off-limits" by mainstream Indologist, it has never been given its proper place in the history of Indian literature. What is known tends to derive often from the misused and misunderstood *Kāmasūtra*, made famous from the oft-reprinted translation of Sir Richard Burton and F. F. Arbuthnot.

Hendriksen was succeeded by **Christian Lindtner** in 1986. This bright and promising young scholar focused on Buddhist philosophical traditions, with a special emphasis on the Mahāyāna school of Mādhyamaka. Although Lindtner left his post prematurely in 1992, he continued to contribute to the field of Buddhist Studies with publications of books and articles.

In 1972, the Parliments' "bifag" or "småfags ordning"[12] came into effect in Denmark, with minor modifications in 1975 and 1979. After modifications in 1975 and again in 2011, the small-subject of Indian studies was divided between Aarhus University, where Hindi is taught along with subjects related to modern India, and Copenhagen University, where Sanskrit and Middle Indic languages are taught along with subjects related to ancient and classical India.

After a brief pause in the teaching of Indology at the University of Copenhagen from 1992 to 1997, **Kenneth Zysk**, PhD from the Australian National University and DPhil from the University of Oslo, was appointed as the new lektor in Indology on 1 November 1997, with the special charge to re-establish teaching and research in classical Indian languages and culture.

Now housed at the Institut for Tværkulturalle og Regionale Studier,[13] the section of Indology at the University of Copenhagen has set special focus on manuscript studies and the history of Indian science, which involves an international team of scholars

[12] "The (funding) schema for the small-academic subjects".

[13] "The Department of Cross-cultural and Regional Studies".

working at present on Indian medicine, astral sciences, and grammar.

Jesper Friis Lærnes, PhD-student, is exploring the early recasts of Pāṇini's grammatical aphorisms and Kenneth Zysk is completing a major work on Indian physiognomy (*Strīpuruṣalakṣaṇaśāstra* or *Sāmudrikaśāstra*, after its semi-mythical founder Samudra) and, with Tsutoma Yamashita from Kyoto is producing a critical edition and translation of Jajjaṭa's early medical commentary on the *Carakasaṃhitā*. His work on Indian physiognomy has already revealed possible important structural similarities to the physiognomic literature from ancient Mesopotamia and Greece, and linguistic connections to the literature of early Mahāyāna Buddhism.

Through the long history of Indology in Denmark, one aspect has remained constant: the emphasis on superior teaching and research in the classical languages and cultures of India. While programmes in Indology are rapidly disappearing from the curricula of western universities, it continues to be recognized as an important subject of study at the University of Copenhagen.

REFERENCES

PAULY, Else 1992. Indisk filologi. In: Poul Johannes Jense & Leif Grane (eds.), *Københavns Universitet, 1479–1979*, VIII: 511–566. Copenhagen: Sads Forlag.

SIMPSON, J. A. & E. S. C. WEINER 1989. *The Oxford English Dictionary*. 2nd edition. Oxford: Clarendon Press.

Vore Gamle Tropekolonier, VI: *Dansk Ostindien 1732–1776*; VII: *Dansk Ostindien 1777–1845*. Copenhagen: Fremad, 1966–67.

ZVELEBIL, K. V. 1974. *Tamil Literature*. (A History of Indian Literature, X.1.) Wiesbanden: Otto Harrasowitz.

ZYSK, Kenneth 2010. Carsten Niebuhr og Rasmus Rask i Indien. Sådan kom indologie til Danmark. In: *Tværkultur*. Årbog for ToRS-2010: 19–25. Copenhagen: Københavns Universitet, Institut for Tværkulturelle og Regionale Studier (ToRS).

Bibliography of the History of Indology

Collected by
KLAUS KARTTUNEN

Biographies, bibliographies, etc. of individual scholars are usually left out. An asterisk (*) indicates a source I have not seen. Tibetology and Iranian studies are included as same scholars were often interested in both.

I. GENERAL

a. On the history of Indology and of Asian studies in general

*ALLCHIN, F. R. & D. K. CHAKRABARTI (eds.) 1979. *A Source-Book of Indian Archaeology*, I: *Background, Early Methods. Geography and Early Man. Domestication of Plants and Animals.* Delhi. [Early Methods, pp. 57–101.]

ALLEN, Charles 2002. *The Buddha and the Sahibs. The Men Who Discovered India's Lost Religion.* London.

ASSAYAG, Jackie & Roland LARDINOIS & Denis VIDAL 1997. *Orientalism and Anthropology. From Max Müller to Louis Dumont.* (Pondy Papers in Social Sciences, 24.) Pondichéry, 2nd impression 2001.

BAILEY, Greg 1995. The fundamental problems of contemporary Indology. In: *International Conference on Sanskrit and Related Studies. September 23–26.1993* [Proceedings] (Cracow Indological Studies, 1): 15–26. Cracow.

BAILEY, H. W. 1972. A half-century of Irano-Indian studies. *JRAS* 1972: 99–110.

BAKKER, Hans & Martin GOSMAN (eds.) 1988. *De Oriënt, droom of dreiging?: het Oosten in Westers perspectief.* Kampen.

BARTHOLD, W. 1913. *Die geographische und historische Erforschung des Orients mit besonderer Berücksichtigung der russischen Arbeiten*. Übers. von E. Ramberg-Figulla. (Quellen und Forschungen zur Erd- und Kartenkunde, 8.) Leipzig. [Translation of the first edition of Bartol'd 1925.]

—— 1947. *La découverte de l'Asie. Histoire de l'orientalisme en Europe et Russie*. Traduit du russe et annoté par B. Nikitine. Paris. [Translation of Bartol'd 1925.]

*BARTOL'D, V. V. 1925. *Istorija izucheniya Vostoka v Evrope i Rossii*, II. (Izdanie Leningradskogo Vostochnogo instituta imeni A. S. Enukidze, 7.) Leningrad. [1st edition: St. Petersburg 1911, cf. Barthold.]

BEDEKAR, V. V. (ed.) 1984. *Proceedings and Papers of the Seminar on Sanskrit Outside India*. Thane.

BENFEY, Theodor 1869. *Geschichte der Sprachwissenschaft und orientalischen Philologie in Deutschland seit dem Anfang des 19. Jahrhunderts mit einem Rückblick auf die früheren Zeiten*. (Geschichte der Wissenschaften in Deutschland, 8.) München.

BHATTACHARYYA, Narendra Nath 1981. *History of Researches on Indian Buddhism*. New Delhi.

Bio-bibliographie de 134 savants. (Acta Iranica, 20 / 4ème série, vol. 1.) Leiden 1979. [On Iranian studies.]

Bollettini del Quarto Congresso internazionale degli Orientalisti. Firenze 1878.

*BOOTH, Arthur John 1902. *The Discovery and Decipherment of the Trilingual Cuneiform Inscriptions*. Cambridge MA.

BORST, A. 1957–63. *Der Turmbau von Babel. Geschichte der Meinungen über Ursprung und Vielfalt der Sprachen und Völker*, I–VI. Stuttgart.

BUCKLAND, C. E. 1905. *Dictionary of Indian Biography*. [Reprint: Varanasi 1971; contains mainly, but not solely, British people.]

BUDGE, E. A. Wallis 1925. *The Rise and Progress of Assyriology*. London.

BURGESS, James 1893. Archaeological research in India. In: *Actes du huitième Congrès international des orientalistes tenu en 1889 à Stockholm et à Christiania*, III: 3–48.

*BURNELL, A. C. 1879. On some early references to the Vedas by European writers. *Indian Antiquary* 8: 98–100.

*CALAND, W. 1918. *De Ontdekkingsgeschiedenis van den Veda*. (Mededeelingen der Koninklijke Nederlandsche Akademie van Wetenschappen, Afd. Letterkunde 5. reek, deel 3.) Amsterdam. [Cf. Zachariae 1921.]

CALLEWAERT, Winand M. & Shilanand HEMRAJ 1982. *Bhagavadgītānuvāda. A Study in Transcultural Translation*. Ranchi.

CHAKRABARTI, Dilip K. 1988. *A History of Indian Archaeology from the Beginning to 1947*. Delhi.

—— 1997. *Colonial Indology. Sociopolitics of the Ancient Indian Past.* Delhi.

CHANDRASEKHAR, A. 1974. The history of linguistic studies in Malayalam. *Vishveshvaranand Indological Journal* 12: 48–67.

CHINMULGUND, P. V. & V. V. MIRASHI (eds.) [1970]. *Review of Indological Research in Last 75 Years. M. M. Chitraoshastri Felicitation Volume.* Poona n.d. [cf. Mylius, *Wissenschaftliche Zeitschrift der Karl-Marx-Universität Leipzig* 24(2) (1975): 222–224.]

CLARKE, J. J. 1997. *Oriental Enlightenment. The Encounter Between Asian and Western Thought.* London.

CUST, Robert N. 1879. Notice on the scholars who have contributed to the extension of our knowledge of the languages of British India during the last thirty years. *JRAS* N.S. 11: 61–71.

DALMIA, Vasudha 2003. *Orienting India. European Knowledge Formation in the Eighteenth and Nineteenth Centuries.* New Delhi.

*DANDEKAR, R. N. (ed.) 1942. *Progress of Indic Studies 1917–1942* (Government Oriental Series, B8.) Poona.

DAWSON, W. R. & E. UPHILL 1972. *Who Was Who in Egyptology.* 2nd revised edition. London.

DOBLHOFER, Ernst 1957. *Zeichen und Wunder. Die Entzifferung verschollener Schriften und Sprachen.* Wien. [DTV-edition: München 1964.]

DODSON, Michael S. 2007. *Orientalism, Empire, and National Culture. India 1770–1880.* Basingstoke.

DOGRA, R. C. 1988. *Catalogue of the Early Printed Books on South Asia.* New Delhi.

DREW, John 1987. *India and the Romantic Imagination.* Delhi.

DUCHESNE-GUILLEMIN, J. 1958. *The Western Response to Zoroaster.* Oxford.

DUGAT, Gustave 1868–1870. *Histoire des orientalistes*, I–II. Paris. [Mainly on his contemporaries, with a long introduction about earlier history.]

EICHHORN, Johann Gottfried 1807. *Geschichte der Litteratur von ihrem Anfang bis auf die neuesten Zeiten*, V.1: *Geschichte der neuern* [sic] *Sprachenkunde*, 1. Göttingen.

**Eminent Orientalists. Indian, European, American.* Madras n.d. (25 biographies written by South Indian authors, from Jones and Wilkins to Keith and Lévi; cf. J. Charpentier, *Orientalistische Literaturzeitung* 32 (1929): 201).

Encyclopaedia of Tamil Literature, I. Madras 1990. (Especially V. M. Gnanapragasam & M. Mathialagan, Contribution of foreign scholars to Tamil, pp. 367–379).

*FIGUEIRA, Dorothy M. 1990. *Translating the Orient. The Reception of Sakuntala in Nineteenth-Century Europe.* Albany NY.

FOUCAUX, Philippe-Édouard 1875. Rapport sur les études bouddhiques [depuis 1852]. In: *I Congrès international des orientalistes, Paris 1873*, II: 409–423.

*FILLIOZAT, Jean 1953. Les premières étapes de l'indianisme. *Bulletin de l'Association Guillaume Budé* 3: 80–96.

—— 1973. La place des études tamoules dans l'indologie. *Indologica Taurinensia* 1: 47–60.

FIRTH, J. R. 1936. Alphabets and phonology in India and Burma. *BSOS* 8: 517–546.

FLÜGEL, Gustav 1834. Orientalische Studien, Literatur, Hülfsmittel. In: J. S. Ersch & J. G. Gruber (eds), *Allgemeine Encyclopädie der Wissenschaften und Künste*, III.5: 194–245. Leipzig.

FÜCK, J. 1955. *Die arabischen Studien in Europa bis in den Anfang des 20. Jahrhunderts*. Leipzig.

GEIGER, W. & E. KUHN (eds.) 1896–1904. *Grundriss der iranischen Philologie*, I–II. Strassburg. [K. F. Geldner, Geschichte der Awestaforschung, II: 40–46].

GEORGE, K. M. 1970. Contribution of the West to the study of Malayalam grammar. In: *Pratibhānam. A Collection of Research Papers Presented to Dr. P. K. Narayana Pillai on His 60th Birthday*: 129–135. Trivandrum.

—— 1971. The contribution of the West to the scientific study of Malayalam. In: *Dr. V. Raghavan Shashtyabdapurti Felicitation Volume*: 223–135. Madras.

GILDEMEISTER, Johannes 1847. *Bibliothecae Sanskritae sive recensus librorum sanskritorum hucusque typis bel lapide exscriptorum critici specimen*. Bonnae ad Rh.

GNANAPRAGASAN, V. M. & M. MATHIALAGAN 1990. Contribution of foreign scholars to Tamil. In: John Samuel (ed.), *Encyclopaedia of Tamil Literature*, I: 367–379. Madras.

GRIERSON, G. A. (ed.) 1898/1903–1928. *Linguistic Survey of India*, I–XII (19 parts). Calcutta. [With much historical informations in introductions and bibliographies, especially in the Hindi volume.]

GUBERNATIS, Angelo de 1872. Cenni sopra alcuni indianisti viventi. *La Rivista Europea* 3(4): 44–59, 265–273, 448–463.

HALBFASS, Wilhelm 1988. *India and Europe. An Essay in Understanding*. Albany, NY. [German original: *Indien und Europa: Perspektiven ihrer geistigen Begegung*. Basel 1981.]

*HARDY, E. 1901. Zur Geschichte der vergleichenden Religionsforschung. *Archiv für Religionswissenschaft* 4: 45–66, 97–135, 193–228.

HEYNE, A. 1912. *Orientalistisches Datenbuch. Eine Sammlung von Geburts- und Todesdaten von Orientalisten seit den Anfängen der Orientalischen Sprachwissenschaft bis auf die Gegenwart.* Leipzig.

Historiographia linguistica 1/1974–.

HODGEN, Margaret T. 1964. *Early Anthropology in Sixteenth and Seventeenth Centuries.* Philadelphia.

HOPKIRK, Peter 1980. *Foreign Devils on the Silk Road. The Search for the Lost Cities and Treasures of Chinese Central Asia.* London.

—— 1982. *Trespassers on the Roof of the World. The Race for Lhasa.* Oxford.

INDEN, Ronald 1990. *Imagining India.* Oxford.

Indian Studies Abroad. London 1964.

Internationales Taschenbuch für Orientalisten 1907, 1910.

International Who's Who in Asian Studies. 1975–76.

DE JONG, J. W. 1974. A brief history of Buddhist studies in Europe and America. *The Eastern Buddhist* 7(1): 55–106 & 7(2): 49–82. (Also in book form: Varanasi 1976; cf. de Jong 1987).

—— 1984–85. The study of the Mahābhārata. A brief survey. *Hokke bunka kenkyū (Risshōdaigaku hokekyō bunka kenkyūjo)* 10 (1984): 1–19 & 11 (1985): 1–22.

—— 1987. *A Brief History of Buddhist Studies in Europe and America.* 2nd revised & enlarged edition. (Bibliotheca Indo-Buddhica, 33.) Delhi. [Cf. de Jong 1974.]

KARTTUNEN, Klaus 1992. *Itää etsimässä. Eurooppalaisen Aasian-tutkimuksen vaiheita.* Helsinki. ['In Search for the East. A History of European Research on Asia'.]

—— 1995. The Rāmāyaṇa in the 19th century European literature and scholarship. In: G. Pollet (ed.), *Indian Epic Values. Rāmāyaṇa and Its Impact. Proceedings of the 8th International Rāmāyaṇa Conference, Leuven, 6–8 July 1991* (Orientalia Lovaniensia Analecta, 66) 115–125. Leuven.

—— 1997. The Mahābhārata in early Western Indology. *Bulletin des Études Indiennes* 13–14 (1995–96): 245–268.

—— 2004. Expansion of Oriental studies in the early 19th century. In: A. Panaino & A. Piras (ed.), *Schools of Oriental Studies and the Development of Modern Historiography* (MELAMMU Symposia, 4): 161–167. Milano.

—— 2010. Some thoughts about Edward Said, Hindutva, and Western Indology. In: Iwona Milewska (ed.), *Future of Indology* (Cracow Indological Studies, 10): 265–275. Krakow.

KEJARIWAL, O. P. 1988. *The Asiatic Society of Bengal and the Discovery of India's Past*. Delhi.

KERN, H. 1880. Begin en voortgang der Oostersche studiën in Europa. *Jaarboek der Universiteit te Leiden* 1880. [Kern's *Verspreide Geschriften*, 13: 69–93. 's-Gravenhage 1929.]

KING, Richard 1999. *Orientalism and Religion. Postcolonial Theory, India and 'The Mystic East'*. London.

KIRFEL, W. 1915. Die Anfänge des Sanskrit-Druckes in Europa. *Zentralblatt für Bibliothekswesen* 32: 274–280. [= *Kleine Schriften* 1976: 375–381.]

KOPF, David 1969. *British Orientalism and the Bengal Renaissance. The Dynamics of Indian Modernization 1773–1835*. Berkeley.

LACH, Donald F. 1965–77. *Asia in the Making of Europe*, I–II (5-parts). Chicago.

LACH, Donald F. & Edwin J. VAN KLEY 1993. *Asia in the Making of Europe*, III. Chicago.

LEUMANN, Ernst 1909. *Unvergessene, gestorben in den Jahren 1891–1908. Lebensdaten, Bilder und Beileidbriefe*. Strassburg.

LONG, J. 1864. Ueber den Stand der Sanskrit-Studien im heutigen Indien. *ZDMG* 18: 343–345.

LUBAC, Henri de 1952. *La rencontre du bouddhisme et de l'occident*. Paris.

MACGREGOR, John 1970. *Tibet. A Chronicle of Exploration*. London. [Written under pseudonym.]

MAYRHOFER, Manfred 1983. Sanskrit und die Sprachen Alteuropas. Zwei Jahrhunderte des Widerspiels von Entdeckungen und Irrtümern. *Nachrichten von der Akademie der Wissenschaften zu Göttingen, Philologisch-historische Klasse* 1983(5): 121–154.

*MEENAKSHISUNDARAN, K. 1979. *The Contribution of European Scholars to Tamil*. Madras.

MESSERSCHMIDT, Leopold 1903. *Die Entzifferung der Keilschrift*. (Der alte Orient, 5.2.) Leipzig.

MISHRA, Madhusudan 2003. *Vedic Scholars from the West*. Delhi.

MITTER, P. 1977. *Much Maligned Monsters. History of European Reactions to Indian Art*. Oxford.

MOHL, J. 1879–80. *See II.12.a. France.*

MOSES, Mohandas & Achala MOULIK 2009. *Dialogue of Civilizations. William Jones and the Orientalists*. New Delhi.

MYLIUS, Klaus 1966. Der gegenwärtige Stand und die weiteren Aufgaben der Vedaforschung. *Mitteilungen des Instituts für Orientforschung* 12: 329–334.

—— 2001. Einige Aufgaben der Jinismus-Forschung zu Beginn des 3. Jahrhundert. In: K. Karttunen & P. Koskikallio (eds.). *Vidyārṇavavandanam*.

Essays in Honour of Asko Parpola (Studia Orientalia, 94): 387–395. Helsinki.

NAIR, P. Thankappan 1973. Malayalam grammars by Carmelites. *International Journal of Dradidian Linguistics* 2: 127–140.

OATEN, Edward Farley 1909. *European Travellers in India*. London.

Orientalische Bibliographie, 1–23. Berlin 1887–1909/11.

PEDERSEN, Holger 1931. *The Discovery of Language. Linguistic Science in the Nineteenth Century*. Translated by J. W. Spargo. Bloomington, IN. [Reprint: 1962.]

PEIRIS, William 1973. *The Western Contribution to Buddhism*. Delhi. [Very unreliable!]

PHILIPS, C. H. (ed.) 1961. *Historians of India, Pakistan and Ceylon*. London.

Picturesque Asia. (Illustrated and annotated catalogue of the antiquarian department of E. J. Brill, 569.) Leiden 1988.

POLIAKOV, Leon 1972. *Le mythe aryen. Essai sur les sources du racisme et des nationalismes*. Paris.

RAGHAVAN, V. 1956. *Sanskrit and Allied Indian Studies in Europe*. Madras.

*—— (ed.) 1979. *"Vasudhaiva kuṭumbakam". International Sanskrit Conference. March 26th–31st, 1972*, I.2: *Sanskrit and Indology in Centres Outside India, Contributions of Haryana, Tamil Nadu*. New Delhi.

RENOU, Louis 1928. *Les maîtres de la philologie védique*. (A.M.G., Bibl. d'Etudes, 38.) Paris.

—— 1950. *Sanskrit et culture. L'apport de l'Inde à la civilisation humaine*. Paris.

ROY, Sourindranath 1961. *The Story of Indian Archaeology*. New Delhi.

SAID, Edward 1978. *Orientalism*. New York.

*SANDBERG, Samuel Louis Graham 1904. *The Exploration of Tibet. Its History and Particulars, 1623–1904*. Calcutta.

Sanskrit Outside India. See Bedekar, V. V.

Sanskrit Studies Outside India. (News Bulletin No. 2. Fourth World Sanskrit Conference, Weimar/ G.D.R. May 23–30, 1979.) Weimar 1979.

**Sanskrit Studies Outside India 1979–1981* (Fifth World Sanskrit Conference, Varanasi, India: October 21–26, 1981.) Delhi 1981.

Sanskrit Studies Outside India. (On the occasion of 10th World Sanskrit Conference, Bangalore, Jan 3–9, 1997.) New Delhi 1997.

SCHIERLITZ, Ernst 1927. *Die bildlichen Darstellungen der indischen Göttertrinität in der älteren ethnographischen Literatur*. Diss. München [On the period 1651–1810.]

SCHOEBEL, Charles 1875. Rapport sur les progrès des études indiennes depuis 1867. In: *I Congrès international des orientalistes, Paris 1873*, II: 355–377.

*SCHROEDER, Leopold von 1895. Über die Entwicklung der Indologie in Europa und ihre Beziehungen zum allgemeinen Völkerkunde. *Mitteilungen der anthropologischen Gesellschaft in Wien* 25: 1–8.

SCHWAB, Raymond 1950. *La renaissance orientale*. Paris. [English translation: *The Oriental Renaissance. Europe's Rediscovery of India and the East 1680–1880*. New York 1984.]

SENGUPTA, Gauranga Gopal 1996. *Indology and Its Eminent Western Savants. Collection of Biographies of Western Indologists*. Calcutta.

SINGH, Upinder 2005. *The Discovery of Ancient India. Early Archaeologists and the Beginnings of Archaeology*. Delhi.

SITRAMPALAM, S. K. 1986. Survey of archaeological studies in Sri Lanka. *BDCRI* 45: 123–135.

STERNEMANN, R. (ed.), *Bopp-Symposium 1992 der Humboldt-Universität zu Berlin. Akten der Konferenz vom 24.3.–26.3.1992 aus Anlaß von Franz Bopps zweihundertjährigem Gebirtstag am 14.9.1991* (Indogermanische Bibliothek, dritte Reihe.) Heidelberg.

TADDEI, M. (ed.) 1995. *Angelo De Gubernatis. Europa e Oriente nell'Italia umbertina*, I. (Collana "Matteo Ripa", 10.) Napoli.

—— 1997. *Angelo De Gubernatis. Europa e Oriente nell'Italia umbertina*, II. (Collana "Matteo Ripa", 13.) Napoli.

—— 1998. *Angelo De Gubernatis. Europa e Oriente nell'Italia umbertina*, III. (Collana "Matteo Ripa", 15). Napoli.

—— 2001. *Angelo De Gubernatis. Europa e Oriente nell'Italia umbertina*, IV. (Collana "Matteo Ripa", 17). Napoli.

**Tamil Studies Abroad*. Kuala Lumpur 1968.

THOMSEN, Vilhelm 1902. *Sprogvidenskabens historie*. København. [In German by H. Pollack: *Geschichte der Sprachwissenschaft*. Halle 1927; in Russian by R. Shor: *Istoriya yazykovedeniya*. Moscow 1938.]

TRAUTMANN, Thomas R. 1997. *Aryans and British India*. Berkeley, CA.

—— (ed.) 2009. *The Madras School of Orientalism. Producing Knowledge in Colonial India*. New Delhi.

VACEK, Jaroslav & Jan DVOŘÁK (eds.) 1998. *Trends in Indian Studies. Proceedings of the ESIS*. Prague.

VATER, J. S. 1847. *Litteratur der Grammatiken, Lexika und Wörtersammlungen in aller Sprachen der Erde*. Zweite, völlig umgearbeitete Ausgabe von B. Jülg. Berlin.

WAHL, Samuel Friedrich Günther 1784. *Allgemeine Geschichte der morgenländischen Sprachen und Litteratur*. Leipzig.

*WEINBERGER-THOMAS, Catherine (ed.) 1988. *L'Inde et l'imaginaire.* (Purushartha, 11.) Paris.

*WELBON, G. R. 1968. *The Buddhist Nirvāṇa and Its Western Interpreters.* Chicago. [Cf. J. W. de Jong, *Journal of Indian Philosophy* 1 (1972): 396–403.]

WEZLER, Albrect 1993. Towards a reconstruction of Indian cultural history. Observations and reflections on 18th and 19th century Indology. *Studien zur Indologie und Iranistik* 18: 305–329.

WINDISCH, Ernst 1917–20. *Geschichte der Sanskrit-Philologie und indischen Altertumskunde*, I–II. (Grundriss der Indo-Arischen Philologie und Altertumskunde, I.I.B.) Strassburg (1917) – Berlin & Leipzig (1920).

—— 1921. *Philologie und Altertumskunde in Indien. Drei nachgelassene Kapitel des III. Teils der Geschichte der Sanskrit-Philologie und indischen Altertumskunde.* (Abhandlungen für die Kunde des Morgenlandes, 15.3.) Leipzig.

WINTERNITZ, Moritz 1908–20. *Geschichte der indischen Literatur*, I–III. Leipzig [Also a revised English edition.]

—— 1935. Indien und der Westen. *Archiv Orientální* 7: 280–301 [= *Kleine Schriften* 1991: 845–866; English tr. in *Visvabharati Quarterly* N.S. 2(4), 1937: 1–24.

WÜST, W. 1929. *Indisch.* (Grundriss der indogermanischen Sprach- und Altertumskunde – Geschichte der indogermanischen Sprachwissenschaft, II.4.1.) Berlin & Leipzig.

*X 1888. L'enseignement du sanscrit et de la grammaire comparée dans les universités d'Europe et d'Amérique. *Revue internationale de l'enseignement* 8(10): 361–366.

YOUNG, Richard F. 1979. Church Sanskrit. An approach of Christian scholars to Hinduism in the 19th century. *WZKS* 23: 205–231.

ZACHARIAE, Theodor 1908. Hanscrit. *WZKM* 22: 86–103. [= *Kleine Schriften* 1920: 17–33.]

—— 1910. Vertia eine Bezeichnung der Jainas. *WZKM* 24: 337–344. [= *Kleine Schriften* 1920: 41–47).

—— 1921. Review of Caland 1918, *Göttingische Gelehrte Anzeigen*: 148–165. [= *Opera minora* 1976, II: 766–783.]

—— 1926. Zur Frühgeschichte der Sanskritphilologie. *Zeitschrift für Indologie und Iranistik* 4: 223–238. [= *Opera minora* 1976, II: 812–827.]

—— 1933. Berichte über die Jainas bei Autoren des 16. und 17. Jahrhunderts. In: *Festschrift Moriz Winternitz 1863–23 Dez.–1933*: 174–184. Leipzig. [= *Opera minora* 1976, II: 934–184).

ZENKER, Th. 1846–61. *Bibliotheca orientalis. Manuel de bibliographie orientale*, I–II. Leipzig.

ZVELEBIL, Kamil 1956. One hundred years of Dravidian comparative philology. *Archiv Orientální* 24: 599–609.

b. Biographical directories, university histories etc.

Biographie universelle ancienne et moderne, 1–85. Paris 1811–62 (Main part 1–52 [1811–28]; 53–55 Partie mythologique [1832–33]; 56–85 Supplement [1834–62]).

Bursians Jahresberichte = Conrad Bursian (ed.), *Jahresbericht über die Fortschritte der klassischen Altertumswissenschaft*. Göttingen 1873ff.

DUNKEL, J. G. W. 1753–60. *Historisch-kritische Nachrichten von verstorbenen Gelehrten und deren Schriften. Insonderheit aber Denenienigen, welche in der allerneuesten Ausgabe des Jöcherischen Allgemeinen Gelehrten-Lexikons entweder gänzlich mit Stillschweigen übergangen, oder doch mangelhaft und unrichtig angeführt werden*, I.1–III.4. Cöthen & Dessau. [Reprint: Hildesheim 1968.]

Encyclopaedia Judaica, I–XVI. Jerusalem 1971–72.

GORTON, John 1833. *A General Biographical Dictionary*. A new edition, continued to the year 1833, I–III. London.

*GÖTTEN, Gabriel Wilhelm 1735–37. *Das jetztlebende gelehrte Europa*. Braunschweig & Zelle.

GUBERNATIS, Angelo de 1879. *Dizionario biografico degli scrittori contemporanei*. Firenze.

—— 1891. *Dictionnaire international des écrivains du jour*, I–III. Florence 1891.

*—— 1905. *Dictionnaire international des écrivains du monde latin*. Rome & Florence.

Index bio-bibliographicus notorum hominum, Pars C, Corpus alphabeticum I. Sectio generalis. 1–. Osnabrück 1974–. [Most recent volume 182, 2014, up to Müller.]

JÖCHER, Christian Gottlieb 1750–51. *Allgemeine Gelehrten-Lexicon*, I–IV. Leipzig.

JÖCHER, Christian Gottlieb & J. Chr. ADELUNG 1784–87. *Fortsetzungen und Ergänzungen zu Christian Gottlieb Jöchers Allgemeinem Gelehrten-Lexicon*, I–II. Leipzig.

JÖCHER, Christian Gottlieb & H. W. ROTERMUND 1810–19. *Fortsetzungen und Ergänzungen zu Christian Gottlieb Jöchers Allgemeinem Gelehrten-Lexicon*, III–VI. Delmenhorst (III) & Bremen.

JÖCHER, Christian Gottlieb & H. W. ROTERMUND 1897. *Fortsetzungen und Ergänzungen zu Christian Gottlieb Jöchers Allgemeinem Gelehrten-Lexikon.* Mit einem Anhang enthaltend die für die 2. Ausgabe des 3. Bandes (K) bestimmten Verbesserungen und Zusätze aus den Handexemplar des Verfassers, VII. Hrsg. von Otto Günther. Leipzig.

Lexicon grammaticorum. Who's Who in the History of World Linguistics. Tübingen 1996.

Minerva. Jahrbuch der gelehrte Welt, 1–30. 1891–1932.

Nouvelle biographie générale, 1–46. Paris 1855–66.

c. Monastic orders and missions (Biographical registers)

*AMBROSIUS À S. TERESIA 1940. *Bio-bibliographia missionaria Ordinis Carmelitarum Discalceatorum (1584–1940).* Rome.

*—— 1944. *Nomenclator Missionariorum Ordinis Carmelitarum Discalceatorum.* Rome.

*BERNARDUS A BONONIA 1747. *Bibliotheca scriptorum Ordinis Minorum s. Franciscani Capucinorum retexta.* Venice.

BESSE, Léon 1918. Liste alphabétique des missionaires du Carnatic de la compagnie de Jésus au XVIIIe siècle. *Revue historique de l'Inde française* 2: 175–242.

KOCH, Ludwig, S.J. 1934. *Jesuiten-Lexicon.* Paderborn.

Lexicon capuccinum. Promptuarium historico-bibliographicum ordinis fratrum minorum capuccinorum (1525–1950). Rome 1951.

SOMMERVOGEL, Carlos 1890–1900. *Bibliothèque de la Compagnie de Jésus,* I: *bibliographie.* Bruxelles & Paris [Reprinted: 1960.]

d. History of missions (with no attempt at completeness)

*BROWNE, G. 1859. *The History of the British and Foreign Bible Society. From Its Institution in 1804, to the Close of Its Jubilee in 1854,* I–II. London.

CHARPENTIER, Jarl 1923. Arbeten rörande Indiens religioner och språk under 1500- och 1600-talen. *Svenska Orientsällskapets Årsbok* 1: 12–26.

DAHLMANN, J. 1891. *Die Sprachkunde und die Missionen. Ein Beitrag zur Charakteristik der älteren katholischen Missionstätigkeit (1500–1800).* (Ergänzungshefte zu den "Stimmen aus Maria-Laach", 50.) Freiburg i. Br.

DELACROIX, D. (ed.) 1956–59. *Histoire universelle des missions catholiques,* I–IV. Paris.

FELIX, Rev. Father, O.C. 1912. Remarks on the Tibetan manuscript vocabularies in Bishop's College, Calcutta. *JASB* N.S. 8: 379–397.

*FERROLI, P. D., S.J. 1939–51. *The Jesuits in Malabar,* I–II. Bangalore.

*GABRIELI, G. 1931. *Gli studi orientali e gli ordini religiosi*. (Il Pensiero Missionario, dell'Unione Missionaria del Clero in Italia, 3.) Roma.

*GUZMAN, Luis de 1891. *Historia de las misiones de la Compañía de Jesus en la India Oriental, en la China y Japon, desde 1540 hasta 1600*. Bilbao.

HOSTEN, Henry 1911–30. A series of articles about the history of Jesuit missions in India and other Asian countries published in the *JASB*.

*JANNE, P. A. 1915. *Die katolischen Missionen in Indien, China und Japan*. Paderborn.

*LAIRD, M. A. 1972. *Missionaries and Education in Bengal, 1793–1837*. Oxford.

*LAUNAY, A. 1898. *Histoire des missions de l'Inde*. Paris.

*MACLAGAN, Sir Edward 1932. *The Jesuits and the Great Mogul*. London.

NAIR, P. Thankappan 1973. Malayalam Grammars by Carmelites. *International Journal of Dravidian Linguistics* 2: 127–140.

ODDIE, Geoffrey A. 2006. *Imagined Hinduism. British Protestant Missionary Constructions of Hinduism, 1793–1900*. New Delhi.

PLATTNER, F. A. 1950. *Jesuits Go East*. Dublin [*German original: *Jesuiten zur See. Der Weg nach Asien. Ein Beitrag zur Geschichte der Entdeckungen*. Zürich [1946]; *French version: *Quand l'Europe cherchait l'Asie*. Paris 1954.]

SWEETMAN, Will 2003. *Mapping Hinduism. 'Hinduism' and the Study of Indian Religions, 1600–1776*. (Neue Hallesche Berichte, 4.) Halle.

*TOSCANO, G. M. 1951. *La prima missione cattolica Tibet*. Roma.

*WESSELS, C. 1924. *Early Jesuit Travellers in Central Asia, 1603–1721*. The Hague.

ZACHARIAE, Theodor 1913. Aufführung von Jesuitendramen in Indien. *Archiv für das Studium der neueren Sprachen und Literaturen* 130: 32–33. [= *Kleine Schriften* 1920: 197–205; cf. *Archiv für das Studium der neueren Sprachen und Literaturen* 155 (1929): 251–253. (= *Opera minora* 1976, II: 891–893).]

ŽUPANOV, Ines G. 1999. *Disputed Mission. Jesuit Experiments and Brahmanical Knowledge in Seventeenth-Century India*. Delhi.

II. HISTORY OF INDOLOGY IN ASIA

1. India

N.B. Section I. includes much that could also be given here.

*BHANDARKAR, S. R. 1906. *The Present Condition of Sanskrit Studies in India.* Bombay.

BRAHMACHARI, U. N. 1932. Some aspects of the Asiatic Society. Past, present, and future. *JASB* N.S. 28, Proceedings for 1931: x–xli.

CASARTELLI, L. C. 1893. The literary activities of the Parsis durig the past ten years in Avestic and Pehlevi studies. *Transactions of the 9th International Congress of Orientalists, Held in London 1892*, Vol. II, Section VII: Persia & Turkey: 528–536.

CHINMULGUND & V. V. MIRASHI (eds.) [1970]. *Review of Indological Research in Last 75 Years. M. M. Chitraoshastri Felicitation Volume.* Poona.

DANDEKAR, R. N. 1949. Indology in India. Retrospect and prospect. In: *Actes du XXIe Congrès international des Orientalistes, Paris 1948*: 179–184. Paris.

*GUPTA, S. S. 1965. *Folklorists of Bengal.* Calcutta. [Lal Beharí Day, S. C. Mitra, D. C. Sen, D. M. Majumdar, G. S. Dutt, C. K. Deo et al.]

*MODI, J. J. 1911. Short history of the society. *Journal of the Anthropological Society of Bombay*, Extra No.

RAGHAVAN, V. 1964. *Indological Studies in India.* Delhi.

RENOLD, Leah 2005. *A Hindu Education. Early Years of the Banaras Hindu University.* New Delhi.

Sanskrit Studies in India. (On the occasion of 10th World Sanskrit Conference 1997.) Editor K. K. Mishra. New Delhi.

*SARKAR, J. N. & J. C. JHA 1963. *History of the Patna College.* Patna.

SIRCAR, D. C. (ed.) 1969. *Pracyavidyātaraṅgiṇī. Golden Jubilee Volume of the Department of Ancient Indian History and Culture.* Calcutta. [With a number of biographical sketches.]

Who's Who of Sanskrit Scholars in India 1991. Ed. by K. C. Dutt. Delhi 1994.

2. China

BAPAT, P. V. & J. N. TAKASAKI 1959. Progress of Buddhist studies in Ceylon, Burma, Thailand, Cambodia, Laos, Vietnam, China and Japan. In V. P. Bapat, *2500 Years of Buddhism*: 370–383. Delhi. Also available in: *Buddhism Today* (http://www.buddhismtoday.com/index/world.htm).

*CHI Hsien-lin 1981. Minami Ajia shokoku to bukkyōgaku ni taisuru Chūgoku no kenkyū ['The South Asian and Buddhist studies in China']. Translated by Chin Shêng-pao. *Ōsaki Gakuhō* 134: 51–69.

HUANG Xinchuan 1984. Sanskrit studies in China. In: V. V. Bedekar (ed.), *Proceedings and Papers of the Seminar on Sanskrit Outside India*: 67–69. Thane.

3. Japan

DOI, Toshio 1983. *The Study of Language in Japan. A Historical Survey.* 4th edition. Tokyo.

HARA, Minoru 1985. *Studies on Indian Philosophy and Literature in Japan, 1973–1983.* (Asian Studies in Japan, 1973–1983, II.21.) Tokyo.

*HIRAKAWA, Akira & E. B. CEADEL 1955. Japanese research on Buddhism since the Meiji period. *Monumenta Nipponica* 11: 221–246, 397–424.

*KAWASAKI, Shinjo 1977. *Indian Buddhism.* (Oriental studies in Japan: Retrospect and prospect, 1967–72, II.2.) Tokyo.

*MAYEDA, Sengaku 1974. *Indian Philosophy and Literature.* (Oriental studies in Japan in Retrospect and Prospect 1963–1972, II.21.) Tokyo.

—— 1984. Growth and practice of Sanskrit studies in Japan. In: V. V. Bedekar (ed.), *Proceedings and Papers of the Seminar on Sanskrit Outside India*: 65–66. Thane.

MAYEDA, Sengaku & Junzō TANIZAWA 1989. Studies on Indian philosophy in Japan 1963–1987. *Acta Asiatica* 57: 61–100.

NAGAO, Gadjin 1975. Reflections on Tibetan studies in Japan. *Acta Asiatica* 29: 107–128.

NAKAMURA, Hajime 1956. Indian studies in Japan. *Indo-Asian Culture* 4(4): 425–439.

ŌHASHI, Yukio 1987. Sanskrit study in Japan. *Vishveshvaranand Indological Journal* 22 (1984): 164–168.

OJIHARA, Yutaka 1979. Sanskrit studies in Japan. In: *Sanskrit Studies Outside India* (News Bulletin No. 2. Fourth World Sanskrit Conference, Weimar/G.D.R. May 23–30, 1979): 86–98. Weimar.

*OTA, Kiyoshi & Masataka IKEDA 1982. Pāli Buddhist studies in Japan. *Pārikagu Bukkyō Bunkagaku* 6(1) (1981–82): 7–32.

YAMAZAKI, Toshio & Gen'ichi YAMAZAKI 1982. Postwar Japanese studies in the socio-economic history of Ancient India. *Acta Asiatica* 43: 81–91.

YUYAMA, Akira 1993. An appraisal of the history of Buddhist Sanskrit studies in East Asia. *Studies on Buddhism in Honour of A. K. Warder*: 194–203. Toronto.

4. Mongolia

YONDON, B. 1979. Sanskrit studies in **Mongolia**. In: *Sanskrit Studies Outside India* (News Bulletin No. 2. Fourth World Sanskrit Conference, Weimar/G.D.R. May 23–30, 1979): 104–116. Weimar.

5. South-East Asia and Indonesia

BAPAT, P. V. & J. N. TAKASAKI 1959. Progress of Buddhist studies in Ceylon, Burma, Thailand, Cambodia, Laos, Vietnam, China and Japan. In V. P. Bapat, *2500 Years of Buddhism*: 370–383. Delhi. Also available in: *Buddhism Today* (http://www.buddhismtoday.com/index/world.htm).

*MALO, V. D. 1974. ['On the history of Pāli studies in Burma']. In: *V. S. Vorob'ev -Desyatovskij Memorial Volume*': 159–172.

*SADDHATISSA, H. 1980a. Pāli Buddhist studies in Cambodia. In: *W. Rahula Volume*: 242–250.

*—— 1980b. Pāli Buddhist studies in Thailand today. In: *Nyanatiloka Centenary Volume*: 31–46. Kandy.

SHASTRI, Satya Vrat 1979. Sanskrit studies in Thailand. In: *Sanskrit Studies Outside India* (News Bulletin No. 2. Fourth World Sanskrit Conference, Weimar/G.D.R. May 23–30, 1979): 163–167. Weimar.

—— 1997. Sanskrit studies in Thailand. In *Sanskrit Studies Outside India*: 86–96. New Delhi.

*UMIE, Hiroki & Shigeki KUDO 1963. Biruma no bukkyō kenkyū jōkyō. *Indogaku shi ronshū* 4–5: 88–92. [The state of Buddhist studies in Burma.]

6. South Asia outside India

BAPAT, P. V. & J. N. TAKASAKI 19??. Progress of Buddhist studies in Ceylon, Burma, Thailand, Cambodia, Laos, Vietnam, China and Japan. *Buddhism Today*: c. 12 pages (http://www.buddhismtoday.com/index/world.htm).

BHOWMICK, D. K. 1996. Sanskrit studies in Bangladesh. *Journal of the Department of Sanskrit (Rabindra Bharati University, Calcutta)*, 5 (1991–93): 60–77.

*DEVENDRA, D. T. 1959. Seventy years of Ceylon archaeology. *Artibus Asiae* 22: 23–40.

*—— 1969. *Story of Ceylon Archaeology*. Colombo.

GODAKUMBURA, C. E. 1969. History of archaeology in Ceylon. *Journal of the Ceylon Branch of the Royal Asiatic Society* 13: 1–38.

HANDURUKANDE, Ratna 1994. Orientalia in the University. *Sri Lanka Journal of Humanities* 17–18 (1991–92): 266–342.

HETTIARATCHI, M. D. E. 1949. The philological work being done in Ceylon. In: *Actes du XXIe Congrès des orientalistes, Paris 1948*: 184–187. Paris.

*KASHIWARA, Shingyo 1984. Suriranka no bukkyō kenkyū jijō. *Bukkyōgaku Seminā* 40: 83–88. [Buddhist studies in Sri Lanka.]

PARANAVITANA, K. D. 1986. Scholar monks of the nineteenth century and the tragic transformation of Ven. Kapugama Dhammakkhanda Thero. *Journal of the Royal Asiatic Society of Sri Lanka* 28 (1985–86): 123–164.

*PEREIRA, S. G. 1941. *The Jesuits in Ceylon. In the XVI and XVII Centuries.* Madura.

SITRAMPALAM, S. K. 1986. Survey of archaeological studies in Sri Lanka. *BDCRI* 45: 123–135.

TILAKASIRI, J. 1979. Sanskrit studies in Sri Lanka (1977–78). In: *Sanskrit Studies Outside India* (News Bulletin No. 2. Fourth World Sanskrit Conference, Weimar/G.D.R. May 23–30, 1979): 131–134. Weimar.

Sri Lanka, see under South Asia outside India

Thailand, see under South-East Asia and Indonesia

III. HISTORY OF INDOLOGY IN EUROPE AND AMERICA

***Argentina**, see under South and Central America*

1. Australia

a. Indology and Oriental studies

BAILEY, Greg 1993. Sanskrit studies in Australia. *Newsletter of the International Association of Sanskrit Studies* 4: 13–16.

BAILEY, Greg & Purushottam BILIMORIA 1997. Sanskrit studies in Australia. In: *Sanskrit Studies Outside India. On the Occasion of 10th World Sanskrit Conference 1997*: 1–11. New Delhi.

BISHOP, Enid 1972. *Australian Theses on Asia*. Canberra.

b. General directories

Australian Dictionary of Biography, I–XVII. Melbourne 1966–. [XVI: until 1980; XVII: 1981–90 A–K, 2007] – also online version.

2. Austria

a. Indology and Oriental studies

BOLLA-KOTEK, S. 1951. Veröffentlichungen und Arbeiten österreichischer Orientalisten seit 1945. *Archiv Orientální* 19: 29–31.

FRAUWALLNER, Erich 1961. Geschichte und Aufgaben der Wiener Indologie. *Anzeiger der Österreichischen Akademie der Wissenschaften* 98: 77–95.

JANERT, Klaus L. 1961. *Verzeichnis indienkundlicher Hochschulschriften. Deutschland–Österreich– Schweiz.* Wiesbaden.

LOCHNER VON HÜTTENBACH, Fritz, Freiherr 1976. *Das Fach vergleichende Sprachwissenschaft an der Universität Graz.* Graz.

LOCHNER VON HÜTTENBACH, Fritz, Manfred HUTTER & Walter SLAJE 1991. *Indo-iranische Sprachen und Kulturen. 100 Jahre Forschung und Lehre in Graz.* Graz.

NEUMANN, W. A. 1899. *Ueber die orientalischen Sprachenstudien seit dem XIII. Jahrhunderte, mit besonderer Rücksicht auf Wien.* Wien. [Cf. G. Kampffmeyer, *Orientalische Literaturzeitung* 4 (1901): 107–110.]

*OBERHAMMER, G. 1966. Indologie in Wien. *Wissenschaft und Weltbild* 19: 56–61.

—— 1979. Sanskrit studies in Austria. In: *Sanskrit Studies Outside India* (News Bulletin No. 2. Fourth World Sanskrit Conference, Weimar/ G.D.R. May 23–30, 1979): 8–12. Weimar.

—— 1984. Sanskrit studies in Austria. In: V. V. Bedekar (ed.), *Proceedings and Papers of the Seminar on Sanskrit Outside India*: 15–16. Thane.

—— 1990. Sanskrit studies in Austria. *Newsletter of the International Association of Sanskrit Studies* 3: 23–26.

RAGHAVAN, V. 1956. *Sanskrit and Allied Indian Studies in Europe*. Madras. [Austria, pp. 46–48.]

*WENRICH, J. G. 1822–24. *Commentatio historica qua quantum linguarum orientalium studia Austriae debeant, exponitur*, I–II. Vindobonae.

b. General directories

Österreichische Biographische Lexikon 1815–1950, I–. Graz & Köln 1957–. [Most recent volume XIII, Spanner–Stulli, Wien 2010.]

WURZBACH, Constant 1856–91. *Biographisches Lexikon des Kaiserthums Oesterreich*, I–LX. Wien.

3. Baltic States

a. Indology and Oriental studies

BĚLKA, Luboš 1996. Oriental and Buddhist studies in Estonia. *Archiv Orientální* 64: 399–404.

HALLIK, Martin & Olaf-Mihkel KLAASSEN 2002. *Keiserlik Tartu Ülikool (1802–1918) ja orient. Eesti-Oriendi kultuurisuhete üldisel taustal*. Tartu.

KLAASSEN, Olaf 1988. *Loenguid Eesti afroasiaatika kujunemisloost*. Tartu.

—— 1990. *Aasia ja Aafrika 1918–1945 ning kontaktid eestiga*, I–II. Tartu.

—— 1992. *Aasia ja Aafrika 1900–1918 ning kontaktid eestiga*. Tartu.

—— 1994. *Aasia ja Aafrika 16.–19. sajandil ning kontaktid Eestiga*. Tartu.

b. General directories

Biobibliograficheskij slovar' professorov i prepodavatelej imperatorskago Yur'evskago, byvshago Derptskago, universiteta za sto let' ego sushchestvovaniya (1802–1902), I–II. Yur'ev 1902–03. (Kathedra nemetskago i sravnitel'nago jazykoznaniya, 2: 563–588).

Deutschbaltisches biographisches Lexikon 1710–1960. Wien 1970.

Eesti biograafiline leksikon. General editor A. R. Cederberg. (Akadeemilise ajaloo-seltsi toimitused, 2.) Tartu 1926–29.

RECKE, Friedr. von & K. E. NAPIERSKY 1827–32. *Allgemeines Schriftsteller- und Gelehrten-Lexicon der Provinzen Livland, Estland und Kurland*, I–IV. Mitau. [Fortsetzungen von C. E. Napiersky & Theodor Beise, I–II. Mitau 1859–61. (Neudruck: Berlin 1966).]

Bosnia-Herzegovina*, see under Yugoslavia*

4. Belgium

a. Indology and Oriental studies

CALLEWAERT, W. M. 1984. Sanskrit studies in Belgium. In: V. V. Bedekar (ed.), *Proceedings and Papers of the Seminar on Sanskrit Outside India*: 9. Thane.

POLLET, G. 1984. Growth and practice of Sanskrit studies in Belgium. In: V. V. Bedekar (ed.), *Proceedings and Papers of the Seminar on Sanskrit Outside India*: 1–2. Thane. [= Itihas Patrika 4: 41–42.]

—— 1995. 150 years of Sanskrit studies in Leuven, Belgium (1841–1991). In: G. Pollet (ed.), *Indian Epic Values. Rāmāyaṇa and Its Impact* (Orientalia Lovaniensia Analecta, 66.): 133–135. Leuven.

RAGHAVAN, V. 1956. *Sanskrit and Allied Indian Studies in Europe*. Madras. [Belgium: 16–18.]

RIES, J. 1979. Sanskrit studies in Belgium. *Sanskrit Studies Outside India* (News Bulletin No. 2. Fourth World Sanskrit Conference, Weimar/G.D.R. May 23–30, 1979.): 194–195. Weimar.

*ROELANDTS, K. 1981. De taalkunde in België sinds 1830. *Verslagen en Mededelingen van de Koninklijke Academie voor Nederlandse Taal- en Letterkunde* 1981(2): 146–176.

*RYCKMANS, G. 1932. Les langues orientales. In: *Liber Memorialis. Le Ve centenaire de la Faculté de Théologie de l'Université de Louvain 1432–1932*: 101–117 (esp. 116–117). Bruges & Louvain.

*—— 1947. L'orientalisme en Belgique. *Revue générale belge* 23: 724–738 (esp. 726, 733–734).

—— 1966. L'orientalisme à Louvain avant 1936. *Le Muséon* 69: 13–33 (Indo-Iranian studies on pp. 25–28); also published in *Universitas Catholica Lovaniensis. Trentième anniversaire de l'Institut orientaliste*. Louvain 1966: 9–23 (21–23).

b. General directories

Biografisch Archief van de Benelux. München 1992. Cards 1–756 (microfiche, now also online, complete).

Biographie nationale de Belgique, I–XXVIII. Bruxelles 1866–1944; XXIX–XLIV = Supplement 1–16 (1957–86).

Dictionnaire des Belges. Par Paul Legrain. Bruxelles 1981.

Nationaal biografisch Woordenboek (Koninklijke vlaamse Academiën van België), I–. Brussel 1964–. [Most recent volume XIX, 2009.]

Nouvelle biographie nationale, I–. Bruxelles 1988–. [Most recent volume XII, 2014.]

5. Bulgaria

a. Indology and Oriental studies

EVTIMOVA, Tatyana 1998. Indology in Bulgaria. In: *Trends in Indian Studies. Proceedings of the ESIS*: 79–83. Prague.

PARASCHKEWOW, Boris 1984. Zur Entstehung und Entwicklung der vergleichenden und historischen Sprachwissenschaft in Bulgarien. *Wissenschaftliche Zeitschrift der Humboldt-Universität zu Berlin, Gesellschaft-Sprachwissenschaftliche Reihe* 33(5): 533–535.

6. Canada

a. Indology and Oriental studies

AKLUJKAR, Ashok 1997. Sanskrit studies in Canada. In: *Sanskrit Studies Outside India. On the Occasion of 10th World Sanskrit Conference 1997*: 12–30. New Delhi.

CHAMBERLAIN, H. B. 1983. *Directory of Asia Scholars of Canada / Repertoire des asianistes du Canada*.

GRANOFF, Phyllis 1984. Sanskrit studies in Austria. In: V. V. Bedekar (ed.), *Proceedings and Papers of the Seminar on Sanskrit Outside India*: 43–44. Thane.

b. General directories

Dictionary of Canadian Biography, I–XV. Toronto 1966–2005 [XV: Deaths until 1925] – also Online version.

WALLACE, H. W. 1963. *The Macmillan Dictionary of Canadian Biography*. 3rd revised & enlarged edition. London.

7. Caucasian States

a. Indology and Oriental studies

During Soviet times Caucasian scholars were included in general works, e.g. in the directory of Oriental scholars by Miliband. See Russia.

***Costa Rica**, see under South and Central America*

***Croatia**, see under Yugoslavia*

8. Czechoslovakia (now Czech Republic and Slovakia)

a. Indology and Oriental studies

FILIPSKÝ, J. 1979. Sanskrit studies in Czechoslovakia. In: *Sanskrit Studies Outside India* (News Bulletin No. 2. Fourth World Sanskrit Conference, Weimar/G.D.R. May 23–30, 1979): 15–20. Weimar.

KOSTIĆ, Svetislav & Jan DVOŘÁK (eds.) 1998. *Institute of Indian Studies. Bibliography (with a Historical Survey).* Prague. [Historical Survey by J. Vacek: 12–19.]

*LESNÝ, V. 1920. Počátky studia sanskrtu v čechách. *Listy filologické* 47: 185–194. [The Beginnings of Sanskrit studies among the Czechs.]

OLPT, Miroslac (ed.) 1967. *Asian and African Studies in Czechoslovakia.* Moscow.

Oriental studies in Czechoslovakia. *East Asian Cultural Studies* 3: 10–48. Tokyo 1964.

*POŘÍZKA, V. 1956. A glance at Indian studies in Czechoslovakia. *Journal of the Asiatic Society of Bombay* 30(2): 33–37.

POUCHA, Pavel 1951. L'indianisme et les études tchécoslovaques concernant la Haute Asie et l'Asie centrale. *Archiv Orientální* 19: 182–206.

PREINHALTEROVÁ, Hana 1998. Bengali studies in Prague. In: *Trends in Indian Studies. Proceedings of the ESIS*: 145–149. Prague.

RAGHAVAN, V. 1956. *Sanskrit and Allied Indian Studies in Europe.* Madras. [Czechoslovakia: 49–50.]

RYPKA, J. 1951. L'orientalisme en Tchéchoslovaque. *Archiv Orientální* 19: 15–26.

SEGERT, S. & K. BERÁNEK 1967. *Orientalistik an der Prager Universität*, I: *1348–1848*. Prag.

VACEK 1998. See under KOSTIĆ & DVOŘÁK 1998.

ZBAVITEL, Dušan 1959. *Die Orientalistik in der Tschechoslowakei.* Prag.

b. General directories (see also those of Austria)

Biographisches Lexikon zur Geschichte der böhmischen Länder. Hrsg. Heribert Sturm, I–. München 1979–. [Most recent volume IV.4, 2011, Stefánik–Sterc.]

Československý Biografický slovník. Prague 1992.

Slovenský biografický slovník (od roku 833 do roku 1990), I–VI. Matica Slovenská 1986–94.

9. Denmark

a. Indology and Oriental studies

HAMMERICH, L. L. 1976. Studies of Buddhism in Denmark. *SIAS Newsletters* 10: 2–10.

HOVDHAUGEN, Even, Fred KARLSSON, Carol HENRIKSEN & Bengt SIGURD 2000. *The History of Linguistics in the Nordic Countries*. Helsinki: Societas Scientiarum Fennica.

JENSEN, Jens Juhl 1992. Sammenlignende sprogvidenskab og almen lingvistik. In: Poul Johannes Jense & Leif Grane (eds.), *Københavns Universitet 1479–1979*, VIII: 353–384. Copenhagen.

LINDTNER, Christian 1984. Sanskrit studies in Denmark. In: V. V. Bedekar (ed.), *Proceedings and Papers of the Seminar on Sanskrit Outside India*: 33–38. Thane.

PARPOLA, Asko 1979. Sanskrit studies in Scandinavia. In. V. Raghavan (ed.), *"Vasudhaiva kuṭumbakam" International Sanskrit Conference. March 26th–31st, 1972*, I.2: *Sanskrit and Indology in Centres Outside India, Contributions of Haryana, Tamil Nadu*: 632–648. New Delhi.

PAULY, E. 1979. Sanskrit studies in Denmark. In: *Sanskrit Studies Outside India* (News Bulletin No. 2. Fourth World Sanskrit Conference, Weimar/G.D.R. May 23–30, 1979): 21–25. Weimar.

—— 1986. Indian influence in Danish literature. *World Culture. Proceedings of the Fourth World Sanskrit Conference ... Weimar May 23–30, 1979* (Schriften zur Geschichte und Kultur des alten Orients, 18): 248–252. Berlin.

—— 1992. Indisk filologi. In: Poul Johannes Jense & Leif Grane (eds.), *Københavns Universitet, 1479–1979*, VIII: 511–566. Copenhagen.

RAGHAVAN, V. 1956. *Sanskrit and Allied Indian Studies in Europe*. Madras. [Denmark: 30–31.]

b. General directories

Dansk biografisk Lexikon, tillige omfattende Norge for tidsrummet 1537–1814, I–XIX. Udgivet af C. F. Birka. Kjøbenhavn 1887–1905.

Dansk biografisk Leksikon. Grundlagt af C. F. Birka, redigeret af P. Engelstaft under medvirkning af Svend Dahl, 1–27. København 1933–1944.

Dansk biografisk Leksikon. Tredje udgave. Redaktør Sv. Cedergreen Bech, I–XVI. København 1979–84.

Kraks Blå Bog. København 1910ff.

Magister-Staten. København 1962, 1967.

Scandinavian Biographical Archive. Section A. Denmark, Iceland and Norway. Cards 1–369 A–Å: 370–383, Appendix. London 1989–.

***Estonia**, see under Baltic States*

10. Finland

a. Indology and Oriental studies

AALTO, Pentti 1951. Les études orientales en Finlande. *Archiv Orientální* 19: 79–84.

—— 1961. Suomalaiset itämaiden tutkijoina. In: *Oma maa*, X: 354–366. [The Finns in Oriental Research.]

—— 1971. *Oriental Studies in Finland 1928–1918.* (The History of Learning and Science in Finland 1828–1918, 10b.) Helsinki.

—— 1977. Zur Geschichte der Erforschung des finländischen Zigeunerdialekts. In *Zigeuerkundliche Forschungen*, I (Innsbrucker Beiträge zur Kulturwissenschaft, Sonderheft 42): 71–72.

HALÉN, Harry 1979. *Vieraiden maanosien tutkimuksen henkilökalenteri.* Helsinki. [Personal register of research on foreign continents.]

—— 1990. *Janua Orientis. Luettelo Aasian ja Afrikan kielten ja kulttuurien opettajista ja opetuksesta Turun Akatemiassa sekä Helsingin yliopistossa 1640–1990.* Helsinki, Aasian ja Afrikan kielten ja kulttuurien laitos.

HEIKEL, I. A. 1894. *Filologins studium vid Åbo Universitet.* (Åbo Universitets lärdomhistoria, 5; Skrifter utgifna af Svenska literatursällskapet i Finland, 26.) Helsingfors.

HOVDHAUGEN, Even, Fred KARLSSON, Carol HENRIKSEN & Bengt SIGURD 2000. *The History of Linguistics in the Nordic Countries.* Helsinki: Societas Scientiarum Fennica.

KARTTUNEN, Klaus 2002. South Asian studies in Finland. *Newsletter of the International Association of Sanskrit Studies* 7: 17–25.

—— 2003. *University of Helsinki, Institute for Asian and African Studies, Department of South Asian and Indoeuropean Studies. A Bibliography.*

Published on the occasion of the 12th World Sanskrit Conference, Helsinki, Finland, 14–18 July, 2003. Helsinki.

—— 2011. *Mooseksen kirjoista kungfutselaisuuden klassikoihin ja Jerusalemista Siperian tundralle. Aasian-tutkimuksen vaiheet Suomessa.* (Suomen Itämaisen Seuran suomenkielisiä julkaisuja, 38.) Helsinki. ['From Pentateuch to Confucian Classics and from Jerusalem to the Siberian Tundra. A History of Asian Studies in Finland', pp. 533–546 English summary.]

LÖYTÖNEN, Markku (ed.) 1988. *Màtka-arkku. Suomalaisia tutkimusmatkailijoita.* Helsinki.

PARPOLA, Asko 1979a. Sanskrit studies in Scandinavia. In: V. Raghavan (ed.), *"Vasudhaiva kuṭumbakam" International Sanskrit Conference. March 26th–31st, 1972,* I.2. *Sanskrit and Indology in Centres Outside India, Contributions of Haryana, Tamil Nadu*: 632–648. New Delhi.

—— 1979b. Sanskrit and Sanskrit-related studies in Finland. In: *Sanskrit Studies. Outside India* (News Bulletin No. 2. Fourth World Sanskrit Conference, Weimar/G.D.R. May 23–30, 1979): 26–33. Weimar.

—— 1998. South Asian studies with Indo-European studies. In: H. Halén (ed.), *Institute for Asian and African Studies, University of Helsinki. A Brief Presentation* (Studia Orientalia Supplementa, 1): 33–39. Helsinki.

STENIJ, E. 1925. Die orientalischen Studien in Finnland während des ersten Halbjahrhunderts der Universität zu Helsingfors 1828–1875. *Studia Orientalia* 1: 271–311.

b. General directories

AALTO, Pentti 1980. *Classical Studies in Finland 1928–1918.* (The History of Learning and Science in Finland 1828–1918, 20a.) Helsinki.

Biografinen nimikirja. Elämäkertoja Suomen entisistä ja nykyajoilta. Toim. Suomen historiallinen seura. Helsinki 1879–83.

CARPELAN, Tor 1903. *Finsk biografisk handbok*, I–II. Helsingfors.

CARPELAN, Tor & L. O. Th. TUDEER 1925. *Helsingin yliopisto. Opettajat ja virkamiehet vuodesta 1828*, I–II. Helsinki.

Helsingin yliopisto / Helsingfors Universitet. Opettajat ja virkamiehet / Lärare och tjänstemän 1939–1968. Porvoo 1977.

Kansallinen elämäkerrasto, I–V. Porvoo 1927–34.

Kansallisgalleria. Suuret suomalaiset, I–V. Espoo 1995–97.

RENVALL, Robert A. 1869. *Biografiska anteckningar öfver det Finlands universitets lärare, embets- och tjenstemän från dess flyttning till Helsingfors år 1828 till nuvarande tid.* Helsingfors.

—— 1891. *Finlands universitet 1828–1890. Biografiska uppgifter öfver dess lärare, embets- och tjenstemän.* 2nd revised edition. Helsingfors.

Scandinavian Biographical Archive. Section B. Sweden, Finland. Cards 1–387 A–Ö, 388–444 A–Rag. London 1989–.

Suomen kansallisbiografia, I–X. Helsinki 2003–07.

SOLA, Solmu & L. O. Th. TUDEER 1940. *Helsingin yliopisto. Opettajat ja virkamiehet vuodesta 1828.* Täydennys vuoden 1938 loppuun. Helsinki.

SUNDMAN, C.-E. 1968. *Åbo Akademis lärare och tjänstemän 1918–1968.* Åbo.

—— 1978. *Åbo Akademis lärare och tjänstemän 1968–1978.* Åbo.

11. France

a. Indology and Oriental studies

*BARENTON, H. de 1902. *La France catholique en Orient.* Paris.

BISSOONDAYAL, B. 1962. India as seen by French travellers. *The Indo-Asian Culture* 10(4): 434–443.

BLOCH, Jules 1951. L'indianisme en France depuis 1939. *Archiv Orientální* 19: 114–124.

BONGARD-LEVIN, Grigorij M. & Roland LARDINOIS & Aleksej A. VIGASIN 2002. *Correspondances orientalistes entre Paris et Saint-Pétersbourg (1887–1935).* (Mémoires de l'Académie des inscriptions et belles-lettres, 26). Paris.

BONNEROT, Olivier H. 1988. *La Perse dans la littérature et la pensée françaises au XVIIIe siècle. De l'image au mythe.* Paris.

Cent-cinquantenaire de l'École des langues orientales. Histoire, organisation et enseignement de l'École nationale des langues orientales vivantes. Paris 1948.

**Centenaire de l'École des langues orientales vivantes 1795–1895. Recueil de Mémoires.* Paris 1895.

Chercheurs d'Asie. Répertoire biographique des membres scientifiques de l'Ecole français d'Extrême-Orient 1898–2002. Paris 2002.

Cinquante ans d'orientalisme en France (1922–1972) (Journal Asiatique 261.). Paris 1973.

Cinquantenaire de l'École fraçaise d'Extrême-Orient. *Comptes rendus de l'Académie des Inscriptions et Belles-Lettres* 1952: 125–157.

DÉHÉRAIN, Henri 1938. *Silvestre de Sacy, ses contemporains et ses disciples.* Paris.

DUGAT, Gustave 1868–70. *Histoire des Orientalistes de l'Europe du XIIe au XIXe siècle*, 1–2. Paris.

É.F.E.O. 1906–76. *Comptes rendus de l'Académie des Inscriptions et Belles-Lettres* 1976: 323–343.

FILLIOZAT, Jean 1937. Une grammaire sanscrite du XVIIIe siècle et les débuts de l'indianisme en France. *JA* 229: 275–284.

—— 1957. France and Indology. *The Indo-Asian Culture* 5(3): 296–313.

—— 1964. Indian studies in France. In: *Indian Studies Abroad*: 6–17. London.

—— 1979. Les études indiennes en France. In: *Sanskrit Studies Outside India* (News Bulletin No. 2. Fourth World Sanskrit Conference, Weimar/G.D.R. May 23–30, 1979): 34–39. Weimar.

FILLIOZAT, Pierre-Sylvain 1984. The French Institute of Indology in Pondicherry (Its origin, spirit and programmes). *WZKS* 28: 133–147.

—— 1997. Sanskrit studies in France. In: *Sanskrit Studies Outside India. On the Occasion of 10th World Sanskrit Conference 1997*: 31–39. New Delhi.

FINOT, L. 1926. L'École française d'Extrême-Orient de 1921 à 1925. *Comptes rendus de l'Académie des Inscriptions et Belles-Lettres* 1926: 132–139.

LE CALLOC'H, Bernard 1988. La littérature orientaliste de langue française et Alexandre Csoma de Kőrös. Essai de bibliographie. *JA* 276: 189–200.

Le Collège de France (1530–1930). Livre jubilaire composé à l'occasion de son quatrième centenaire. Paris 1932.

MCGETCHIN, Douglas T. 2003. Wilting florists: The turbulent early decades of the Société Asiatique, 1822–1860. *Journal of the History of Ideas* 64(4): 565–580.

MOHL, Jules 1879–80. *Vingt-sept années d'histoire des études orientales, rapports faits à la Société asiatique de Paris de 1840 à 1867*, I–II. Paris.

*OL'DENBURG, S. F. 1894. Ocherki prepodavaniya vostochnyh jazykov vo Frantsii, Anglii i Germanii. *Zhurnal Ministerstva Narodnogo Prosveshcheniya* 293 (1894[6.2]): 255–275.

*—— 1898. Vostokovedeniya v novykh frantsuzskikh universitetakh. *Zhurnal Ministerstva Narodnogo Prosveshcheniya* 318 (1898[7.4]): 1–4.

*—— 1902. Francuskaja škola Krajnego Vostoka v Sajgone. *Žurnal Ministerstva Narodnago Prosveshcheniya* 340 (1902[3.4]): 47–51.

OLIVIER-UTARD, Françoise 1997. *Politique et archéologie. Histoire de la* Delegation archéologique française en Afghanistan (1922–1982). Paris.

POUILLON, François (éd.) 2008. *Dictionnaire des orientalistes de langue française*. 2nd edition. Paris.

RAGHAVAN, V. 1956. *Sanskrit and Allied Indian Studies in Europe*. Madras. [France: 19–25.]

SCHWAB, Raymond 1950. *La renaissance orientale*. Paris. [English translation: *The Oriental Renaissance. Europe's Rediscovery of India and the East 1680–1880*. New York 1984.]

*VAÏSSE, Léon 1844. Essai sur l'histoire de la philologie orientale en France. In: *Dictionnaire encyclopédique de l'histoire de France*. Paris. [Extrait, 15 p. in 16°.]

b. General directories

Archives biographiques françaises. Fusion dans un ordre alphabétique unique de 180 des plus importants ouvrages de référence biographiques français publiés du 17e au 20e siécle. Rédactrice: Susan Bradley. Cards 1–1048 A–Z, 1049–1073 Supplement. London 1988–90 (microfiche).

Catalogue générale de la librairie française, I–XXXIV. Paris 1867–1945. [1840–1925.]

CHARLE, Christophe 1986. *Les professeurs de la faculté des lettres de Paris*, I: *Dictionnaire biographique 1809–1908*. Paris.

—— 1987. *Les professeurs de la faculté des lettres de Paris*, II: *Dictionnaire biographique 1909–1939*. Paris.

CHARLE, Christophe & Eva TELKÈS 1988. *Les professeurs du Collège de France: Dictionnaire biographique 1901–1939*. Paris.

Dictionnaire de biographie française, I–. Paris 1933–. [Most recent volume XXI, Le Marois – Le Nain, 2011.]

La France protestante ou vies des protestants français qui se sont fait un nom dans l'histoire depuis les premiers temps de la reformation jusqu'à la reconnaissance du principe de la liberté des cultes par l'assemblée nationale, I–X [1846] (reprint: Genève 1966).

Grand dictionnaire universel du XIXe siècle, I–XVII. Paris 1866–77.

Who's Who in France. Paris 1953ff.

12. Germany

a. Indology and Oriental studies

Albert-Ludwigs-Universität Freiburg i. Br. Orientalisches Seminar – Indologie – Publikationen der Institutsmitglieder. Freiburg 1998.

ALSDORF, Ludwig 1960. Indologie in Berlin von 1821–1945. In: H. Leussink & E. Neumann & G. Kotowski (eds.), *Studium Berolinense. Aufsätze und Beiträge zu Problemen der Wissenschaft und der Geschichte der Friedrich-Wilhelms-Universität zu Berlin* (Gedenkschrift der Westdeutschen Rektorenkonferenz und der Freien Universität Berlin zur 150.

Wiederkehr des Gründungsjahres der Friedrich-Wilhelms-Universität zu Berlin, 2): 567–580. Berlin. [Also in *Kleine Schriften.*]

—— 1962. Indian studies in Germany. *The Indo-Asian Culture* 10(3): 296–314 & 10(4): 456–461.

—— 1964. Indian studies in Germany. In: *Indian Studies Abroad*: 18–35. London.

BABINGER, Franz 1957. Ein Jahrhundert morgenländischer Studien an der Münchener Universität. *ZDMG* 107: 241–269.

BEHRMANN, D. 1902. *Hamburgs Orientalisten.* Hamburg .

BENFEY, Theodor 1869. *Geschichte der Sprachwissenschaft und orientalischen Philologie in Deutschland seit dem Anfang des 19. Jahrhunderts mit einem Rückblick auf die früheren Zeiten.* (Geschichte der Wissenschaften in Deutschland, 8.) München.

BENSE, Gertrud 1958. Die vergleichende Sprachwissenschaft in Halle seit F. A. Pott. *Wissenschaftliche Zeitschrift der Martin-Luther-Universität Halle-Wittenberg* 7(4): 901–906.

BRENTJES, Burchard & Hans-Joachim PEUKE 1987. *Wissenschaftsbeziehungen zwischen Halle und Indien in Tradition und Gegenwart.* (Martin-Luther-Universität Halle-Wittenberg. Wissenschaftliche Beiträge, 1987/44 = I 42.) Halle (Saale).

BRÜCKNER, Heidrun, Klaus BUTZENBERGER, Angelika MALINAR & Gabriele ZELLER 2003. *Indien-Forschung im Zeitwandel. Analysen und Dokumente zur Indologie und Vergleichenden Religionswissenschaft in Tübingen.* Tübingen.

DAS, Rahul Peter 1997. The study of classical Indian medicine in Germany. *Journal of the European Āyurvedic Society* 5: 1–18.

Die Deutsche Morgenländische Gesellschaft. Seit 1845 der Erforschung der Sprachen und Kulturen des Orients, Asiens und Afrikas und dem Verstehen des Fremden verpflichtet. D.M.G. 1995.

GATZLAFF, M., B. JÄCKEL, A. KRAUSE, K. MYLIUS, C. H. SCHOLZ & G. SELTER 1975. Südasienwissenschaften der Karl-Marx-Universität – Tradition und Aufgaben. *Wissenschaftliche Zeitschrift der Karl-Marx-Universität Leipzig, Gesellschaft-Sprachwissenschaftliche Reihe* 24(2): 111–127 [Including M. Gatzlaff, Ausgewählte indologische Bibliographie (1960–1974): 213–217.]

GLASENAPP, Helmuth von 1957. The influence of Indian thought on German science, philosophy and literature. *JASB* 3rd series 23(2): 1–10.

—— 1960. *Das Indienbild deutscher Denker.* Stuttgart.

HAHN, Michael 1979. Sanskrit studies in the Federal Republic of Germany and West-Berlin. In: *Sanskrit Studies Outside India* (News Bulletin No. 2.

Fourth World Sanskrit Conference, Weimar/G.D.R. May 23–30, 1979): 40–49. Weimar.

HAUER, J. W. 1927. Zur Geschichte der Professur für vergleichende Sprachwissenschaft und Indologie und des Orientalischen Seminars. In: *Die Philipps-Universität zu Marburg 1527–1927. Fünf Kapitel aus ihrer Geschichte (1527–1866). Die Universität Marburg seit 1866 in Einzeldarstellungen*: 693–695. Marburg.

HERRING, Herbert 1994. Great German Dravidologists. *International Journal of Dravidian Linguistics* 23(2): 53–66.

HILLEBRANDT, Alfred 1911. Sanskrit und vergleichende Sprachforschung. In: *Universität Breslau. Festschrift zur Feier des hundertjährigen Bestehens*, 2): 369–374. Breslau.

HOFFMANN, Paul Th. 1915. *Der indische und der deutsche Geist von Herder bis zur Romantik*. Tübingen.

HOFMANN, Erich 1969. Philologie. In: Karl Jordan & Erich Hofmann (eds.), *Geschichte der Philosophischen Fakultät*, II (Geschichte der Christian-Albrechts-Universität Kiel 1665–1965, 5): 103–251. Neumünster. [5. Sanskrit und vergleichende Grammatik: 235–250.]

JACOBSOHN, Hermann 1927. Zur Geschichte des Lehrstuhls für Indogermanistik. In: *Die Philipps-Universität zu Marburg 1527–1927. Fünf Kapitel aus ihrer Geschichte (1527–1866). Die Universität Marburg seit 1866 in Einzeldarstellungen*: 692–693. Marburg.

JANERT, Klaus L. 1961. *Verzeichnis indienkundlicher Hochschulschriften. Deutschland–Österreich–Schweiz*. Wiesbaden.

JUNGINGER, Horst (ed.) 2008. *The Study of Religion under the Impact of Fascism.* (Numen Book Series, 117.) Leiden.

KAHLE, Paul 1933. Das orientalische Seminar. *Geschichte der Rheinischen Friedrich-Wilhelm-Universität zu Bonn am Rhein*, II: *Institute und Seminare, 1818–1933*: 173–185. Bonn am Rhein. [Including: W. Kirfel, Die indische Philologie im besonderen: 177–185.]

KIRFEL, Willibald 1933. See under Kahle 1933.

LEHMANN, Arno 1968. German Tamil studies. *Wissenschaftliche Zeitschrift der Martin-Luther-Universität Halle-Wittenberg, Gesellschaft-Sprachwissenschaftliche Reihe* 17(6): 139–145.

LEIFER, Walter 1957. Buddhism in Germany. *The Indo-Asian Culture* 5(3): 329–339.

*—— 1971. *India and the Germans*. Bombay.

MCGETCHIN, Douglas T., Peter K. J. PARK & Damodar Sar DESAI (eds.) 2004. *Sanskrit and 'Orientalism'. Indology and Comparative Linguistics in Germany, 1750–1958*. New Delhi.

MANICKAVASAGOM, M. E. 1998. Review of Mohanavelu 1998. *International Journal of Dravidian Linguistics* 27(1): 133–138.

MEHLIG, Johannes 1958. Die Pflege und Tradition der Indologie in Halle. *Wissenschaftliche Zeitschrift der Martin-Luther-Universität Halle-Wittenberg, Gesellschaft-Sprachwissenschaftliche Reihe* 7(4): 891–899.

MODE, Heinz, Hans-Joachim PEUKE & Burchard THALER (eds.) 1966. *Bibliography of Literature on Buddhist Topics Published on the Territory of the G.D.R. Since 1945.* (Supplement to *Buddhist Yearly* 1966.) Halle.

MOHANAVELU, C. S. 1993. *German Tamilology. German Contributions to Tamil Language, Literature and Culture During the period 1706–1945.* Chennai. [Originally diss. Madras.]

MORGENROTH, W. 1976. 150 Jahre Sanskritstudien in Berlin – humanistische Traditionen und Aufgaben der Indologie an der Humboldt-Universität. *Wissenschaftliche Zeitschrift der Humboldt-Universität zu Berlin, Gesellschaft-Sprachwissenschaftliche Reihe* 25: 281–291.

—— 1979. Sanskrit studies in the German Democratic Republic. In: *Sanskrit Studies Outside India* (News Bulletin No. 2. Fourth World Sanskrit Conference, Weimar/G.D.R. May 23–30, 1979): 50–60. Weimar.

MYLIUS, Klaus 1979. Bedeutende Traditionen der Indologie an der Universität Leipzig. *Wissenschaftliche Zeitschrift der Karl-Marx-Universität Leipzig, Gesellschaft-Sprachwissenschaftliche Reihe* 28(1): 47–66.

—— 1995. Die Geschichte der Sanskrit-Philologie an der Universität Leipzig von den Anfängen bis zur Emeritierung von Friedrich Weller 1958. *BDCRI* 54–55 (1994–95): 133–143.

*OL'DENBURG, S. F. 1894. Ocherki prepodavaniya vostochnykh jazykov vo Frantsii, Anglii i Germanii. *Zhurnal Ministerstva Narodnogo Prosveshcheniya* 293 (1894[6.2]): 255–275.

PAREL, A. 1976. Friedrich Schlegel and the beginning of Sanskrit studies in Germany. *Journal of Indian History* 54: 547–565.

PREISSLER, Holger 1995. Die Anfänge der Deutschen Morgenländischen Gesellschaft. Erweiterter Sonderdruck aus der *ZDMG* 145(2).

RABAULT-FEUERHAM, Pascale 2008. *L'archive des origines. Sanskrit, philologie, anthropologie dans l'Allemagne du XIXe siècle.* Paris.

RAGHAVAN, V. 1956. *Sanskrit and Allied Indian Studies in Europe.* Madras. [Germany: 37–45.]

RAU, Wilhelm 1964. *Bilder hundert deutscher Indologen.* (VOHD, Suppl.-Band, 4.) Wiesbaden.

—— 1982. *Bilder 135 deutscher Indologen.* 2. erweiterte und verbesserte Auflage. (Glasenapp-Stiftung, 23.) Wiesbaden.

*REMY, Arthur F. J. 1901. *The Influence of India and Persia on the Poetry of Germany.* (Columbia University Germanic Studies, 1.4.) New York. [Diss.]

RICHTER, E. et al. 1985. Asienwissenschaftliche Forschung und Lehre in Leipzig. *Wissenschaftliche Zeitschrift der Karl-Marx-Universität Leipzig, Gesellschaft-Sprachwissenschaftliche Reihe* 34: 549–567.

RUBEN, Walter 1962. Indological studies in the German Democratic Republic. *The Visvabharati Quarterly* 27(3–4), 1961–62: 197–211.

Sanskrit Studies in the G.D.R. Traditions, Results, Tasks, I–II. Berlin: Humboldt University, Institute of Asian Sciences 1978–79.

SARANGI, A. C. 1984. The Indo-German intellectual relationship. German scholars on Sanskrit studies. In: V. V. Bedekar (ed.), *Proceedings and Papers of the Seminar on Sanskrit Outside India*: 17–21. Thane.

SCHLINGLOFF, D. 1981. *German Indology. A List of Institutions and Persons Concerned with Sanskrit and Allied Studies.* Munich. [Cf. Stache-Weiske 1988.]

—— 1996. *German Indology. A List of Institutions and Persons Concerned with Sanskrit and Allied Studies.* Munich.

—— 2007. *German Indology. A List of Institutions and Persons Concerned with Sanskrit and Allied Studies.* Leipzig.

SCHÖNE, Maria 1975. Die Tradition der Indologie an Alma mater Jenensis. *Wissenschaftliche Zeitschrift der Humboldt-Universität zu Berlin, Gesellschaft-Sprachwissenschaftliche Reihe* 25(3): 309–310.

*SCHUMANN, Hans Wolfgang 1972. *Buddhism and Buddhist Studies in Germany.* Bonn.

—— 1974. *Buddhismus und Buddhismusforschung in Deutschland.* Wien. [Enlarged German edition of Schumann 1972.]

SCHÜTTE, Hans-Wilm 2004. *Die Asienwissenschaft in Deutschland. Geschichte, Stand und Perspektiven.* (Mitteilungen des Instituts für Asienkunde Hamburg, 380.) Hamburg.

SCHWYZER, Eduard 1933. Das sprachwissenschaftliche Seminar. In: *Geschichte der Rheinischen Friedrich-Wilhelm-Universität zu Bonn am Rhein*, II: *Institute und Seminare. 1818–1933*: 150–173. Bonn am Rhein.

SEDLAR, Jean W. 1982. *India in the Mind of Germany. Schelling, Schopenhauer and Their Times.* Washington DC.

*SOMMERFELD, S. 1943. *Indienschau und Indiendeutung romantischer Philosophen.* Zürich.

STACHE-ROSEN, Valentina 1990. *German Indologists.* Second revised edition by Agnes Stache-Weiske. New Delhi. [1st edition: Delhi 1981.]

STACHE-WEISKE, Agnes 1988. *German Indology. A List of Institutions and Persons Concerned with Sanskrit and Allied Studies.* Munich. [Cf. Schlingloff 1981.]

TAUBE, Manfred 1979. Tibetologie und Mongolistik an der Leipziger Universität. *Wissenschaftliche Zeitschrift der Karl-Marx-Universität Leipzig, Gesellschaft-Sprachwissenschaftliche Reihe* 28(1): 33–46.

Universität Hamburg. Institut für Kultur und Geschichte Indiens und Tibets. Publikationen der Institutsmitglieder und Publikationsreihen. Hamburg 1990.

—— id. liber. Hamburg 1995.

Universität München. Institut für Indologie und Iranistik. Publikationen der Institutsmitglieder. München 1987.

*VÄTH, Alfons 1920. *Die deutschen Jesuiten in Indien. Geschichte der Mission von Bombay–Puna (1854–1920).* Regensburg.

*WENDT, Heinrich 1916. *Schlesien und der Orient. Ein geschichtlicher Rückblick.* (Darstellungen und Quellen zur schlesichen Geschichte, 21.) Breslau.

WILHELM, Friedrich 1961. The German response to Indian culture. *JAOS* 81: 395–405.

*WILSON, A. Leslie 1964. *A Mythical Image. The Ideal of India in German Romanticism.* Durham, N.C.

WINDISCH, E. 1917–20. *Geschichte der Sanskrit-Philologie und indischen Altertumskunde,* I–II. (Grundriss der Indo-Arischen Philologie und Altertumskunde I.I.B.) Strassburg 1917; Berlin 1920.

WÖLFFLING, S. 1974. Zur Geschichte der deutschen archäologischen Erforschung Persiens. *Wissenschaftliche Zeitschrift der Martin-Luther-Universität zu Halle-Wittenberg, Gesellschaft-Sprachwissenschaftliche Reihe* 23(4): 63–71.

Zweihundertfünfzig Jahre Halle – Indien anlässlich des fünfundzwanzigsten Jahrestages der Unabhängigkeit Indiens. / 250 Years Halle – India. 25 Years of Indian Independence. Supplement to *Buddhist Yearly* 1972.

b. General directories

Allgemeine Deutsche Biographie, I–LV. Leipzig 1875–1910. [Main part, I–XLV (1875–1900); Addenda XLVI–LIV; LV; now also online version.]

ASEN, Johannes 1955. *Gesamtverzeichniss der Lehrkörpers der Universität Berlin,* I: *1810–1945.* Leipzig.

BADER, Karl 1925. *Lexikon deutscher Bibliothekare.* (Zentralblatt für Bibliothekswesen, Beiheft 55.) Leipzig.

Biographisches Jahrbuch und Deutscher Nekrolog, I–XVIII. Berlin 1897–1917.

Das Grosse Brockhaus.

Deutsche Biographische Enzyklopädie (DBE), I–XIII. München 1995–2003.

Deutsche Biographische Enzyklopädie (DBE). 2. Ausgabe, I–XII. München 2005–08.

Deutscher Biographischer Index, I–IV. Hrsg. W. Gorzny. München 1986.

Deutscher Biographischer Index / German Biographical Index, I–VIII Ed. by Axel Frey. München 1998.

Deutscher Gelehrtenkalender, I–. Berlin 1925–. ["Kürschner".]

Deutscher Literaturkalender. I–. Berlin 1879–. ["Kürschner".]

Deutsches Biographisches Archiv. Eine Kumulation aus 254 der wichtigsten biographischen Nachschlagewerke für den deutschen bis zum Ausgang des neunzehnten Jahrhunderts. Microfiche-Edition. Herausgegeben von Bernhard Fabian. Bearbeitet unter der Leitung von Willi Gorzny. Cards 1–1421 A–Z, 1422–1431 Nachtrag. London 1982.

—— Neue Folge bis zur Mitte des 20. Jahrhunderts. Cards 1–1457 A–Z. München 1989–98.

Deutsches biographisches Jahrbuch, I–XI. Stuttgart 1925–32.

Deutsches Geschlechterbuch, I–. Limburg 1889–. [In early volumes entitled *Genealogisches handbuch bürgerlichen Familien*; most recent Band 221, 2012.]

DRÜLL, Dagmar 1986. *Heidelberger Gelehrtenlexikon 1803–1932*. Heidelberg.

—— 1991. *Heidelberger Gelehrtenlexikon 1652–1802*. Heidelberg.

EBEL, Wilhelm 1962. *Catalogus Professorum Gottingensium 1734–1962*. Göttingen.

GUNDLACH, Franz 1927. *Catalogus Professorum Academiae Marburgensis 1527–1910* (Veröffentlichungen der Historischen Kommission für Hessen und Waldeck, 15.) Marburg.

HAMBURGER, Ge. Chr. vide MEUSEL 1796–1806.

HARTKOPF, Werner 1983. *Die Akademie der Wissenschaften der DDR. Ein Beitrag zu ihrer Gescichte. Biographischer Index*. Berlin. [Brief articles on members of the Academy from its foundation in the early 18th century.]

HENNICKE, K. A. 1811–1813. *Beiträge zur Ergänzung und Berichtigung des Jöcher'schen Allgemeinen Gelehrten-Lexikon's und des Meusel'schen Lexikon's der vom Jahr 1750 bis 1800 verstorbenen teutschen Schriftstellern*, I–III. Leipzig (reprint: Hildesheim 1969).

*LEHNERT, G. & H. HAUPT 1907. Dozentenverzeichniss der Universität Giessen 1607–1907. In: *Der Universität Giessen*, I: 411–467.

MEUSEL, Johann Georg 1796–1806. *Das gelehrte Teutschland oder Lexikon der jetzt lebenden teutschen Schriftsteller*. Angefangen von Ge. Chr.

Hamburger,' fortgesetzt von Joh. Georg. Meusel. 5. vermehrte Ausgabe, I–XII. Lemgo.

—— 1808–1834. A number of supplements to the same. Parts XIII–XXVI. Lemgo.

—— 1802–1816. *Lexikon der vom Jahr 1750 bis 1800 verstorbenen teutschen Schriftstellern*, I–X. Leipzig.

MORTZFELD, P. 1986–2008. *Die Porträtsammlung der Herzog August Bibliothek Wolfenbüttel 1500–1850.* Reihe A. [Abbildungen] 1–28, B. [Text] 1–9, Supplement 1–3. München.

Neue Deutsche Biographie. I–. Berlin 1953–. [Most recent Band XXV, Stadion–Tecklenborg, 2013; also online version.]

*THIESS, Johann Otto 1800–03. *Biographische und bibliographische Nachrichten von allen bisherigen Lehrern der Theologie in Kiel*, I–II. Kiel.

13. Greece

b. General directories

Megas Ellenike Enkyklopaideia, I–XXIV. Athenai 1926–34.

Mega Ellenikon biografikon lexicon, I–V. Athenai [1958]–1962.

14. Hungary

a. Indology and Oriental studies

ARADI, E. 1995. The Rāmāyaṇa in Hungary. In: G. Pollet (ed.), *Indian Epic Values. Rāmāyaṇa and Its Impact* (Orientalia Lovaniensia Analecta, 66): 95–100. Leuven.

BETHLENFALVY, Géza 1980. *India in Hungarian Learning and Literature. With a Bibliography of Translations by Gyula Wojtilla*. New Delhi.

HÁRMATTA, J. 1979. Sanskrit studies in Hungary. In: *Sanskrit Studies Outside India* (News Bulletin No. 2. Fourth World Sanskrit Conference, Weimar/G.D.R. May 23–30, 1979): 78–84. Weimar.

KARSAI, György 1998. Indian studies in Hungary. In: *Trends in Indian Studies. Proceedings of the ESIS*: 109–115. Prague.

PUSKÁS, I. 1995. Indian studies and the Rāmāyaṇa in Hungary. In: G. Pollet (ed.), *Indian Epic Values. Rāmāyaṇa and Its Impact* (Orientalia Lovaniensia Analecta, 66): 137–153. Leuven.

—— 1991. *India bibliográfia / India Bibliography*. Budapest.

RAGHAVAN, V. 1956. *Sanskrit and Allied Indian Studies in Europe*. Madras. [Hungary: 51.]

SIPOS, Stephen 1964. Indian studies in Hungary: In: *Indian Studies Abroad*: 36–40. London.

TERJÉK, J. 1972. Lamaist studies in Hungary. *Acta Orientalia (Academiae Scientiarum Hungaricae)* 26: 384–387.

WOJTILLA, Gy. 1977. Sanskrit literature in Hungary. In: *Studies in Indo-Asian Art and Culture*, V (Śata-Piṭaka Series, 238): 177–182.

b. General directories

Das geistige Ungarn. Biographisches Lexikon, I–II. Hrsg. von Oskar von Krücken & Imre Parlagi. Wien [1918?].

Magyar életrajzi lexikon, I–III. Főszerkesztő Keneyres Ágnes. Budapest 1967–81.

SZINNYEI, József (írta) 1891–1914. *Magyar írók. Élete és munkái*, I–XIV. Budapest (reprint: Budapest 1980–91).

14. Iceland

b. General directories

Merkir íslendingar. Ævisögur og minningargreinar, I–VI. Reykjavík 1947–57.

Merkir íslendingar. Nýr flokkur, I–VI. Reykjavík 1962–67.

Scandinavian Biographical Archive. Section A. Denmark, Iceland and Norway. Cards 1–369 A–Å, 370–383 Appendix. London 1989–.

16. Ireland

a. Indology and Oriental studies

LENNON, Joseph 2004. *Irish Orientalism. A Literary and Intelectual History*. Syracuse.

MANSOOR, M. 1944. *The Story of Irish Orientalism*. Dublin. [Earlier version in **Hermathema* 62 (1943).]

RAGHAVAN, V. 1956. *Sanskrit and Allied Indian Studies in Europe*. Madras. [Eire: 13–15.]

b. General directories

BOYLAN, H. 1988. *A Dictionary of Irish Biography*. 2nd edition. Dublin.

CRONE, John S. 1928. *A Concise Dictionary of Irish Biography*. London.

17. Italy

a. Indology and Oriental studies

BAUSANI, A. 1951. Les études d'iranistique et turcologie en Italie, depuis 1941. *Archiv Orientální* 19: 85–93.

BOTTO, Oscar 1985. Appunti per una storia degli studi buddhisti in Italia. In: *Orientalia Iosephi Tucci memoriae dicata* (Serie Orientale Roma, 56.1): 175–189. Rome.

—— 1997. Sanskrit studies in Italy. In:, *Sanskrit Studies Outside India. On the Occasion of 10th World Sanskrit Conference 1997*: 57–79. New Delhi.

CIMINO, R. M. & F. SCIALPI 1974. *India and Italy*. Rome.

**Contributo italiano alla conoscenza dell'Oriente. Repertorio bibliografico dal 1935 al 1958*. Firenze 1962. [South and Central Asian section by Paolo Daffinà.]

*DE GUBERNATIS, Angelo 1867. *Memoria intorno ai viaggiatori Italiani nelle Indie orientali*. Florence.

—— 1876. *Matériaux pour servir à l'histoire des études orientales en Italie*. Paris.

*—— 1891. Gli studi indiani in Itàlia. *Giornale della Societa Asiatica Italiana* 5: 102–126.

FRANCI, Giorgio Renato (ed.) 1985. *Contributi alla storia dell'Orientalismo*. (Studi e testi orientali, 1.) Bologna.

—— 1991. *La benedizione di Babele. Contributi alla storia degli studi orientali e linguistici, e delle presenze orientali, a Bologna*. (Studi e testi orientali, 3.) Bologna.

GABRIELI, Giuseppe 1935. *Bibliografia degli studi orientalistici in Italia dal 1912 al 1934*. Roma.

Gli studi orientali in Italia durante in cinquantenario 1861–1911 (Bibliografia). (Rivista degli Studi Orientali, 5.) Rome 1913–27. [Indian section by A. Ballini.]

Le Marche e l'Oriente. Una tradizione ininterrotta da Matteo Ricci a Giuseppe Tucci. Atti del Convegno Internazionale Macerata, 23–26 ottobre 1996. A cura di Francesco D'Arelli. Roma 1998.

MARAZZI, U. (ed.) 1984. *La conoscenza dell Asia e dell'Africa in Italia nei secoli XVIII e XIX*, I.1–2. Napoli.

—— 1985. *La conoscenza dell Asia e dell'Africa in Italia nei secoli XVIII e XIX*, II.1–2. Napoli.

—— 1989. *La conoscenza dell Asia e dell'Africa in Italia nei secoli XVIII e XIX*, III.1–2. Napoli.

*N[EUBAUER]. A. 1888. Oriental studies in Italy. *Academy* 1.12.1888: 357–358.

NICOLINI, Nicola 1942. *L'Istituto Orientale di Napoli. Origini e statuti. Studi e documenti*, I. Rome.

PENSA, Corrado 1964. Indian studies in Italy. In: *Indian Studies Abroad*: 41–48. London.

PORRU, G. 1940. *Studi d'indianistica in Italia del 1911 al 1938*. Firenze. [Bibliography.]

*PREDARI, F. 1842. *Origine e progresso dello studio delle lingue orientali in Italia*. Milano.

RAGHAVAN, V. 1956. *Sanskrit and Allied Indian Studies in Europe*. Madras. [Italy: 55–59.]

SORRENTINO, Antonio 1982. Dravidian studies in Italy. *Annali, Instituto Orientale di Napoli* 42: 617–622.

SORRENTINO, Antonio & Maurizio TADDEI (eds.) 1990. *Napoli e l'India. Atti del Convegno Napoli-Ercolani, 2–3 giugno 1988*. (I.U.O. Dipartimento di studi asiatici, Series Minor, 34.) Napoli.

*TUCCI, Giuseppe 192?. Italian Indology. *Modern Review* 39: 158–161.

—— 1949. *Italia e Oriente*. Milano. [New edition: Roma 2005.]

VALLAURI, Mario 1952. Jain studies in Italy. *East & West* 3: 108–111.

b. General directories

Archivio biografico italiano. Cards 1–1018 A–Z (microfiche). München 1987–91 (online version 2004).

Archivio biografico italiano. Nuova serie. München 1994–97 (& third series, 1998ff.).

Dizionario biografico degli Italiani, I–. Roma 1960–. [Most recent volume LXXX, Ottone–Pansa, 2014.]

Enciclopedia Italiana, I–XXXVI. Milano 1929–38.

*TIPALDO, Emilio de (ed.) 1834–45. *Biografia degli Italiani illustri nelle scienze, lettere ed arte del secolo XVIII, e de'contemporanei*, I–X. Venezia.

***Latvia**, see under Baltic States*

***Lithuania**, see under Baltic States*

18. Luxembourg

b. General directories

Biografisch Archief van de Benelux. München. Cards 1–756. München 1992. [Microfiche, now also online, complete.]

Biographie nationale du pays de Luxembourg depuis ses origines jusqu'à nos jours, I–XXII. Ed. par J. Mersch. Luxembourg 1947–75.

***Mexico**, see under South and Central America*

19. Netherlands

a. Indology and Oriental studies

ARENDONK, C. van 1916. Oriental Literature. In: *Science in the Netherlands*: 121 (?).

BLOM, M. L. B. 1981. *Catalogus van de boeken gepubliceerd door de Utrechtse Indologen*. Leiden.

'Een bescheiden onderkomen'. Historisch overzicht van de studie van de Oostersche talen en kulturen aan de Rijksuniversiteit te Utrecht. Utrecht 1981.

DREWES, G. W. J. 1957. Oriental studies in the Netherlands. An historical survey. *Bulletin Higher Education and Research in the Netherlands* 1(4): 1–19.

GONDA, Jan 1964. *Indology in the Netherlands*. Leiden. [Reprint from *Books on the Orient*.]

—— 1979. Sanskrit studies in Netherlands. *Sanskrit Studies Outside India* (News Bulletin No. 2. Fourth World Sanskrit Conference, Weimar/ G.D.R. May 23–30, 1979): 117–121. Weimar.

DE JONG, Jan Willem 1957. Sanskrit studies in the Netherlands. *The Indo-Asian Culture* 5(4): 421–427.

—— 1964. Sanskrit studies in the Netherlands. In: *Indian Studies Abroad*: 60–64. London.

MUYZENBERG, Hanneke van den & Thomas DE BRUIJN (ed.) 1991. *Waarom Sanskrit? Honderdvijfentwintig jaar Sanskrit in Nederland.* (Kern Institute Miscellanea, 4.) Leiden.

NAT, J. 1929. *De Studie van de oostersche talen in Nederland in de 18. en de 19. eeuw*. Purmerend. [Cf. F. Babinger, *Orientalische Literaturzeitung* 35 [1932]: 537–539.]

ONDAATJE, Mat. P. J. 1865. A tabular list of original works and translations published by the late Dutch Government of Ceylon at their Printing Press at Colombo. *JRAS* N.S. 1: 141–144.

Quatre esquisses détachées aux études orientalistes à Leiden. Leiden 1932 [Including: Arendonk & van Ronkel: Legatum Warnerianum; Vogel: Kern Institute; Duyvendak: Dutch relations with China.]

RAGHAVAN, V. 1956. *Sanskrit and Allied Indian Studies in Europe*. Madras. [Holland: 26–29.]

SCHARPÉ, A. A. M. 1966. *Tentoonstelling. Sanskritkunde in de Nederlanden en in Europa in historisch perspectief.* (Werken uitgegeven door het Rectoraat van de Rijksuniversiteit te Gent, 21.) Leuven.

VOGEL, J. Ph. 1951. The contribution of the University of Leiden to Oriental research. *Indian Art and Letters* 23(2) (1949): 45–59 & separately. Leiden.

*WILLMET, J. 1820. Schets van den staat der Oostersche Litteratuur in Holland, in de achttiende eeuw. *Gedenkschriften in de Hedendaagsche Talen van de Derde Klasse van het Koninklijk Nederlandsche Instituut van Wetenschappen. Letterkunde en Schoone Kunsten*, 2: 139–238. Amsterdam.

b. General directories

VAN DER AA, A. J. 1852–78. *Biographisch Woordenboek der Nederlanden*, I–XXI. Haarlem (reprint: 1969).

Biografisch Archief van de Benelux. München. Cards 1–756. München 1992 (microfiche, now also online, complete).

Biografisch Woordenboek van Nederland. Red. J. Charité, I–. 's-Gravenhage 1979–. [Most recent volume VI, 2008.]

Nieuw Nederlandsch Biografisch Woordenboek, I–IX. Leiden 1911–33.

Wie is dat? The Hague 1931–.

20. Norway

a. Indology and Oriental studies

HOVDHAUGEN, Even, Fred KARLSSON, Carol HENRIKSEN & Bengt SIGURD 2000. *The History of Linguistics in the Nordic Countries*. Helsinki: Societas Scientiarum Fennica.

PARPOLA, Asko 1979. Sanskrit studies in Scandinavia. In: V. Raghavan (ed.), *"Vasudhaiva kuṭumbakam" International Sanskrit Conference. March 26th – 31st, 1972*, I.2. *Sanskrit and Indology in Centres Outside India, Contributions of Haryana, Tamil Nadu*: 632–648. New Delhi.

RAGHAVAN, V. 1956. *Sanskrit and Allied Indian Studies in Europe*. Madras. [Norway: 32–33.]

b. General directories

Aschehougs Konversasjons Leksikon, I–VI. Oslo 1907–13 (and several new editions).

Norsk biografisk Leksikon, I–XIX. Kristiania/Oslo 1923–83.

Scandinavian Biographical Archive. Section A. Denmark, Iceland and Norway. Cards 1–369 A–Å, 370–383 Appendix. London 1989–.

***Peru**, see under South and Central America*

21. Poland

a. Indology and Oriental studies

Bibliografia polskich prac orientalistycznych (1945–1955). (Polska Akademia Nauk, Komitet Nauk Orientalistycznych.) Warszawa 1957.

KUSIO, Joanna 1999. Dravidian studies in Poland. In: *'On the Understandig of Other Cultures' – Materials of the International Conference on Sanskrit and Related Studies to Commemorate the Centenary of the Birth of Stanisław Schayer (1899–1941), Warsaw University, Poland 1999*: 49–52. Warsaw.

MEJOR, Marek 1997. A note on Buddhist studies in Poland. *Studia Indologiczne* 4: 125–133.

MILEVSKA, Iwona 1995a. Sanskrit studies in Poland (with special reference to scientific research on the Rāmāyaṇa). In: G. Pollet (ed.), *Indian Epic Values. Rāmāyaṇa and Its Impact* (Orientalia Lovaniensia Analecta, 66): 127–131. Leuven.

—— 1995b. Sanskrit studies in Kraków. In: *International Conference on Sanskrit and Related Studies. September 23–26.1993 (Proceedings)* (Cracow Indological Studies, 1): 5–11. Cracow.

PIEKARSKI, Przemysław 1998. Polish Indology – the present and the future. In: *Trends in Indian Studies. Proceedings of the ESIS*: 141–143. Prague.

POBOŻNIAK, T. 1979. Sanskrit studies in Poland. In: *Sanskrit Studies Outside India* (News Bulletin No. 2. Fourth World Sanskrit Conference, Weimar/G.D.R. May 23–30, 1979): 123–130. Weimar.

*—— 1983. Indian studies in Poland. In: *Oriental Studies in the Sixty Years of Independent Poland.* Warszawa.

—— 1984. History of Indian studies in Poland. In: V. V. Bedekar (ed.), *Proceedings and Papers of the Seminar on Sanskrit Outside India*: 39–41. Thane.

*REYCHMAN, Jan 1949. Tłumacze języków wschodnich w Polsce XVIII w. *Przegląd Orientalistyczny* 1: 83–90.

—— 1950a. *Znajomość i nauczanie językow orientalnych w Polsce XVIII w.* (Prace wrocławskiego towarzystwa naukowego, Seria A, 35.) Wrocław.

*—— 1950b. Tradycje ślaskiej orientalistyki. *Przegląd Orientalistyczny* 2: 71–86.

—— (ed.) 1966. *Szkice z dziejów polskiej orientalistyki*, II: *Zakład orientalistyki Polskiej Akademii nauk*. Warszawa. [Cf. Glaesser, *East & West* 16 (1966(: 164–166.]

*RUTKOWSKA, Tatiana 1976. Powojenna indologia polska – 1945–1975. *Przegląd Orientalistyczny* 100(4).

Selected bibliography of Polish Indologists connected with Sanskrit studies in Kraków. In: *International Conference on Sanskrit and Related Studies. September 23–26.1993 (Proceedings)* (Cracow Indological Studies, 1): 301–306. Cracow.

SŁUSZKIEWICZ, Eugeniusz 1959. Indic studies in Poland. *The Indo-Asian Culture* 7(4): 412–422.

—— 1961-62. India as seen by Polish travellers upto the 19th century. *The Indo-Asian Culture* 9(4): 385–403 & 10(3): 336–339.

—— 1964. Indian studies in Poland. In: *Indian Studies Abroad*: 65–72. London.

STASIK, Danuta 1999. Hindi studies at the Oriental Institute of the University of Warsaw. In: *'On the Understandig of Other Cultures' – Materials of the International Conference on Sanskrit and related Studies to Commemorate the Centenary of the Birth of Stanisław Schayer (1899–1941), Warsaw University, Poland 1999*: 53–57. Warsaw.

STRELCYN, Stefan (ed.) 1957. *Szkice z dziejów polskiej orientalistyki*, I. Warszawa.

SUDYKA, Lidia 1995. Translations and Adaptations of Rāmāyaṇa in Poland. In: G. Pollet (ed.), *Indian Epic Values. Rāmāyaṇa and Its Impact* (Orientalia Lovaniensia Analecta, 66): 89–93. Leuven.

*WAŁKÓWSKA, H. 1983. Oriental studies in Wrocław. In: *Oriental Studies in the Sixty Years of Independent Poland*. Warszawa.

WALTER, Elżbieta 1999. Bengali studies in Warsaw. In: *'On the Understandig of Other Cultures' – Materials of the International Conference on Sanskrit and related Studies to Commemorate the Centenary of the Birth of Stanisław Schayer (1899–1941), Warsaw University, Poland 1999*: 42–48. Warsaw.

WÜTHRICH-SARNOWSKA, Maria Mariola 1996. Polish translations of the Bhagavadgītā. *Asiatische Studien/Études Asiatiques* 50: 673–679.

b. General directories

Polski Słownik Biograficzny, I–. Kraków (since 1950s Wrocław – Warszawa – Kraków) 1935–. [Most recent volume XLIX, 2013–14, up to Szyjewski.]

***Portugal**, see under Spain and Portugal*

22. Romania

a. Indology and Oriental studies

AL-GEORGE, Sergiu 1986. La résonnance de la pensée indienne dans la culture roumaine. In: W. Morgenroth (ed.), *Sanskrit and World Culture. Proceedings of the Fourth World Sanskrit Conference of the International Association of Sanskrit Studies, Weimar May 23–30, 1979* (Schriften zur Geschichte und Kultur des alten Orients, 18): 225–229. Berlin.

BANATEANU, Vlad 1959. First Indianists of the XIX century Rumania. *The Indo-Asian Culture* 7(3): 275–282.

—— 1962. Indian studies in Rumania in the past and in the present. *The Visvabharati Quarterly* 27(3–4), 1961–62: 239–259.

—— 1964. First Indianists of the XIX century Rumania. In: *Indian Studies Abroad*: 90–94. London.

CIURTIN, Eugen 2003. *Histoire de l'image et de la mémoire de l'Asie dans la culture roumaine du 17e siècle à 1940*. PhD dissertation.

HITCHINS, Keith 1965. Reflections of India in Rumanian popular literature, XVI to XVIII centuries. *The Indo-Asian Culture* 14: 106–126.

POGHIRC, Cicerone 1972. Sanskrit studies in Romania. *Cultural Forum* (India) 15(1): 48–54. [Cf. *Studiile sanscrite în România. *Analele Universităţii Bucureşti, Limbi clasice şi orientale* 21 (1972): 109–119; one of these is in his *collected articles: 493–503.]

ROSU, Arion 1960. India in Rumanian culture. *The Indo-Asian Culture* 8(3): 276–291.

VIANU, Tudor 1957. Indian echoes in Rumanian literature. *The Indo-Asian Culture* 6(2): 180–190.

b. General directories

Dictionar enciclopedic romin, I–. Bucureşti 1962ff.

Dicţionarul literaturii Române de la origini pînà la 1900. Bucureşti 1979.

IONESCU, Şerban N. 1994. *Who Was Who in Twentieth-Century Romania*. New York.

23. Russia

a. Indology and Oriental studies

ALAEV, L. B. 1963. Izuchenie istorii Indii v SSSR v 1917–1934 godakh. *Narody Azii i Afriki* 1963(2): 160–172.

BARTHOLD, W. 1913. *Die geographische und historische Erforschung des Orients mit besonderer Berücksichtigung der russischen Arbeiten.* Übers. von E. Ramberg-Figulla. (Quellen und Forschungen zur Erd- und Kartenkunde 8.) Leipzig. [Translation of the first edition of Bartol'd 1925.]

—— 1947. *La découverte de l'Asie. Histoire de l'orientalisme en Europe et Russie.* Traduit du russe et annoté par B. Nikitine. Paris. [Translation of Bartol'd 1925.]

*BARTOL'D, V. V. 1925. *Istoriya izucheniya Vostoka v Evrope i Rossii*, II. (Izdanie Leningradskogo Vostochnogo instituta imeni A. S. Enukidze, 7.) Leningrad. [Cf. Barthold.]

*BAẒIYANTS, A., N. KUZNETSOVA & L. KULAGINA 1969. *Aziatskij Muzej – Institut vostokovedeniya AN SSSR 1918–1968.* Moskva.

BESKROVNYJ, V. M. 1957. Iz istorii izucheniya zhivykh indijskikh yazykov v Rossii v XIX veke. *Vestnik Leningradskogo Universiteta* 1957(8): 37–50.

Bibliografiya Indii, dorevolyutsionnaya i sovetskaya literature na russkom yazyke i yazykakh narodov SSSR, original'naya i perevodnaya. Moskva 1976.

Bibliografiya Indii 1968–1975. Sovetskaya i perevodnaya literatura. Moskva 1982.

BOGOLYUBOV, M. N. 1960. Iranskoe yazykoznanie v Leningrade (1917–1957). *Uchenye zapiski Instituta vostokovedov* 25: 303–318.

BONGARD-LEVIN, G. 1979. Sanskrit and ancient Indian studies in the USSR. In: *Sanskrit Studies Outside India* (News Bulletin No. 2. Fourth World Sanskrit Conference, Weimar/G.D.R. May 23–30, 1979): 144–162. Weimar.

BONGARD-LEVIN, Grigorij & A. VIGASIN 1984. *The Image of India. The Study of Ancient Indian Civilisation in the USSR.* Moscow.

BONGARD-LEVIN, Grigorij M., Roland LARDINOIS & Aleksej A. VIGASIN 2002. *Correspondances orientalistes entre Paris et Saint-Pétersbourg (1887–1935)* (Mémoires de l'Académie des inscriptions et belles-lettres, 26.) Paris.

BULICH, S. K. 1904. *Ocherk istorii yazykoznaniya v Rossii*, I: XIII v. – 1825. Sankt-Peterburg. [Chapter XIII: Izuchenie vostochnykh yazykov v XVIII v. pri preemnikakh Petra I: 365–529; reprint: Specimina philologiae slavicae, 83. München 1989.]

DORN, Bernhard 1840. Ueber die hohe Wichtigkeit und die nahmhaften Fortschritte der asiatischen Studien in Russland. In: *Recueil des actes des séances publiques de l'Académie impériale des sciences de St.-Petersbourg* 1839 (1840): 55–114.

Dvadtsatipyatiletie imperatorskogo Novorossijkogo universiteta. Istoricheskaya zapiska. Odessa 1890. [Sravnitel'noe yazykovedenie i sanskritskij yazyk: 271–280.]

ÈRMAN, V. G. 1960. Izuchenie drevnej Indii v Leningrade. *Uchenye zapiski Instituta vostokovedov* 25: 150–161.

GOPAL, Surendra 1967. Indian studies in Russia. *Journal of Indian History* 45: 569–582.

—— 1972. Indian studies in Soviet Central Asia. *Indo-Asian Culture* 20(2): 19–33.

Istoriya otechestvennogo vostokovedeniya s serediny XIX veka do 1917 goda. Moskva 1997.

KAL'YANOV, V. I. 1957. Ob izuchenii sanskrita v Sovetskom Soyuze. *Vestnik Leningradskogo Universiteta* 1957(8): 23–36.

—— 1962. Izuchenie sanskrita v Rossii. In *Uchenye zapiski Leningradskogo Gosudarstvennogo Universiteta* (Seriya vostokovedcheskikh nauk, 14 [304]): 140–167.

*KOTSCHETOW, A. N. 1967. Die buddhistische Forschung in der UdSSR. *Buddhist Yearly* 1967: 86–118.

KOVALEVSKIJ, A. P. 1961. Izuchenie Vostoka v khar'kovskom universitete i v Khar'kove v XVIII – XX vekakh. In: *Antologiya literatur vostoka*: 9–121. Khar'kov.

*KRACHKOVSKIJ, I. Yu. 1950. *Ocherki po istorii russkoj arabistiki*. Moskva. [Cf. Kratschkowski 1957.]

KRATSCHKOWSKI, I. J. 1957. *Die russische Arabistik. Umrisse ihrer Entwicklung*. Übersetzt und bearbeitet von Otto Mehlitz. Leipzig. [Translation of Krachkovskij 1950.]

LIVOTOVA, O. È. & V. B. PORTUGAL' 1966. *Vostokovedenie v izdaniyah Akademii nauk 1726–1917. Bibliografiyá*. Moskva.

MILIBAND, Sofiya D. 1976. *Biobibliograficheskij slovar' sovetskikh vostokovedov*. Moskva. [1st edition 1975.]

—— 1995. *Biobibliograficheskij slovar' otechestvennykh vostokovedov*. I–II. Moskva. [Revised & enlarged edition; new edition 2008.]

—— 1997. Dopolneniya i ispravleniya k "Biobibliograficheskij slovar' otechestvennykh vostokovedov". *Vostok* 1997(3): 201–221; 1997(5): 198–216; 1997(6): 200–212 (A–O).

—— 1998. Dopolneniya i ispravleniya k "Biobibliograficheskij slovar' otechestvennykh vostokovedov" *Vostok* 1998(1): 210–217; 1998(4): 200–205; 1998(6): 190–200 (P–S).

—— 1999. Dopolneniya i ispravleniya k "Biobibliograficheskij slovar' otechestvennykh vostokovedov" *Vostok* 1999(3): 210–214 (T).

NADEL', H. S. 1964. Indologiya v Kharkovskom universitete za poltora veka. Istoriko-bibliograficheskij ocherk. *Narody Azii i Afriki* 1964(2): 169–173.

Ocherki po istorii russkogo vostokovedeniya, I–VI. Moscow 1953–63.

*OL'DENBURG, S. F. 1919. Aziatskij muzej 1818–1918. *Bibliotechnoe obozrenie*, I: 144–148.

*—— 1927. Vostokovedenie. *Akademiya nauk SSSR za desyat' let (1917–1927)*: 140–154. Leningrad.

ORANSKIJ, Iosif M. 1975. Altiranische Philologie und altiranische Sprachwissenschaft in der UdSSR (1917–1970). *Altorientalische Forschungen* 2: 139–179.

*R[ICHTER], A. [von] 1825. O sostoyanii vostochnoj slovesnosti v Rossii. *Aziatskij Vestnik*.

ROERICH, G. N. 1945. Russian Indology. *The Journal of the Greater India Society* 12: 69–98.

**Rol' russkoj nauki v razvitii mirovoj nauki i kul'tury*. (Uchenye zapiski, vypusk 107, tom III, kniga 2.) Moskva 1946. [N. K. Dmitriev on Turkology, B. V. Miller on Iranistics, and I. Yu. Krachkovskij on Arabistics.]

SHAMOV, G. F. 1959. Sanskritologiya v Kazanskom universitete v pervoj polovine XIX v. *Problemy vostokovedeniya* 1959(3): 117–122.

SEREBRYAKOV, I. D. 1976. Kontakty i sotrudnichestvo mezhdu indogami Rossii i Germanii v XVIII–XIX vekakh. Neskol'ko zamechanii k istorii indologii v Evrope. *Wissenschaftliche Zeitschrift der Humboldt-Universität zu Berlin, Gesellschaft-Sprachwissenschaftliche Reihe* 25: 311–313.

STACY, R. H. 1985. *India in Russian Literature.* Delhi.

*STARIKOV, A. A. 1960. Vostochnaya filologiya v Moskovskom universitete. *Ocherki po istorii russkogo vostokovedeniya* 3: 126–146. Moskva.

VASIL'KOV, Ya. V., A. M. GRISHINA & F. F. PERCHENOK 1990. Repressirovannoe vostokovedenie. Vostokovedy, podvergshiesya repressiyam v 20e–50e gody. *Narody Azii i Afriki* 1990(4): 113–125 & 1990(5): 96–106.

VESELOVSKIJ, N. I. 1880. Svedeniya ob offitsial'nom prepodavanii vostochnykh yazykov v Rossii. In: *Trudy tret'yago mezhdunarodnogo s"ezda orientalistov v S.-Peterburge 1876 (Travaux de la troisième session du Congrès international des orientalistes, St.-Pétersbourg 1876)*, I: 97–256. St. Petersburg.

VIGASIN, A. A. 2008. *Izuchenie Indii v Rossii (ocherki i materialy).* Moskva.

WAFA, A. H. & L. A. GORDON 1964. Indian studies in the U.S.S.R. In: *Indian Studies Abroad*: 118–123. London.

YERMOSHKIN, Nikolai 1967. *Buddhism and Buddhists in the USSR*. Moscow.

ZHUKOVSKAIA, N. L. & Tracy SCHWARZ 1979. Research on Lamaism in the USSR: 1917–1976. *The Canada-Mongolia Review / La Revue Canada-Mongolie* 5: 37–49. [Annotated translation of Zhukovskaya 1977.]

*ZHUKOVSKAYA, N. L. 1977. Izuchenie lamaizma v SSSR (1917–1976). *Narody Azii i Afriki* 1977(2): 187–196. [Cf. Zhukovskaia & Tracy 1979.]

ZOGRAF, G. A. 1960. Stanovlenie novoindijskoj filologii v Leningrade. *Uchenye zapiski Instituta vostokovedov* 25: 162–176.

b. General directories

Biobibliograficheskij slovar' professorov i prepodavatelej imperatorskogo Yur'evskogo, byvshego Derptskogo, universiteta za sto let' ego sushchestvovaniya (1802–1902), I–II. Yur'ev 1902–03. [Katedra nemetskogo i sravnitel'nogo yazykoznaniya: II: 563–588.]

Biobibliograficheskij slovar' professorov i prepodavatelej imperatorskogo Kazanskogo universiteta (1804–1904) v dvukh chastyakh, I–II. Kazan 1904.

Biobibliograficheskij slovar' professorov i prepodavatelej imperatorskogo Moskovskogo universiteta. Moskva 1855.

Biobibliograficheskij slovar' professorov i prepodavatelej imperatorskogo S.-Peterburgskogo universiteta za istekshuyu tret'yu chetvert' veka ego sushchestvovaniya 1869–1894, I–II. S.-Peterburg 1896–98.

**Materialy dlya biograficheskogo slovarya dejstvitel'nkyh chlenov Akademii Nauk*, II. Petrograd 1917.

Russkij biograficheskij slovar', I–XXV. 1896–1918 (reprint: New York 1962).

***Serbia**, see under Yugoslavia*

***Slovakia**, see under Czechoslovakia*

***Slovenia**, see under Yugoslavia*

24. South and Central America

a. Indology and Oriental studies

ALTUCHOW, N. 1979. [Short notes.] In: *Sanskrit Studies Outside India* (News Bulletin No. 2. Fourth World Sanskrit Conference, Weimar/ G.D.R. May 23–30, 1979). Weimar. [Argentina: 5–6, Brazil: 13, Costa Rica: 14, Peru: 122, Uruguay: 189–190.]

DA FONSECA, Carlos Alberto 1984. The study of Sanskrit in Brazil. In: V. V. Bedekar (ed.), *Proceedings and Papers of the Seminar on Sanskrit Outside India*: 56–60. Thane.

*JOSHI, Rasik Vihari 1971. Sanskrit studies in Mexico. *Dr V. Raghavan Shashtyabdapurti Felicitation Volume*: 285–289. Mylapore.

MORA, Juan Miguel de 1979. Sanskrit studies in Mexico. In: *Sanskrit Studies Outside India* (News Bulletin No. 2. Fourth World Sanskrit Conference, Weimar/G.D.R. May 23–30, 1979): 99–103. Weimar.

—— 1983. Sanskrit studies in Latin America. *JAOS* 103: 615–616.

—— 1984. Sanskrit studies in Latin America. In: V. V. Bedekar (ed.), *Proceedings and Papers of the Seminar on Sanskrit Outside India*: 3–5. Thane.

TOLA, Fernando 1982. Quinta Conferencia Mundial de Sánscrito. *Papeles de la India* 10–11 (1981–82): 12–23. [La Indologia en Latinoamérica: 17–20.]

*URQUIDI, Victor L. & LA LAMA, Graciela de 1970. [Title unkown]. *Journal of Oriental Research* 36. [Cf. *Papeles de la India, I.1 (1972): 60–70.]

b. General directories

Archivo biográfico de España, Portugal e Iberoamérica. Cards 1–1048 A–Z, 1049–1143 Supplemento. München 1990 (microfiche).

Archivo biográfico de España, Portugal e Iberoamérica, Nueva Serie. Cards 1–1018 Aanda–Camilo (microfiche, also third series and online version).

Indice biográfico de España, Portugal e Iberoamérica / Indice biográfico de Espanha, Portugal e Ibero-América / Spanish, Portuguese and Latin-American Biographical Index / Spanischer, Portugiesischer und Ibero-amerikanischer Biographischer Index. Ed. V. Herrero Mediavilla & L. R. Agnayo Nayle, I–IV. München 1990.

25. Spain and Portugal

a. Indology and Oriental studies

AMZALAK, Moses Bensabat 1928. *The Oriental Studies in Portugal. Address Presented at the General Meeting of the XVIIth International Congress of Orientalists*. Lisbon. [14 p.]

CORREIA-AFONSO, John (ed.) 1981. *Indo-Portuguese History. Sources and Problems*. Bombay.

GERSON DA CUNHA, J. 1880. Materials for the history of Oriental studies amongst the Portuguese. In: *Atti del 4. congresso internazionale degli orientalisti tenuto in Firenze nel settembre 1878*, II: 179–219. Firenze.

RAGHAVAN, V. 1956. *Sanskrit and Allied Indian Studies in Europe*. Madras. [Spain and Portugal: 60.]

RIVIERE, Juan Roger 1964. Indian studies in Spain. In: *Indian Studies Abroad*: 95–96. London.

SALDANHA, Mariano 1936. História de Gramática Concani. *BSOS* 8(2–3 [Grierson Volume]): 715–735.

DA SILVA 1875. Les études orientales chez les Portugais. In: *Compte-rendu de premier Congrès international des orientalistes, Paris 1873*, II: 463–471.

b. General directories

Archivo biográfico de España, Portugal e Iberoamérica. Cards 1–1048 A–Z, 1049–1143 Supplemento. München 1990 (microfiche).

Archivo biográfico de España, Portugal e Iberoamérica, Nueva Serie. Cards 1–1018 Aanda–Camilo (microfiche, also third series and online version).

Enciclopedia Universal Ilustrada, I–LXX. Madrid n.d.–1930; Apendice, 1–10 (then biennial supplement volumes).

Grande Enciclopédia Portuguesa e Brasileira, I–XL. Lisbon 1935–60.

Indice biográfico de España, Portugal e Iberoamérica / Indice biográfico de Espanha, Portugal e Ibero-América / Spanish, Portuguese and Latin-American Biographical Index / Spanischer, Portugiesischer und Ibero-amerikanischer Biographischer Index. Ed. V. Herrero Mediavilla & L. R. Agnayo Nayle. I–IV. München 1990.

26. Sweden

a. Indology and Oriental studies

CALLMER, Christian 1985. *In orientem. Svenskars färder och forskningar i den europeiska och asiatiska Orienten under 1700-talet.* (Asiatica Suecana, 2.) Stockholm.

CHARPENTIER, Jarl 1924. Indologiska studier i Sverige. *Svenska Orient-sällskapets Årsbok* 2: 55–72.

Faculty of Arts at Uppsala University. History, Art and Philosophy. (Acta Universitatis Upsaliensis. Uppsala University 500 Years, 5.) Uppsala 1976.

Faculty of Arts at Uppsala University. Linguistics and Philolophy. (Acta Universitatis Upsaliensis. Uppsala University 500 Years, 6.) Uppsala 1976.

HOVDHAUGEN, Even, Fred KARLSSON, Carol HENRIKSEN & Bengt SIGURD 2000. *The History of Linguistics in the Nordic Countries*. Helsinki: Societas Scientiarum Fennica.

JUNTUNEN, Mirja 1997. Sanskrit studies in Sweden. In: *Sanskrit Studies Outside India. On the Occasion of 10th World Sanskrit Conference 1997*: 80–85. New Delhi.

LIENHARD, Siegfried 1979. Sanskrit studies in Sweden. In: *Sanskrit Studies Outside India* (News Bulletin No. 2. Fourth World Sanskrit Conference, Weimar/G.D.R. May 23–30, 1979): 135–143. Weimar.

PARPOLA, Asko 1979. Sanskrit studies in Scandinavia. In: V. Raghavan (ed.), *"Vasudhaiva kuṭumbakam" International Sanskrit Conference. March 26th–31st, 1972*, I.2: *Sanskrit and Indology in Centres Outside India, Contributions of Haryana, Tamil Nadu*: 632–648. New Delhi.

RAGHAVAN, V. 1956. *Sanskrit and Allied Indian Studies in Europe*. Madras. [Sweden: 34–36.]

SEGERSTEDT, Torgny T. 1976. Professuren i sanskrit med jämförande indoeuropeisk språkforskning. In: *Acta Universitatis Upsaliensis. Skrifter rörande Uppsala universitet*, B. Inbjudningar: 12–19. Uppsala.

b. General directories

Biographiskt Lexicon öfver namnkunnige svenska män, I–XXIII. Upsala & Örebro 1835–1857. [Cf. *Svenskt biografiskt Lexikon*.]

Göteborg Högskolas Matrikel. 1891–1916. Utg. af L. Wåhlin och J. V. Johansson. Göteborg 1916.

Göteborg Högskolas Matrikel. 1916–1941. Av S. Hallberg. (Göteborg Högskolas Årsskrift, 48.) Göteborg 1942.

Göteborg Högskolas Matrikel. 1942–1954. Av N. Sandberg. Göteborg 1957.

Lunds Universitets Matrikel 1834–47. Av Eva Gerle. Lund 1978.

Lunds Universitets Matrikel. Biografiska uppgifter öfver Universitetets styresmän, lärare och tjenstemän. 1879. Lund 1879.

[Lunds Universitets Matrikel.] *Biographiske underrättelser on professorer vid kongl. Universitetet i Lund, ifrån dess inrättning till närvarande tid*. Af M. L. Ståhl. Christianstad 1834.

Lunds Universitets Matrikel. Af C. af Petersens och A. Malm. Lund 1899.

Lunds Universitets Matrikel. Läsåret 1924–1925. Utg. av A. Malm och P. Wilner. Lund 1925.

Lunds Universitets Matrikel. 1939. Utg. av W. Norlind och B. Olsson. Lund 1939.

Lunds Universitets Matrikel. 1949–1950. Utg. av W. Norlind och M. Persson. Lund 1951.

Lunds Universitets Matrikel. 1959–1960. Utg. av W. Norlind och M. Persson. Lund 1962.

Nordisk Familjebok, I–XX. Stockholm 1876–99 (and new editions).

Scandinavian Biographical Archive. Section B: *Sweden, Finland*. Cards 1–387 A–Ö, 388–444 A–Rag. London 1989–.

Stockholm Högskolas Matrikel. 1887–1927. Utg. av Elise Adelsköld. Stockholm 1978.

Stockholm Högskolas Matrikel. 1928–1950. Utg. av Elise Adelsköld. Stockholm 1984.

Stockholm Högskolas Matrikel. 1951–1960. Utg. av Elise Adelsköld. Stockholm 1987.

Svenska män och kvinnor, I–VIII. Stockholm 1942–55.

Svenskt biografiskt lexikon, Ny följd. I–X. Örebro & Stockholm 1857–1907 [Cf. *Biographiskt Lexicon öfver namnkunnige svenska män*.]

Svenskt biografiskt lexikon, I–. Stockholm 1918–. [Up to Stålhammar, 2013.]

Upsala Academies Matrikel 1832. Utg. af C. H. Ekstrand. Upsala 1832.

Upsala Academies Matrikel 1841. Utg. af Aug. Th. Låstbom. Upsala 1841.

Upsala Universitets Matrikel. Utg. af J. von Bahr och Th. Brandberg. Upsala 1896.

Uppsala Universitets Matrikel. Utg. af Th. Brandberg och J. von Bahr. Upsala 1906.

Uppsala Universitets Matrikel. Höstterminen 1916. Utg. af Th. Fries och E. von Döbeln. Upsala 1917.

Uppsala Universitets Matrikel. Höstterminen 1926. Utg. av Th. Fries och E. von Döbeln. Upsala 1927.

Uppsala Universitets Matrikel. Höstterminen 1936. Utg. av Th. Fries & E. von Döbeln. Upsala 1937.

Uppsala Universitets Matrikel. 1937–1950. Utg. av Å. Dintler & Sune Lindqvist. Uppsala 1953.

Uppsala Universitets Matrikel. 1951–1960. Utg. av Å. Dintler & L. Grönberg. Uppsala 1953.

Vem är det? Stockholm 1912–.

Vem är hon? Stockholm 1988.

(In addition, those scholars who were also priests, can be searched in the directories ["Herdaminne"] of Swedish dioceses. Some of these also include schoolteachers:)

27. Switzerland

a. Indology and Oriental studies

HORSCH, Paul 1964. Sanskrit studies in Switzerland. In: *Indian Studies Abroad*: 97–103. London.

JANERT, Klaus L. 1961. *Verzeichnis indienkundlicher Hochschulschriften. Deutschland–Österreich–Schweiz*. Wiesbaden.

RAGHAVAN, V. 1956. *Sanskrit and Allied Indian Studies in Europe*. Madras. [Switzerland: 52–54.]

SCHELLER, M. 1951. Der heutige Stand der schweizerischen Orientalistik. *Archiv Orientální* 19: 271–275.

Who's Who in Asian Studies in Switzerland 1989. Geneva 1989.

b. General directories

**Biographisches Lexikon verstorbener Schweizer*, I–VIII. Zürich 1947–82.

BONJOUR, Edgar 1971. *Die Universität Basel von den Anfängen bis zur Gegenwart 1460–1960*. 2nd revised edition. Basel.

Dozenten der Bernischen Hochschule. Bern 1984.

Historisch-biographisches Lexikon der Schweiz, I–VII. Basel & Neuenburg 1921–34; Supplement, Neuenburg 1934.

Schweizer Lexikon, I–VI. Luzern 1991–93.

Schweizerisches Zeitgenossen-Lexikon. 2nd edition. Bern 1932. [1st ed. 1921.]

STELLING-MICHAUD, S. 1976. *Le livre du recteur de l'Académie de Genève (1559–1878)*, V. Genève.

28. Ukraine (see also Russia)

a. Indology and Oriental studies

Dvadtsatipyatiletie imperatorskogo Novorossijkogo universiteta. Istoricheskaya zapiska. Odessa 1890. [Sravnitel'noe yazykovedenie i sanskritskij yazyk: 271–280.]

KOVALEVSKIJ, A. P. 1961. Izuchenie Vostoka v khar'kovskom universitete i v Khar'kove v XVIII–XX vekakh. In: *Antologiya literatur vostoka*: 9–121. Khar'kov.

NADEL', H. S. 1964. Indologiya v Kharkovskom universitete za poltora veka (Istoriko-bibliograficheskij ocherk). *Narody Azii i Afriki* 1964(2): 169–173.

29. United Kingdom

a. Indology and Oriental studies (including British scholarly activity in India)

ALLEN, Charles 2002. *The Buddha and the Sahibs. The Men who Discovered India's Lost Religion*. London.

ARBERRY, A. J. 1938. *The Library of the India Office. A Historical Sketch*. London. [Cf. R. Fick, *Göttingische Gelehrte Anzeigen* 1939: 464–469.]

—— 1942. *British Contributions to Persian Studies*. London.

—— 1943. *British Orientalists*. London.

—— 1960. *Oriental Essays. Portraits of Seven Scholars*. London. [Simon Ockley, William Jones, E. W. Lane, E. H. Palmer, E. G. Brown, R. A. Nicholson and A. J. Arberry.]

*BISWAS, Hari Charan 1909. Some English Orientalists. *Calcutta Review* 1909: 64–98. [Halhed, Wilkins, Colebrooke, Jones.]

BOWEN, John 1955. The East India Company's education of its own servants. *JRAS* 1955: 105–123.

BRAHMACHARI, U. N. 1932. Annual address, 1931–32. *JASB* N.S. 28, (Proceedings for 1931): x–xli.

BROUGH, John 1979. Sanskrit studies in Great Britain. In: *Sanskrit Studies Outside India* (News Bulletin No. 2. Fourth World Sanskrit Conference, Weimar/G.D.R. May 23–30, 1979): 70–77. Weimar.

BUCKLAND, C. E. 1905. *Dictionary of Indian Biography*. London (reprint: Varanasi 1971).

CHATTERJEE, Sir Atul & Sir Richard BURN 1943. *British Contributions to Indian Studies*. London.

DUNDAS, Paul 2006. Sanskrit studies in Britain. *Newsletter of the International Association of Sanskrit Studies* 8: 21–24.

FOSTER, William (ed.) 1921. *Early Travels in India 1583–1619*. London.

*HIGGINBOTTOM, J. J. 1874. *Men Whom India Has Known. Biographies of Eminent Indian Characters*. Madras. ["Indian" here means British in India.]

HOERNLE, A. F. Rudolf 1885. *Centenary Review of the Asiatic Society of Bengal From 1784–1883*, II. *Archæology, History, Literature, &c.* Calcutta.

Indian studies in Britain. In: *Indian Studies Abroad*: 1–5. London 1964.

*JAVADI, H. 1987. *Persian Literary Influence on English Literature*. (Middle Eastern Series, 17.) Piedmont.

*KEAY, John 1979. *The Gilgit Game. Explorers of the Western Himalayas 1865–95*. London.

KEJARIWAL, O. P. 1988. *The Asiatic Society of Bengal and the Discovery of India's Past 1784–1838*. Calcutta.

KOPP, D. 1969. *British Orientalism and the Bengal Renaissance. The Dynamics of Indian Modernization 1773–1835*. Berkeley.

*LAMB, Alastair 1960. *Britain and Chinese Central Asia. The Road to Lhasa, 1767–1905*. London.

*MARSHALL, P. J. (ed.) 1970. *The British Discovery of Hinduism in the Eighteenth Century*. Cambridge.

*OL'DENBURG, S. F. 1894. Ocherki prepodavaniya vostochnykh yazykov vo Frantsii, Anglii i Germanii. *Žhurnal Ministerstva Naródnago Prosveshchenija* 293 (1894[6.2]): 255–275.

PRASAD, Ram Chandra 1980. *Early English Travellers in India.* 2nd revised edition. Delhi (1st ed. 1965).

RAGHAVAN, V. 1956. *Sanskrit and Allied Indian Studies in Europe.* Madras. [Great Britain: 61–77.]

REAY, lord 1920. The Presidential Adress. *JRAS* 1920: 411–421. [On the history of the Society.]

RENDALL, Jane 1982. Scottish Orientalism. From Robertson to James Mill. *The Historical Journal* 25(1): 43–69.

*ROWE, R. 1892. *Famous British Explorers and Navigators, from Drake to Franklin.* London.

SARKAR, Gopal Ch. 1997. *Encyclopedia of British Indologists.* Calcutta.

SIMMONDS, Stuart & Simon DIGBY (eds.) 1979. *Royal Asiatic Society. Its History and Treasures.* Leiden.

Statement [about the situation of Oriental studies in the U.K.]. *JRAS* N.S. 19 (1887): 344–349 + an Appendix of three tables.

THOMPSON, Stephen 1984. Sanskrit in Britain. In: V. V. Bedekar (ed.), *Proceedings and Papers of the Seminar on Sanskrit Outside India*: 16–64. Thane.

*TURNER, R. L. 1943. *Memorandum on the Present State of Indian Studies in Great Britain.* London. [26 p.]

YOHANNAN, J. D. 1977. *Persian Poetry in England and America. A 200-Year History.* Delmar N.Y.

b. General directories

British Biographical Archive. A One-Alphabet Cumulation of 324 of the Most Important English-Language Reference Works Originally Published Between 1601 and 1929. Microfiche Edition. Managing Editor: Laureen Baillie. Editor: Paul Sieveking. Cards 1–1213 A–Z, 1214–1236 Appendix. London 1984.

—— Series 2. *A Supplementary Series Gathered from 268 Sources Which both Complements the Material Already Published in the British Biographical Archive and Extends the Period Covered to 1960.* Microfiche edition. Managing Editor: David Bank. Editor: Anthony Esposito. Cards 1237–1466 A–Ez. London 1991–.

British Biographical Index. Eds. D. Bank & A. Esposito, I–IV. London 1990.

CHAMBERS, Robert 1870. *A Biographical Dictionary of Eminent Scotsmen*. New Edition, revised throughout and continued by Thomas Thomson, I–III. London (reprint: Anglistica & Americana, 105, Hildesheim 1971).

Dictionary of National Biography, I–LVIII. London 1885–1900. Supplement volumes.

Dictionary of Welsh Biography down to 1940. Cardiff & Oxford 1959.

FOSTER, John 1888. *Alumni Oxonienses. The Members of the University of Oxford 1715–1886: Their Parentage, Birthplace, and Year of Birth, With a Record of Their Degrees*, I–IV. Oxford (reprint: Nendeln, Liechtenstein 1968).

—— 1891. *Alumni Oxonienses. The Members of the University of Oxford 1500–1714: Their Parentage, Birthplace, and Year of Birth, With a Record of Their Degrees*, I–IV. Oxford (reprint: Nendeln, Liechtenstein 1968).

Oxford Dictionary of National Biography. From the Earliest Years to the Year 2000, I–LIX; Supplement volume (2001–2004) 2004.

VENN, J. & J. A. VENN 1922–27. *Alumni Cantabrigienses. A Biographical List of All Known Students, Graduates and Holders of Office at the University of Cambridge. From the Earliest Times to 1751*, I–IV. Cambridge.

VENN, J. & J. A. VENN 1940–54. *Alumni Cantabrigienses. A Biographical List of All Known Students, Graduates and Holders of Office at the University of Cambridge. From 1752 to 1900*, I–VI. Cambridge.

Who's Who. London 1897–.

Who Was Who. London 1929–.

***Uruguay**, see under South and Central America*

30. USA

a. Indology and Oriental studies

BENDER, E. 1979. Sanskrit studies in United States. In: *Sanskrit Studies Outside India* (News Bulletin No. 2. Fourth World Sanskrit Conference, Weimar/G.D.R. May 23–30, 1979): 168–188. Weimar.

BROWN, W. Norman 1964. South Asian studies in the United States. In: *Indian Studies Abroad*: 104–117. London.

ELDER, Joseph W., Edward C. DIMOCK, Jr. & Ainslie T. EMBREE (eds.) 1998. *India's Worlds and U.S. Scholars 1947–1997*. New Delhi.

POLEMAN, H. L. 1948. Middle Eastern studies. *Archiv Orientální* 16: 213–224.

PREBISH, Charles S. 1994. The academic study of Buddhism in the United States. A current analysis. *Religion* 24: 271–278.

RAGHAVAN, V. 1975. *Sanskrit and Allied Indian Studies in U.S.* Gauhati.

ROCHER, Rosane 1997. Sanskrit studies in United States. In: *Sanskrit Studies Outside India. On the Occasion of 10th World Sanskrit Conference 1997*: 97–152. New Delhi.

YOHANNAN, J. D. 1977. *Persian Poetry in England and America. A 200-Year History.* Delmar NY.

YUYAMA, Akira 2003. Groundwork layers for Buddhist Sanskrit philology in America. In: *Annual Report of The International Research Institute for Advanced Buddhology at Soka University for the Academic Year 2002*: 321–339.

b. General directories

American Biographical Archive. Cards 1–1806 A–Z, 1807–1842 Appendix (microfiche).

BRIGGS, Ward W., Jr. (ed.) 1994. *Biographical Dictionary of North Americal Classicists.* Westport, CT.

Directory of American Scholars. A Biographical Directory. Lancaster, PA 1942ff.

Dictionary of American Biography, I–XX. London 1928–36 + Index Volume 1937.

National Cyclopædia of American Biography, I–XLIX. New York 1898–1966.

Who Was Who in America. Historical Volume 1607–1896. Revised Edition. Chicago, IL 1967 (also other volumes).

31. **Yugoslavia** (former, with Bosnia-Herzegovina, Croatia, Macedonia, Montenegro, Serbia and Slovenia)

a. Indology and Oriental studies

JAUK PINHAK, Milka 1979. Sanskrit studies in Yugoslavia. In: *Sanskrit Studies Outside India* (News Bulletin No. 2. Fourth World Sanskrit Conference, Weimar/G.D.R. May 23–30, 1979): 191–193. Weimar.

*KATIČIĆ, Radoslav 1972. Sanskrit studies in Yugoslavia. *Cultural Forum* 48: 45–46. (?)

MATIŠIĆ, Zdravka 1976. Über die Sanskritstudien an der Universität Zagreb. *Wissenschaftliche Zeitschrift der Humboldt-Universität zu Berlin, Gesellschaft-Sprachwissenschaftliche Reihe* 25: 297–299.

VYNCKE, F. 1973. L'évolution du śanscritisme et de l'indianisme en Yugoslavie. *Annuaire de l'Institut de Philologie et d'Histoire Orientales et Slaves* 20 (1968–72): 523–536. Bruxelles.

b. General directories

Enciklopedija Jugoslavije, I–VIII. Zagreb 1955–71 (2nd edition: 1980–90).

Hrvatski biografski leksikon, I–. Zagreb 1983–. [Most recent volume VIII, 2013, Kr–Li.]

Slovenski biografski leksikon, I–IV. Ljubljana 1925–1990.

INDEX